GENTLE RE

Gentle Regrets
Thoughts from a life

ROGER SCRUTON

continuum

Continuum
The Tower Building, 11 York Road, London SE1 7NX
80 Maiden Lane, Suite 704, New York, NY 10038

www.continuumbooks.com

First published 2005
Reprinted 2006

British Library Cataloguing in Publication Data
A catalogue record for this book is available from the British Library.

ISBN 08264-8033-0

Typeset in Sabon by BookEns Ltd, Royston, Herts.
Printed and bound in Great Britain by
MPG Books Ltd, Bodmin, Cornwall

Contents

Preface

'How did you come to be what you are?' This question is often asked of me, and from time to time I have found myself revisiting the past in an attempt to answer it. These autobiographical excursions have usually formed part of some larger intellectual enterprise and, in bringing them together in this book, my intention has been not to dwell on them, but to understand the concrete beginnings of some fairly abstract ideas.

Wisdom is truth that consoles. There is truth without wisdom, as we know from the many mad scientists who are running loose in our world. And there is consolation without truth, as we know from the history of religion. Whatever its defects, my life has enabled me to find comfort in uncomfortable truths. Whether this counts as wisdom I do not know; but it encourages me to provide some of the personal background from which my worldview arose.

I have described one or two influential friends and companions, mentioned others, but in no way attempted to name all the people who have been important to me. More people than I deserve have offered me love and friendship, and if I do not mention them by name, it is because this book is not a record of my *éducation sentimentale* but an attempt to explain a particular conservative outlook.

Some of the material that follows has been adapted from previously published articles, and I am grateful to the editors of *Books and Company*, *City Journal*, *BBC Music Magazine*, *New Criterion and Nexus* for the relevant permissions.

Malmesbury, January 2005

1
How I Discovered Books

Although my father was a teacher, books did not play a large part in our home. Those that could be found in the house were of a useful or improving kind: encyclopaedias, the Bible, Palgrave's *Golden Treasury*, some gardening books, the Penguin *Odyssey*, and memoirs of the Second World War. By way of shielding herself from my father's gloom, my mother dabbled a little in exotic religions, which meant that pamphlets by Indian gurus would from time to time occupy the front room table. But neither she nor my father had any conception of the *book*, as a hidden door in the scheme of things that opens into another world.

My first inkling of this experience came from Bunyan. The year was 1957. I was 13, a day boy at our next-door grammar school, where I learned to distinguish books into two kinds: on the syllabus; and off it. *Pilgrim's Progress* must surely have been off the syllabus; nothing else can account for the astonishment with which I turned its pages. I was convalescing from flu, sitting in the garden on a fine spring day. A few yards to my left was our house – a plain whitewashed Edwardian box, part of a ribbon development that stretched along the main road from High Wycombe halfway to Amersham. To the right stood the neo-Georgian Grammar School with its frontage of lawn. Opposite was the ugly new housing estate that spoiled our view. I sat in a nondescript corner of post-war England; nothing could conceivably happen in such surroundings, except the things that happen anywhere: a bus passing, a dog barking, football on the wireless, shepherd's pie for tea.

And then suddenly I was in a visionary landscape, where even the most ordinary things come dressed in astonishment. In

Bunyan's world words are not barriers or defences, as they are in suburban England, but messages sent to the heart. They jump into you from the page, as though in answer to a summons. This, surely, is the sign of a great writer, that he speaks to you in your voice, by making his voice your own.

I did not put the book down until I had finished it. And for months afterwards I strode through our suburb side by side with Christian, my inner eye fixed on the Celestial City.

Two years later, when I was studying A-level science, my parents decided to move. They had found a house in Marlow, smaller, quieter and quainter than Amersham Road. The owners – a retired couple called Deas who were emigrating to Canada – drove over to discuss the deal. I was left sitting in the same spot in our garden, drinking tea with their son.

Since Bunyan, few books off the syllabus had passed through my hands. Nevertheless, I had heard rumours of the artistic temperament, and something about Ivor Deas made me suspect that he suffered from this obscure but distinguished ailment. He was a bachelor of some 40 years, still living with his parents. His face was pale and thin, with grey eyes that seemed to fade away when you looked at them. His alabaster hands with their long white fingers; his quiet voice; his spare and careful words; his trousers, rubbed shiny at the knees; and his Adam's apple shifting up and down like a ping-pong ball in a fountain – all these seemed totally out of place in our suburb and conferred on him an air of suffering fragility that must surely have some literary cause. He sat in silence, waiting for me to speak. I asked him his occupation. He responded with an embarrassed laugh.

'Librarian,' he said, and I looked at him amazed. To think of it – a real librarian, in our garden, sitting over a cup of tea! What could I say to him? There was an uncomfortable silence as I searched my mind for topics. Mozart was my latest passion, and eventually I asked the librarian if he knew *Don Giovanni*, from which opera I had just acquired a long-playing record of extracts. He looked at me for a moment, eyes wavering, neck wobbling, hands clutching his knees. Then suddenly he began to speak, quietly, almost tonelessly, as though confessing to some dreadful crime.

'Of course it's a conundrum, isn't it – such a perfect work of art, not a note or a word out of place, and yet Mozart feels free to add two arias, just like that, because the tenor asks for them! Purists would cut these arias: they hold up the action, destroy the artistic integrity. But music like "Dalla sua pace" – would you remove such a jewel just because – well, I mean, just because it stretches the crown? So to speak.'

Having delivered himself of this weighty utterance he stared down sadly into his teacup, a posture that he maintained in silence until his parents emerged from the house. I was stunned by his words. No track on the treasured LP had stirred me more deeply than 'Dalla sua pace', and the thought that something so beautiful could also be a problem, that a composer might actually think of adding or subtracting it for the sake of the whole, filled me with an astonished sense of the labour, the complexity, the sheer holiness of art. As they were leaving he turned to me and said

'I hope you enjoy Marlow library. I worked hard on it.'

'And will you still be there?' I asked, astonished to have met not only a librarian, but a *town* librarian.

He gave me a frightened look.

'Oh no. I shall be going with them,' he nodded over his shoulder, 'to Canada.'

'Come along, Ivor,' his mother shouted. She was a large, formidable-looking lady, with permed grey hair and layers of woollen clothing in maroon and mauve. With a nod and a gulp the librarian disappeared into the back of the family car, and that was the last I saw of him.

But it was not the last of his influence. In those days immigration from Britain was encouraged by the Canadian government, which subsidized the cost. Mrs Deas was able to take her furniture and knick-knacks, down to the last Bambi on the mantelpiece. But, as she explained to my mother, Ivor's books would cause them to go over the weight limit. So would we mind if they were left behind? If we had no use for them they could always be given to the RSPCA.

The first book that I picked from Ivor's collection was a volume of letters by Rainer Maria Rilke. Needless to say, I had never heard of this writer, but I was attracted by his name. 'Rainer' had a faraway, exotic sound to it; 'Rilke' suggested knighthood and chivalry. And 'Maria' made me think of a being more spiritual than material, who had risen so high above the scheme of things as no longer to possess a sex. I read the book with a feeling of astonishment, just as I had experienced two years before through Bunyan. An air of sanctity, a reckless disregard for the world and its requirements, seemed to radiate from those mysterious pages. Here was a man who wandered outside society, communing with nature and his soul. I did not suspect that Rilke was a shameless sponge; I could not see that these letters, which seem to be all giving, are in fact all taking, the work of a spiritual vampire. To me they exemplified another, higher mode of being, of which I had no precise conception, but for which I tried to find a name: 'aesthetic' sounded right at first; but then 'ascetic' seemed just as good, and somewhat easier to say. Eventually I used both words interchangeably, satisfied that between them they captured the mysterious vision that had been granted to me, but withheld from those coarser beings – my parents and sisters, for instance – who had no knowledge of books.

Thanks to Rilke, I embarked on the aesthetic, or ascetic, way of life. The first requirement was to fall in love with someone pure and inaccessible, for whom I could suffer in silence. One of my class-mates seemed a promising candidate: he was handsome, thoughtful, showed a faint interest in music, sought my good opinion. But when I asked him to read Rilke's letters he protested that he didn't have time. I fixed my eye instead on a girl whom I had seen in Marlow church. She wore a white mackintosh and a white silk scarf, and her neatly plaited hair and cream-coloured cheeks radiated child-like piety. I knew nothing about her, except that she came from Marlow Bottom. When I confided this fact to my sister, whose curiosity had been aroused by my ostentatious sighs, she roared with laughter, and promptly named the object of my passion 'Big Bertha of Marlow Bottom'. Such taunts notwithstanding, Big Bertha, who was in fact small and delicate, sustained my reading for several months. Then one evening I caught sight of her in a doorway, snogging lasciviously with a man in jeans. I revised my conception of the ascetico-aesthetic life, with love excised from it.

By now I had discovered Dante, in the Temple Classics edition that Ivor Deas had annotated in a fine italic hand. This was my introduction to symbolism; I formed the conclusion that symbols put us in touch with our real selves, and that our real selves are vastly more interesting than the pretend-selves we adopt for others' consumption. The theory was confirmed by a reading of Robert Graves's *White Goddess* – surely the most dangerous way for a child to discover poetry, but incomparable in its excitement.

Graves challenged me to read more widely. I began to explore Ivor's other domain, the public library, to whose Eng. Lit. section he had clearly devoted the greater part of his time. All the poets, critics and novelists had found a place in those unvisited rooms, from the windows of which you could see the high wall of a secluded Victorian mansion, occupied, as it happened, by the ageing C. K. Scott Moncrieff. It was months before I was to know the significance of that name. But the books that Ivor had collected at public expense, and which I read, usually four at a time, on a table between the bookshelves, were now inextricably fused in my mind with the view of that high brick wall. Wisteria swarmed over the top of it, and a great cedar tree rose in the garden, resting its branches on the coping-stones and hiding the house from view. I read like an alchemist, searching for the spell that would admit me to that secret world, where shadows fall on tonsured lawns, and the aesthetic (or was it ascetic?) way of life occurs in solemn rituals after tea.

Soon order of a kind was established in my literary thinking. Thanks to Mr Broadbridge, a Leavisite master, those in our sixth form who were doing A-level English came to literature only after being steeped in the vinegar of *Revaluation*. I too, though studying natural sciences, felt the force of Mr Broadbridge's edicts, issued in classrooms three corridors away. Once again, books were divided into those on the syllabus and those off it – the only change being that the syllabus was now indefinitely large. Whatever the charms of Rilke and Graves, they were definitely off the syllabus. Dante was OK, because Eliot said so. But Dante had to be approached through *The Sacred Wood*, and the going was hard. As for Kafka and Kierkegaard, who had also captured my imagination, they were apologists for sickness, tempters who must be banished by those for whom 'life is a necessary word'. The severity of Dr Leavis appealed to me, since it made my literary excursions into sins. I went on reading Rilke and Kafka, with a renewed sense of being an outsider, obscurely redeemed by the crime that condemned me. And to this day I remain persuaded that it is not life that is the judge of literature, but the other way round.

One of the poets on the Leavisite index was a favourite of Ivor's. His copy of Shelley, which I still possess, is annotated in every margin. On its title page is Ivor's name – George Ivor Deas, or Georgius Ivorus Decius as he there expresses it, by way of preface to some lines of Ovid. On the next page, in Ivor's italic hand, is a sonnet dated 23 February 1945. It captures, in its stilted way, the premonition that all of us feel when the first enthusiasms of youth begin to wane:

Evolution

In youth he shouts to the stars – 'There is no God!'
Laughs till Faith withers in his laughter's flame;
Cries that Law libels Freedom without blame,
That Order sweats and weeps and smells of blood;
Says Life's a dull game played with smudged old cards;
And Death's humiliation, no one's gain;
Envies those lunatics who dare be sane
In handcuffs, elbowed on by bored young guards.

Older, with steel of need and flint of fear,
Strikes God ablaze again through the bare sky;
Drugs with a sleepy Faith Life's apathy;
Makes hope his soul and Death a doorway near;
Pats Law and Order on their snarling crest,
And lives a meek Assenter with the rest!

The meek assenter who slipped away to Canada at his mother's command, leaving his life behind, was my saviour. Librarians like Ivor made fortresses of books, where taste and scholarship survived and could be obtained free of charge. For those born into bookless homes, but awoken by chance to literature, the public library was a refuge, a place where you could come to terms with your isolation. It was made so by people like Ivor.

I recently had cause to remember him. I had been looking for Wagner's writings from Paris – a collection of wonderful essays and stories, the kind of book that every library should possess, if only to offer a true record of our culture. At last I obtained the book from a dealer's catalogue. On the title page, at the very place where George Ivor Deas would have copied out his name, is a red stamp: 'Discarded by the Hackney Library Services'.

2
How I Discovered my Name

An important part of every writer's task is to use proper names judiciously. Shakespeare's names – Ophelia, Prospero, Caliban, Portia, Bottom, Titania, Malvolio – summon character and plot, and also seem to light up regions of the human psyche, so that we can say, knowing what we mean and without other words to express it, 'I am not Prince Hamlet, nor was meant to be'. And what poem makes greater use of a name than the one from which I have just quoted? 'The Lovesong of J. Alfred Prufrock': all the existential hesitation of the protagonist is foreshadowed in the title, which illustrates the deep-down impossibility of anyone called J. Alfred Prufrock uttering a plausible love song. Christopher Ricks shows this with characteristic élan in *T. S. Eliot and Prejudice*: '"I'm in love." "Who's the lucky man?" "J. Alfred Prufrock" – impossible.'

Shakespeare's genius is revealed not only in his choice of names, but in his ability to take the names prescribed by his sources, and make them become the characters who wear them: Antony and Cleopatra, for example, both so swelled with erotic recklessness by Shakespeare that it is not surprising that Dryden called his version of the story *All for Love*, and allowed the names to creep in later. With what fine sense of drama does the poet display the dying Antony through his name, while Cleopatra is eclipsed by a title:

Ant. Peace!
Not Caesar's valour hath o'erthrown Antony,
But Antony's hath triumph'd on itself.
Cleo. So it should be, that none but Antony

Should conquer Antony, but woe 'tis so!
Ant. I am dying, Egypt, dying . . .

When treating of erotic love Shakespeare makes play with the very act of naming, reminding us that the arbitrariness of names stems from the attempt to record what is not arbitrary at all but unique and therefore inexpressible. Juliet, having learned that Romeo bears the hated name of Montague, attempts to separate him in thought from his name:

What's in a name? That which we call a Rose,
By any other word would smell as sweete,
So *Romeo* would, were he not *Romeo* call'd,
Retaine that dear perfection which he owes
Without that title. *Romeo*, doffe thy name,
And for thy name which is no part of thee,
Take all my selfe.

As the tragedy shows, it is precisely this that Romeo cannot do. To doff his name is to doff his destiny as the child of his parents and the heir to their burden of revenge. As the two lovers are entangled in the web of disaster, their names gather the resonance of their passion, and that which they at first strive to doff is at last engraved in marble on their common tomb. Thus, before the end of the scene Juliet is already saying:

Bondage is hoarse, and may not speake aloud,
Else would I teare the Cave where Echo lies,
And make her airie tongue more hoarse than myne,
With repetition of my *Romeo*.

Romeo's rejection of the claims of Rosaline is expressed in his forgetting her name, and when Romeo later rages against his name –

O tell me, friar, tell me
In what vile part of this Anatomie
Doth my name lodge? Tell me that I may sack
The hateful mansion

III,iii

– his words show the futility of his effort to excise this thing, which is the focal point of Juliet's passion. 'In the name,' wrote

Hegel, 'the individual as pure individual is "weighed", not only in "his" consciousness, but in the consciousness of all.' (*Phenomenology of Spirit*)

Shakespeare's plays are works of philosophy – philosophy not argued but shown. Other writers, less concerned with the finer points of metaphysics, have nevertheless busied themselves with the impossible task of presenting an individual essence in a name. Dickens is a master of this, so too is Henry James. In Dickens the effect is mostly comic: in James it is often turned to tragic purpose, as when American innocence, encapsulated in a bright-eyed, honest name like Milly Theale or Daisy Miller, is turned inwards and destroyed by old-world moral artifice. A writer's heraldic talent may be revealed in plain syllables – Tom Jones, Moll Flanders – or in a label that invites social and linguistic diagnosis: Rougon-Macquart, Buddenbrooks or Proust's tantalizing Charlus, revealed after many hundreds of pages to be only the least and most obscure of the Baron's titles. A name acquired by marriage is particularly significant, since it resounds with the choice that introduced it. Flaubert begins his great novel in the first person plural, placing Charles Bovary both inside the mind and outside the story, observed like a curious insect under the microscope, so that his surname fills with honest clumsiness and well-meant social failure. And then suddenly the writer withdraws, the 'we' evaporates, and this yoke is clamped around the neck of Emma.

Writers are connoisseurs of names. They jot them down from noticeboards and newspapers, from small ads and telephone directories. And to each they try to affix an image or a story; the name in the phonebook is a glimpse through curtains of a private space as yet unentered by the narrator. But what about the writer's own name? A *nom de plume* is a mask, like Stendhal, and it is chosen as a *writer's* name, the name of that all-seeing eye on the edge of things, the consciousness that observes but is no part of the action. To live with such a name is not to gain a personality but to renounce it, to become the narrator of a supreme fiction, and so to fictionalize oneself. The *nom de plume* conceals the other name, the unchosen patronymic in which lives the real human essence – the Henri Beyle or Eric Blair who is not Prince Hamlet nor was meant to be.

Even without the device of a *nom de plume*, there is room for the literary imagination. You can address your readers from the formal posture of a surname, or you can offer a glimpse of your intimate self, the self that is known to those who truly live with it. Suppose T. S. Eliot had written Tom Eliot on his title pages – like Thom Gunn or Ted Hughes. Would his poetry still retain the hieratic, suffering detachment that is so important to its sense? Or suppose, conversely, that *Ariel* had been the work of one S. Plath. How then could we take seriously the knife-like accusations, the sense of intimacy as horrible as the hands of the Inca priest seizing the heart of a living victim?

Daddy, I have had to kill you ...

Not, surely, the words of S. Plath, but a cry from the depths of Sylvia. Who is Sylvia, what is she, That all our swains commend/condemn her? The answer is there on the page.

Spelling, too, matters. Thom Gunn is decidedly not Tom Gunn. The inaudible 'h' suggests a softness, a sensibility, to which only those who relish the written word are fully attuned. 'H' is for 'homosexual': it reveals to the eye, while hiding from the ear, the flesh beneath the biker's jacket.

Initials used by a woman writer are like the George Eliot of our greatest philosophical novelist – a masculine disguise, calculated both to exploit and to challenge the supposed ascendancy of men. (I say 'supposed', but of course if enough people suppose that it is so, then it is so.) And if such a writer reveals in every line and every word that she is first of all a woman, and only by default and in unguarded moments a dispassionate narrator (dispassionate narrators being mostly of the masculine gender, if not of the male sex), the result is unsettling and even incongruous. It was a relief to discover that A. L. Kennedy is called Alison. If someone asked me who wrote *So I am Glad*, I would now without thinking say Alison Kennedy, the very same Alison Kennedy who wrote *On Bullfighting*. But no such writer appears in the library catalogues.

The use of initials is to some extent a matter of fashion. Maybe it is no accident that T. S. Eliot, W. H. Auden, W. B. Yeats and D. H. Lawrence were of the same period and the same cultural milieu, or that they all made such an impression on F. R. Leavis who, with his wife Q. D., felt called upon to judge them. But that is not the whole story. In an age of first names initials remain a useful tool: they suggest coolness and objectivity. Novelists who see through their characters, as A. N. Wilson does, are well advised to keep their first names to themselves; a poet like C. H. Sisson, for whom the human world is only a point of departure for the empty courtroom where God once sat in judgement, ought to be wary of letting us call him Charles. And, while on the subject of religious poetry, how wrong it would be to call Gerard Manley Hopkins G. M. – for here is a poet whose religion consists in letting his heart flow out, rather than in fastidiously withdrawing it.

But what about the names themselves – not first names only, but surnames too? For those addicted to words, the surnames of writers take on the sense of their writings. Wittgenstein, for me, has the sound of a frozen mountaineer, poised on the apex of an argument and remaining there, aloof, uncomforted and alone. Dickens – whose name is proverbial in English – has the sound of an old-fashioned haberdashery: an accumulation of oddments, some still useful, others left behind by fashion or piled in a heap of unvisited history, like the objects in Mrs Jellaby's cupboard. Lawrence roars like a lion, and yawns like one too; while Melville is not the noise of Captain Ahab stomping his wooden peg on the deck above, but the melancholy sound of a quiet harbour, where the sheets smack in the breeze and a clerk sucks his pen at a counting desk above the quay.

As for the first names of writers, they matter in another way: for they are the private aspect of a name that has chosen to go public. Acquiring the right surname is hard; but at least people don't blame you for it. Acquiring the right first name is easier, since your parents often give you a choice, and there are nicknames galore to replace them. But for this very reason you stand accused of your first name. It is your fault that you are Agatha, Gramophone or Quin.

Names have fatally affected my literary career. My mother was born and bred in the genteel suburbs of London, cherishing an ideal of gentlemanly conduct and social distinction that my father set out with considerable relish to destroy. She saw in me her great hope of rescue from the Lawrentian wildness of Jack Scruton, and of a return to the quiet tea-parties and box-lined gardens of Upper Norwood. She therefore decided that I should be called Vernon, after a distant cousin who looked sweet and poetic in photographs, but whose greatest merit was that he had emigrated to Canada before he could reveal how few real merits he had.

My father, who perhaps saw in this name a fitting revenge for my existence, acquiesced in his wife's desire. However, a residual tenderness towards his son reminded him of the misery that would be faced by a boy with a cissy name, if he could not fight his way to another one. He therefore insisted also on Roger, after Sir Roger de Buslingthorpe, who lay in effigy in the church next to the farm where I was born. Furthermore it was mercifully agreed between my parents that, while I was to be called Vernon by all my relations, Roger would be the first name on my birth certificate and, as it were, the official title that I would one day win through my deeds.

I was a timid child, who keenly felt the double injury of red hair and a cissy name. The critical moment came aged ten, during last year at primary school. A large boy called Herman, whose misfortune was also contained in a name, and who therefore became the school bully by way of compelling us to respect him, kicked me as I sat down for morning assembly, launching into a diatribe against red hair with every word of which I fully concurred. I gave him to understand that, had it been possible to vote for the abolition of red hair, I would have been first to raise my hand. To my dismay, however, Herman was not satisfied with this general apology for my condition, and indicated that I must meet him in the playground during break, so that my head could be bashed in and the problem of red hair solved for good and all.

'There's no helping it,' said my friend Brian (the only one in the playground who was more timid than I). 'He's after you. If not today then tomorrow. Best to get it over with.' News of the impending fight spread rapidly through the school and at the appointed hour the spectators gathered into a ring. Brian pushed me forward and my antagonist strode out from the crowd with flaring nostrils, fists up and big lips parted in a sneer. I closed my eyes, shielded my face with my left hand, and stretched my right arm out to protect myself. Herman came forward at a run, with blood-curdling shrieks and flailing arms. I stood rooted to the spot, the sounds of Herman's war-dance filling my ears, my outstretched fist trembling in the air before me. After what seemed like an age, there was a staggering blow to my knuckles. I opened my eyes to discover Herman recoiling backwards, lips split open and blood pouring over his chin. With a howl of dismay he pirouetted through the crowd, and fled to the headmaster's office to report my crime.

It seemed unjust at the time that I should be caned and Herman comforted. But it added to a reputation that had already spread through the school as quickly as the newest cigarette card, and I resolved at once to exploit my eminence as the conqueror of Herman. I went from gang to gang in the playground, escorted by Brian (now promoted to first lieutenant), and informing my respectful listeners that henceforth I was not Vernon but Roger, that all uses of my former name, which had been no more than a disguise adopted for secret service reasons, would be as severely punished as remarks about red hair. Obedience was immediate and universal, and henceforth I was Roger to everyone, including my family, who were told that the choice was simple: either they ceased to call me Vernon, or I went to live with the gypsies.

Inside, however, just behind the egg-shell armour of Roger's belligerence, Vernon peered out at the world. His name had been excised from the public record – even his initial was no longer used – and his perfunctory funeral had been announced and completed. But he remained, a quiet, timorous creature who still suffered from the fact of having red hair. Roger went to the local grammar school keen to prove his reality, and promptly made a reputation for himself as a rebel, with a talent for home-made bombs. But with the onset of puberty, and the discovery of books, Vernon saw his chance. He was not allowed to use his name, of course, since that would have undermined five years of patient labour. But he was allowed to whisper his literary ambitions, since Roger had fallen into the trap of sharing them. We looked around for precedents, and could find no Roger among the novelists and poets. Indeed the only Roger in the whole of literature seemed to be Sir Roger de Coverley, the ineffectual squire of Addison and Steele. Nor did we at first find any Vernons.

Then one day an anthology of modern verse came into our hands. There, right up among the gods, next to Ezra Pound and T. S. Eliot, was someone called Vernon Scannell. We were not to know that this Vernon had begun life as a professional boxer, no doubt in an attempt to erase the stigma of his name. All that we understood was the irrebuttable proof that writers could be called

Vernon. Even if he published under the name Roger Scruton, therefore, it was agreed that Vernon would be the real author of our words. Everything that I have written that has come from the heart rather than the head has been the work of someone officially dead aged ten.

Not that the relation between Roger and Vernon has been an antagonistic one. Labouring under shared disadvantages, and joined inseparably by fate, they have had to get on. Vernon, they knew, was an impossible name, like St Evremond or J. Alfred Prufrock. They knew too that no writer could make a convincing show of Roger, and despite these facts they were determined to be a writer.

To those difficulties must be added the even more crushing disadvantage of their surname. There are surnames designed for a literary career: Wordsworth, for example, Metastasio or Hölderlin. But most writers have to make do with the same accidental surnames as the rest of us. These, roughly speaking, are of two kinds: names that denote a trade; and names that denote a place. The first can generally be relied upon, since the natural flow of human life has made them smooth with use and versatile. Smith, Baker, Thatcher, Porter: all such names trip off the tongue, their menial meaning forgotten, eagerly presenting themselves for more interesting work. Place names are more tricky. If too well known – like Liverpool, Somerset or Shrewsbury – they sound like aristocratic titles. If too rustic – like Lobthorpe, Ordsall or Dowdeswell – they suggest characters out of Thomas Hardy, or the *nom de plume* of someone who would like to have been Hardy but lacks his talent.

Many French place names owe their magical and euphonious character to the fact that they are the linguistic relics of Latin saints. Thus the steady flow of piety and dialect has turned Sanctus Sidonius into Saint-Saëns, itself the ideal name for a conservative composer. From the earthy St Gengoux to the seraphic St Exupéry, whose remains now lie in ocean's depths, these names express the archaeological reality of a nation rooted in a place, a faith and a tongue.

Our place names are equally historic, but fatally distorted by their heathen roots. One such name is Scruton – Scrofa's Tun – named from a Viking chieftain whose distinguishing feature was not red hair but dandruff. The sound can be rectified by no efforts of elocution. In whatever tone of voice Scruton sounds mean and censorious. Scourge, Scrooge, Scrotum and Scrutiny all tumble like black scarabs from the mouth that utters it. I am convinced that the hostile reception encountered by even my most forgiving works has been due, not to the conservative voice that speaks through them (which is Vernon's voice, not Roger's), but to the scraping steel of this scalpel-like surname. I was not surprised to find Sue Townsend using it for her nasty headmaster in the Adrian Mole stories. And I am sure that its subliminal effect is one cause of the enormous surprise that people feel, on meeting me, to discover that I am approximately human.

Maybe I should have adopted a *nom de plume* like Stendhal, or even let it be known that Scruton *is* a *nom de plume*, the deliberately forbidding mask adopted by a mild-mannered humanist who regrets the words that truth compels from him. For good or ill, however, I stuck with my family name, took comfort from the fact that others had learned to live with it – the photographer Roger Scruton, for example – and reminded myself that it had the merit, like Dracula, Heliogabalus and Rasputin, of being unforgettable.

This problematic surname, which I could by then neither discard nor amend, was much on my mind during the eighties, when my writings were routinely greeted with anger or ridicule. One summer day I stepped from an aeroplane in Adelaide, where I was due to give a lecture to a small gathering of local conservatives. I was depressed by the reception of my latest book, *Sexual Desire*, and depressed too that I had had to fly all the way to Australia to find an audience. It was quite clear to me that I had made a mistake in pursuing Vernon's literary ambition, while choosing Roger's method of advancing it.

The first thing I saw on emerging into the Arrivals Hall was a placard on which SCRUTON had been written in bold gothic letters. I had to fight the urge to apologize for this name, which had begun to sound in my ears like the growls of a bogeyman. To my surprise, however, a middle-aged man emerged from behind the placard and apologized for nobbling me. He wore blue plastic sandals, khaki shorts and a hideous orange shirt, above the open collar of which his leathery neck stretched and gobbled impatiently. On top was a large Anglo-Saxon head, precariously balanced, in which the pink-veined blueish eyes stared fixedly like headlights.

'Mr Scruton,' he cried as he shook my hand. 'Welcome to Adelaide. I just had to come to meet you. I am a Scruton aficionado, a Scruton fanatic. I collect everything to do with Scruton – everything!'

Taken aback, I stuttered out my gratitude. Maybe Scruton wasn't such a hideous name after all. Maybe it was the kind of name a writer could justify, a name with a genuine appeal for a narrow range of discriminating readers. Maybe Scruton would earn its place in the cannon along with other names beginning in 'Sc', for example ... well, for example, Scannell. I shook the proffered hand warmly and asked him which of my books he enjoyed.

'See here,' he said, ignoring me, 'I brought you the Scruton catalogue. I've got another copy. This one's yours.'

He reached into a grubby satchel that swung from his left arm, took out a large green folio and thrust it towards me with a comradely smile. On the woven paper cover was written:

> ***The Scruton Estate***
> *between*
> *Northallerton and Bedale*
> *and close to*
> *Leeming Bar*

Inside, it announced that by order of the Executors of Mrs M. E. J. A. Coore, deceased, the Scruton Estate, comprising Scruton Hall, five farms, innumerable cottages, smallholdings, woodland, and 1,111 acres – in short, the whole village of Scruton – was to be auctioned in 38 lots at the Golden Lion Hotel, Northallerton, on Wednesday 15 July 1953. There was a photograph of the magnificent Queen Anne Hall, and an emotionless Pevsner-like description of its state-rooms and corridors, patrolled only by ghosts, some of them perhaps my ancestors, and one, Mrs Coore, the bearer of four inscrutable initials. Each cottage and farm and field was described in the same archaeological tone: it was as though the Germans had won the war, and a dutiful officer were sending an inventory to his distant commander-in-chief. To an Englishman attuned to recent history it was a funeral oration, a lament in auctioneer's jargon for our destroyed spiritual home.

We stood in the searing light of the Arrivals Hall, my official hosts now striding towards me with relieved and eager gestures. I turned the pages of the auctioneer's text while my companion gave a running commentary. He had many photographs of the village as it was, of the cottages and farms, of people who had lived there. He had collected memorabilia: maps, church guide-books, local histories. The hall had been bought by an American and taken brick by brick to Virginia. But my companion had rescued some of it – two bricks and a door handle. Yes, he had been there, before the village had been torn down, purchased some bits and pieces from one of the cottages. Nothing amazing, only a few mugs and plates and an old picture. Also the bricks left lying where the Hall had stood. He had letters written to his own great-great-grandfather from the people back home, describing life in the village. Yes, he could claim a distant connection. In so far as he came from anywhere – and the point of Australia is that you come from nowhere – he was a Scrutonian.

'But of course,' he added, 'that's not what makes you an addict. As you know.'

I didn't know.

'You mean that it was a kind of symbol of the old country – England as it was – until the modern world caught up with it?'

'Naaa!' he said. 'Villages like that are two a penny. It's the *name* – your name.'

The official welcome party now surrounded me, and it turned out that my companion was a part of it. As we left the airport he walked with us in silence, sometimes smiling at me, as though to remind me of a shared and secret passion.

Returning to England I decided to investigate my right to the Scruton name. I discovered that my grandfather was described on his birth certificate as Lowe, which was his mother's unmarried name. She had called her illegitimate child Scruton for reasons that she never imparted, being permanently drunk by the time anyone thought to inquire of her. I made up a story that would connect me to that precious document in which an English village – my village – was offered for sale. My grandfather, I put it out, had been conceived in Scruton when my great-grandmother had been in service there. She had drifted to Manchester, pregnant and rejected, in search of support.

This story gave me the kudos of bastardy, the glamour of poverty and a wonderfully succinct family tree. And I discovered another curious fact. The journalist George Gale, who as a young man had looked just like me, with the same crowning disability of bright red hair, revealed that the squires of Scruton Hall, before Mrs M. E. J. A. Coore acquired the right to it, were the Gales, his ancestors: good-for-nothing drunks and womanizers, whose features were replicated all over the Yorkshire dales.

Often, when appalled by the sound of Scruton and tempted by Lowe, I pick up the green auctioneer's catalogue and turn the pages. And there I read the name Scruton, attached not to a person but to a house, a village and a farm, to cottages and fields and woodlands, to those ancient demesnes where Scrofa shook out his dandruff, and where his descendants ploughed the fields. Scruton becomes united in my imagination to the real, historical England; it seems right then to call myself Scruton, and to be re-possessed by my name.

And suppose that I am really Lowe, or rather, to resurrect what I assume to be the original spelling, Löwe. What better *nom de plume* for a writer of German-Jewish ancestry, whose theme is England, than the name of an old Yorkshire village that has now been razed to the ground?

3
How I Discovered Culture

I grew to immaturity in the sixties, when disorder was the order of the day. Like most of my generation, I was a rebel – but a meta-rebel, so to speak, in rebellion against rebellion, who devoted to shoring up ruins the same passionate conviction that my contemporaries employed in creating them. How this happened is a mystery. I have gained nothing whatsoever from my anti-antinomian stance, and discarded my socialist conscience only to discover that a socialist conscience was the one thing required for success in the only spheres where I could aspire to it. When I revisit the overgrown path of my adolescence, I am puzzled by those signposts that I so gravely mistook, those invitations I read as warnings, and those desolate tombstones I took for shrines. Only in one particular did I conform to what was then expected, and this was in behaving gratuitously as a swine.

The secret pact between Roger and Vernon did not mitigate or interrupt this swinishness. Roger was the visible occupant of the citadel and Vernon an invisible anchorite, walled up somewhere in the crypt, responding with a fastidious shrug to the rumours of his twin's atrocities. Roger had the usual ready-made excuse. He was a victim of oppression, a prisoner struggling to be free. But the one thing he hated most was worn excuses. Besides, his rebellion was from the first a kind of paradox. He was searching the world for that impossible thing: an original path to conformity.

The desire for this impossible thing was implanted by my father. We had moved to Marlow, I had entered the sixth form, had become immersed in books and friends and music, had begun to behave as though a world of opportunities lay before me – opportunities that Jack Scruton, although a man of great energy and intellect, had never enjoyed. Often we would take the same bus home from school – I from the school that gave me all that I wanted, he from a school that gave him nothing at all. Relations were strained, and we never sat together. However, it seemed right to tell him, when I met him at the bus stop one day, that I had gained a place at Cambridge; he looked at me in silence, and then walked away. He came home late that night, surly, taciturn and drunk. For months he found it impossible to speak to me, except in angry monosyllables. I was forcing him to re-live his great misfortune, which was that of being taken from school at the age of 14 by a violent and illiterate father, to be compelled to work at menial jobs in the fruit market, until able to save himself through the RAF.

It seemed to me, as a result of my father's implicit condemnation, that I could be myself only at school, by acting out the part of Roger. And I was fortunate in that the school had been installed in our town like some regal signpost, pointing away from the suburbs to the glowing city on the hill. High Wycombe Royal Grammar School was contained in a neo-Georgian building of brick, dating from the 1920s. It stood on the crown of Amersham Hill, fronted by a stretch of green lawn and surmounted by a white clock tower that imparted to the façade a vaguely nautical appearance. The classrooms had tall sash windows, sturdy old-fashioned desks of beechwood, in which many generations of schoolboys had scratched their names, and panelled doors with brass handles. The masters wore gowns and the Head, Mr Tucker, would take Assembly in a mortarboard, the tassel of which dangled next to his glasses like a twirling spider on its thread.

Mr Tucker was ambitious for the school, and had consciously re-designed it on the model of Eton. There were rival 'houses', with boarders under the jurisdiction of Housemasters. We had 'rugger' rather than football; there was a cricket pavilion and fives courts and all the military apparatus associated with a flourishing cadet corps. Discipline was strict, with a spartan regime for the boarders and corporal punishment administered fairly (that is to say, liberally) throughout the school. Improving forms of torture were offered by the school chaplain, the boarding-house Matron, the Deputy Head and other ingenious specialists. We did not go as far as Eton in the way of uniforms, but any boy seen wearing the school blazer out of school without the cap was liable to be punished.

I approved of such things in general and rebelled against them in particular – that is to say, in the particular case of Roger. I esteemed my school as a futile prolongation of the war-time ethos, and was deeply attached to my physics master, Mr Chapman, an old colonial whom I have described elsewhere and who implanted in me the sublime and unbelievable vision that was England, while also providing my first *impressions d'Afrique*.[1] This inner endorsement of my surroundings provoked, however, the swinish desire to disrupt them. I was an accomplished fouler of the nest, and used my knowledge of chemistry to blow up small but significant parts of the school facilities with chlorate bombs and nitrogen tri-iodide. I refused categorically to attend the cadets or to take part in organized sport, and treated my lessons as unnecessary, now that I had gained a place at Cambridge. Mr Tucker insisted that I stay on at school, since he wanted me to try for a scholarship, and, besides, I was far too young to be anywhere else. But this seemed to me like a licence to misbehave and I treated it accordingly.

It was important, however, to misbehave in an interesting way: not merely to skive off sports and cadets, but to do so while ostentatiously playing the piano in the hall. I was helped in this ambition by a remarkable boy who was also, like me, waiting around to take the scholarship exam, he having gained admission to Cambridge when only 15. Dave was an instinctive musician, who had passed all the available piano examinations by the time he was 14, and could even play the Bartók Sonata. On Thursday afternoons, when the rest of the school paraded in their uniforms, we shook the hall with the four-hand version of *The Rite of Spring*, he playing impeccably, I rejoicing in the fact that wrong notes scarcely mattered. Dave had taken English and German at A-level, had acquired a Leavisite censoriousness in all matters to do with culture, and constantly surprised me with his views. His father was manager of a paper mill, and he had been brought up

1 See *England: An Elegy*, London, 2000, Chapter 2

as a quiet conformist, who was to all outward appearances a law-abiding and meticulously respectable Christian. He was an only child but discouraged, nevertheless, from bringing his uncouth friends to the smart house in which he lived with his snobbish parents and where – if truth were known – he would have liked to smash everything save the piano. Like Nietzsche, he hid behind his meek exterior a seething rebellious heart, an excoriating sarcasm towards all established things, and a nihilistic view of the world according to which nothing meant anything save art. Dave encouraged my misdemeanours and took a kind of vicarious delight in them. He himself, however, stayed out of trouble, and none of the masters guessed that he longed for nothing in this world save destruction – a destruction that he wrought at last upon himself.

Like many Englishmen of my generation, I had entered grammar school with the sense that I was taking my first step toward a scientific career. Neither I nor my parents had had a clear notion of what this involved, but it had been established in our minds that the future, and therefore the money, lay with science. This had partly reconciled my father to the inevitable outcome of my schooling, which was that I would rise above my station. Accordingly, I had found myself specializing in science subjects from the age of eleven, with only Latin and English Literature to nurture the soul. Of course, Roger thrived on science, which provided the tools for his belligerence. But Vernon was waiting his chance.

All had gone reasonably smoothly until I discovered books, and Vernon began to peep from beneath his coffin lid. I became obsessed with the idea of a knowledge beyond science, beyond calculation, beyond our attempts to gain mastery over the future. Practicalities and plans were an offence to the aesthetico-ascetic worldview, and the very concept of the future had no place in the other knowledge that lurked in the heart of books. Yet this knowledge justified every effort on the part of the one who pursued it, as Rilke had pursued it through the written word, and Rodin through those sacred but sensual forms that illustrated the book of Rilke's letters in Ivor Deas's bookcase.

The real me, I decided, existed in those hours when literature and philosophy passed through my hands uncomprehended. And because I understood nothing, every word was invested with enormous power – a power of destiny, as though my life now ran in channels marked out for it by visionaries who had 'foreseen and foresuffered all'. An air of holiness, a reckless disregard for the world and its requirements seemed to radiate from those mysterious pages. They referred me to a place where justification was no longer needed and where it was sufficient just to be.

At the same time, a sadness grew in me, a sense that something was wrong with the world. Science, progress and money had prevented people from observing this thing; I too had been blind to its existence, so lost had I been in the world's concerns. But my feeling testified to its reality. Sadness looked out at me from art and literature, like the pitying face of a painted saint. I encountered it in the words of Rilke, I saw it in the mad paintings of Van Gogh, and I heard it, via Mr Chapman's gramophone, in the infinite, still spaces of Beethoven's last quartets – spaces made through sound, in which, however, there reigns a greater silence than can be heard in any desert.

This sadness made no difference to Roger's rebellious demeanour. But Vernon nurtured it. Vernon, in fact, was longing to come to the window of Roger's body and timidly venture a wave. It was Dave who first responded. Roger, Dave discovered, was an artificial being, a Frankenstein's monster invented in the same laboratory as the nitrogen tri-iodide that he sprinkled about the school. True, I confessed. And I went on to reveal that Roger's real inventor was devoted, ridiculous though it may seem, to things of the spirit. Vernon longed for nothing more than a life among books and art and music. Dave's response was to look at me intently through his thick spectacles and command me, in his breaking treble voice, not to read Spengler's *The Decline of the West*. As long as I kept away from that book, I might still be saved. But if I so much as touched it, he warned, I was doomed forever.

I went straight to the public library and found the volume. (Dave, I discovered later, had his own tattered copy, which he pored over nightly.) The title alone was intoxicating. Indeed, for several days I did not advance very far beyond it. Those five words told me that the sense of decline that troubled me was no personal foible but the sign of a cosmic tragedy that was playing itself out in me. It linked my own paltry emotions to the destiny of civilization itself. I had been caught up in a drama of untold proportions and, just as the heart of the worshipper leaps to discover God's personal interest in him; just as the psychoanalytic patient feels a renewed will to live on learning that his petty suffering conforms to some universal archetype; so did I become happy in my mournful emotions, knowing that it was not I, but culture itself, that was alive in them, and also dying there. I became more fully wedded to despair, in the very act of discovering that the despair was not mine. And when, a few days later, Dave forbad me to read another of his favourite books – Erich Heller's *Disinherited Mind* – I was able to add a second sloganizing title to the one that had first impressed me. I felt that I possessed, at last, the secret of my *Weltschmerz*. I was disinherited, like all my generation, from – from what? I had no name for this legacy, from which I was now cut off, save 'culture'.

Culture was the awareness beyond science, which had been intimated in my first encounter with books. I thought of it as a kind of self-sufficient knowledge, not tainted like science by the separation of the knower from the known. It lives in us, and us in it; and what is living must also die. Its concern is not being but becoming; not mechanism, cause and experiment, but life, history and destiny. Those ideas came to me by a kind of osmosis from Spengler, who also told me that I had already been initiated into culture, since it was this that had made me sad. My experience of art came to me with a sense of loss, a knowledge that I was among the last to whom it would be offered, and that, with the passing of my generation, the light of civilization would be extinguished forever and all meaning gone from the world. Unlike the cheerful scientific view of things that I learned in my formal classes – the view of a constantly accumulating store of knowledge, whose application would ensure the mental and physical progress of mankind – the image that I acquired from Spengler was of an inheritance more easily lost than won, and never more easily than through the heedless pursuit of objective knowledge.

> *'One day the last portrait of Rembrandt and the last bar of Mozart will have ceased to be – though possibly a coloured canvas and a sheet of notes may remain – because the last eye and the last ear accessible to their message will have gone.'*

When I first came across those words, I knew so little about Western culture (although the thesis of its decline was already an immovable part of my mental equipment) that I could hardly be said to have believed them. Nevertheless, I greeted them as a revelation. Like Pound, whose poems I was reading at the time, I was a 'barbarian let loose in a library', who took from what he read just so much as was necessary to satisfy his own emotions.

From Spengler I took two further things, besides the view of culture to which I have alluded. First, the cyclical theory of history, and second, the idea that such a theory could not be established by scientific argument. This second idea, far from being a refutation of Spengler's theory, struck me as a refutation of science: a proof that the real truths, those we understand and accept in the life-process itself, are inaccessible to scientific method. How impressive, indeed, was the opening chapter of *The Decline of the West*, in which mathematics is thrown from its pedestal. The theory that had been offered to me as a paradigm of objective certainty and the heart of scientific knowledge was placed beside the 'Magian' mathematics of Arabia and the 'Apollinian' mathematics of Euclid. It was shown (by reasoning that only later did I see to be entirely fraudulent) to be of no greater and no lesser validity than they, and to derive its value not from its status as objective science but from its ability to give form and expression to the Faustian spirit that lives and thrives in all the great creations of our culture, and whose death-pangs had been foretold in me. Spengler offered not a science of history but a philosophy – and the philosophy of history, he claimed, was the only possible philosophy for our times. Accordingly, when I went at last to university, I changed the direction of my studies from natural science (the price of my admission) to philosophy – a subject that, I supposed, counted Nietzsche and Spengler among its greatest masters.

The university I attended was Cambridge, and the philosophy I studied was that bequeathed by Russell, Wittgenstein and Moore. I was taught that neither Spengler nor Nietzsche was a philosopher in anything but a metaphorical sense; that both had an extremely weak grasp of the logical principles my lecturers were impressing on me; and that in neither thinker's theories was truth accorded a position comparable to that occupied by empty rhetoric. I resisted such conclusions, of course, but with a dwindling self-confidence and a sense of defeat. Little by little, thanks in part to my own scientific training, whose preconceptions were now fortified by the truths of logical analysis (truths that are denied only by those who do not understand them), I gave in to analytical philosophy; and when, at the end of my first year of studies, I returned to the book that had first set me on their path, I found in it nothing more than megalomaniac fantasies, implausible analogies and false distinctions founded neither in logic nor in fact.

However, the new philosophy I studied proved no more satisfactory to me than the science it had replaced. Still, it seemed to me, there was another and more important way of seeing things, a view onto the world for which the word 'culture' remained the most appropriate description. And still there was contained, in this other perspective, an experience of human value, together with the painful recognition of its mortality. I was never a progressive, nor was I to acquire that cheerful 'clairantism' (as J. L. Austin called it) of the positivists and their successors: the belief that the mystery of things is our own creation, and that it wants only the effort of removing it for science to deliver the full and final truth about our condition. And if I have retained those traces of an *Urverdunkelung*, of an obstinate resistance to enlightenment and a belief in the necessity of culture and in the fact of its decline, it is as much the work of Spengler as of any of the more powerful thinkers who replaced him in my pantheon.

Looking back on *The Decline of the West*, I find one of the strangest creations of the human spirit, monstrous as a Grünewald crucifixion, equally full of exaggerated feeling and a strange, exalted beauty. History is there, but reshaped in the telling of it, moulded into artistic forms and painted over with a passionate chiaroscuro. Art is there too: the prime object of Spengler's reflections and the guiding principle of his argument, which moves with the urgency of poetry and in a style that speaks straight to the heart. Nothing is mentioned that is not touched with the writer's feeling, gathered into the *Sturm und Drang* of an inner drama. The writing is compelling because it is compelled, governed from first to last by a force of emotional necessity. To gain an objective view of such a work is difficult, perhaps impossible. For to what category does it belong? Should we read it as historiography, as philosophy, as poetry, or as prophecy? In fact, Spengler answers a profound need of our culture: the need to bring philosophy, historiography, and art together in a form of speculation that will synthesize their insights and justify the title 'humane'.

Spengler was not, I am happy to say, the only influence during those years at the Royal Grammar School. Dave introduced me to a sixth-form discussion group, through which I became acquainted with the A-level syllabus in English, French and Latin, and fell under the spell of Mr Broadbridge, the Leavisite English master whom I never met, but whose pupils were trained to relay his exhilarating messages. The greatest poet of the twentieth century, T.S. Eliot, had briefly taught English at the RGS, and the prayerful melancholy of *The Waste Land* still seemed to drift about the corridors. Dave took the severe view that all English literature apart from the King James Bible and a couple of Shakespeare plays was rubbish, and that only German literature was relevant to the times in which we lived. But I had another and closer friend, Tom, who was studying Greek and Latin, and who would pour out his romantic heart to me as we sat upstairs in the damp Victorian slum where he lived with his parents. Tom's heroes were Bartók and Yeats and when, on leaving school, we hitch-hiked to Greece together, he taught me to love the ancient Greeks and their civilization as the German Romantics had done, wandering from ruin to ruin crying: '*Schöne Welt, wo bist du?*' Tom wrote poetry and went one step further in the name game than Thom Gunn, signing himself Thomme. But he was not the least bit homosexual, and his feelings for me were both passionate and pure. For several years we corresponded, often in verse, building on the foundations of our adolescent love a wonderful castle of allusions and illusions, in which we could shut out the world and treasure our aloofness. I recall his face and his voice with gratitude, not least because it was through him that I discovered *Four Quartets*, a poem that he was later to dismiss as mere prose, but with which we were constantly wrestling during our last days at school together, since it was such a stunning rebuke to our boyishness. *Four Quartets* engaged immediately with a vestigial Anglican faith, and exerted a shaping influence on my thinking that has been matched only by Wittgenstein, Kant and Wagner, all of whom I was to encounter only later, at Cambridge.

Eliot also saved me from Spengler. *Four Quartets* told me that our culture contains the seeds of its own renewal, that it is a source of meaning and value and that, even at the eleventh hour, it can be received and passed on. And our school was a living illustration of that creed. The RGS had not been infected by the modern heresy that tells us that knowledge must be adapted to the interests of the child. On the contrary: our 'beaks' believed that the interests of the child should be adapted to knowledge. The purpose of the school was not to flatter the pupils but to rescue the curriculum, by pouring it into heads that might pass it on. Of course, you can impart knowledge only to those who are willing to receive it. But that means making a radical distinction – the distinction the egalitarians refuse to make – between those who *can* be taught and those who can't. Even the most rebellious among us shared the assumption on which our education was based, which is that there are real distinctions between knowledge and opinion, culture and philistinism, wit and stupidity, art and kitsch. We were consciously aiming to better ourselves, and even if some of us entertained eccentric views as to what self-improvement might consist in (Roger being particularly disgraceful in this respect), the real goal of education was constantly before our eyes and endorsed by all of us.

This attachment to traditional education did not mean that either we or our teachers were parochial. On the contrary, the writers who exerted the greatest influence on us were Joyce, Eliot and Pound, the first two steeped in the works of Dante, Baudelaire and Flaubert, the third in the Noh plays and the Confucian Odes. Nor did it mean that we were isolated from popular culture. Although Vernon's evenings were devoted to string quartets, Roger's involved rock, R&B and sexual intercourse, which began in 1961, two years before the date allotted by Philip Larkin, though with an unhappiness of which he would surely have approved. Our school contingent arrived in Cambridge in the shape of a pop group, with Dave as lead guitar, myself on piano and Pete, the rhythm guitarist, relaying to us the interesting innovations of a group he knew in Liverpool.

Dave continued to influence me during our undergraduate years. We had gained entry to this wondrous and unfriendly citadel by the same underground passage and faced the same dangers within. And just as I was split between the ambitious

Roger and the meek and retiring Vernon, so was Dave split between the careful conformist who was studying law and intended for a career in the city, and the dark, Faustian aesthete, who despised all worldly success and had sold his soul to the Devil. Dave became the symbol and enactment of my own self-discovery, and I watched in trepidation as he first expanded like a sick flower, then shed his petals.

He had a thin but expressive tenor voice and I would accompany him on the college piano as we worked our way through the Schubert Lieder. His boyish face, with its protruding upper teeth, its residual acne and balding temples, is forever associated in my memory with *Winterreise*, which he would sing as though holding back tears, afterwards curling over his pain and crying 'Fuck! Fuck! Fuck!' before marching in silence to his room, where he kept the whisky that was later to destroy him.

During our first year at Cambridge, when we discovered the blues, Muddy Waters, Ray Charles and Chuck Berry, Dave worked on his guitar at another and deeper level, exploring the twelve-string repertoire, and mastering the superimposed harmonies of the early blues musicians. From a physical point of view Dave had no beautiful attributes, save only his hands, which were articulate, sensitive and strong. He would bend over the guitar and watch those beautiful long fingers as they climbed from string to string and fret to fret like bare-limbed acrobats, coaxing pain, grief and mourning from the instrument, while his half-closed eyes looked down on them with a kind of forgiveness, and his voice sang to them in tones of farewell. It never ceased to amaze me that Dave, who despised popular culture, had nevertheless plunged into it and through it, and had discovered in doing so a source of feeling every bit as intense as the songs of Schubert.

Dave's own attitude to this, however, was revealing. 'Look,' he said to me when I questioned him, 'just about everything is phoney. Almost all blues is phoney. But not quite all. And when you hit gold, the seam runs deep. Finding that seam is hard. You have to work. That kind of work is criticism.'

Thus did Dave reinterpret the message that had been delivered to us at school. A discipline was available that would permit us to absorb the works of our culture, to discriminate between them and to venture safely into hitherto uncharted areas. This discipline was criticism, and it had been brought intensely home to Dave by Mr Broadbridge (who was my teacher only indirectly and only through Dave) that criticism is necessary if the culture is to be protected from decay. I never thereafter lost the sense that if you want to know the meaning of life – of your own life as well as of the lives around you – you should explore your cultural inheritance with a critical eye, so as to repossess the meaning that has been distilled in it. The temptation was not other cultures, whatever they might be, but corruption within our own culture – in particular the ubiquitous diseases of sentimentality and kitsch. My aesthetic ideal remained *Four Quartets*, a work imbued through and through with a religious melancholy, and which also achieved a purity of utterance that set it apart from all the ordinary pleasures of high art.

This attitude was by no means peculiar to me. On the contrary, it belonged to the air we breathed at Cambridge. Nor did we think of it as a political attitude, a way of taking sides in the trivial conflicts (as we saw them) that occupied Members of Parliament. Although our suspicion of kitsch came to us from the arch-conservative T. S. Eliot, we found it endorsed by the quasi-socialist F. R. Leavis, by the liberal Thomas Mann and, in due course, by the Marxists Theodor Adorno and Walter Benjamin. The effort to 'purify the dialect of the tribe' was one that could, and did, unite people of all political persuasions, and the study of culture was something higher and more meaningful than the adoption of any political creed. Culture, we believed, is a form of knowledge, while politics is mere opinion.

Hence, during those Cambridge years I was, although socially estranged (like virtually every grammar-school boy), spiritually at home. The spiritual home in which I existed was what Dave and I called culture, and culture rose around us and above us like a great cathedral, defining a place of judgement, discrimination and allusion, a place where everything connected and where everything was imbued with a significance that made its study worthwhile. It still seems to me that the best form of education in the humanities would be one in which students enter that cathedral, and enter it as we did, with a critical as well as a wondering eye.

But it is no accident that the image of a cathedral presents itself to me. This culture into which we were inducted was not just a by-product of Christianity. Although it rejoiced in its universal vision, its central manifestations derived from the Christian faith. Even the pagan writings of D. H. Lawrence depend for their penetration on a language rooted in the Book of Common Prayer and in the imagery of the Psalms and the Gospels. *Four Quartets* owed its immense power over people of my generation to its ability to summon the ghost of a Christian belief that had all but died in us, but which was seeking to breathe again.

We were, I think, aware of this intimate dependence of our culture on the Christian faith, and our heroes – Eliot, Stravinsky, Messiaen, Matisse – were Christians. But we were also convinced that our culture could be studied, enjoyed and internalized by unbelievers – could become, for them as much as for the committed Christian, a source of meaning, truth and value. Moreover, it never seemed to us that our critical studies were merely subjective, that our tastes were arbitrary or ideologically motivated, still less that in pursuing them we were falling victim to some hidden political agenda. The methods of interpretation and evaluation that we applied, when assessing the sincerity, depth, finesse or emotional truth of a particular poem or painting, seemed to us to deliver clear and absolute answers – or at any rate answers as clear and as nearly absolute as the subject allowed. Indeed, we did not fully endorse the suggestion that there was some 'method' that we used in order to establish the superiority of Mozart over Vivaldi, of Milton over Carew, of Titian over Veronese or, for that matter, of Paul McCartney over Mick Jagger. For that would have implied that someone else could choose some other 'method' and arrive at some other result. It would have implied that the method was something added, chosen by us, in order to decipher a cultural artefact that was otherwise mysterious. The works of our culture were not mysterious to us, but merely deep, in the way that the face of a mother is deep to the eyes of her child.

All that has, of course, been thrown into question, through changes that many would regard as confirming the central thesis of *The Decline of the West*. Yet, despite all that has happened to unsettle our culture, some element of the old critical discipline remains. Returning to RGS to present the prizes 35 years after my expulsion (an understandable response by Mr Tucker who, showing a distinguished guest around the school one Saturday morning, entered the hall to discover the stage on fire, a half-naked girl attempting to extinguish the flames, and that appalling boy Scruton standing listlessly in the wings reciting Samuel Beckett), I found myself confronting a hall full of respectful boys and respectable parents. Two 14-year-olds stood in front of the stage playing the solo parts of the Bach double violin concerto, accompanied by the strings and continuo of the school orchestra. The prizes that I was asked to hand over consisted almost entirely of serious books, including works of poetry and philosophy – yes, books, real books, difficult books, of a kind that I too might have chosen! The racial profile of the school had changed, and the prizewinners with Asiatic features were supported by noticeably larger contingents among the observing families. But all nodded their approval at my brief encomium, in which I described my initiation into culture and thanked the school for the part that it had played. Afterwards we repaired to a marquee, where the school jazz band, under the inspired leadership of a young music master, took us through the big band classics, with a creditable imitation of Glen Miller.

Returning home from that event, full of grateful feelings towards the school where I had been so deliciously unhappy, wondering whether all the subsequent unhappinesses had not also had their roots in my discovery of culture, beset as always by the Wagnerian longing for the love that would redeem unhappiness without posing too great a burden in the way of washing up, nappies, school runs or trips to Disneyland, remembering too that those boys who had received their prizes from my hands would soon be attending universities where high culture and all that it meant would be sneered at and 'deconstructed', I asked myself why I still retained my trust in this thing that isolated me so effectively from the surrounding social order. There began a train of thought that led me back to that momentous experience when a group of 16-year-olds clubbed together between classes to declare war on kitsch. *That*, it seemed to me now, was the decisive moment, the point of no return.

4
How I Become a Conservative

I was brought up at a time when half the English people voted Conservative at national elections and almost all English intellectuals regarded the term 'conservative' as a term of abuse. To be a conservative, I was told, was to be on the side of age against youth, the past against the future, authority against innovation, the 'structures' against spontaneity and life. It was enough to understand this to recognize that one had no choice, as a free-thinking intellectual, but to reject conservatism. The choice remaining was between reform and revolution. Do we improve society bit by bit, or do we rub it out and start again? On the whole my contemporaries favoured the second option, and it was when witnessing what this meant, in Paris in May 1968, that I discovered my vocation.

In the narrow street below my window the students were shouting and smashing. The plate-glass windows of the shops appeared to step back, shudder for a second, and then give up the ghost, as the reflections suddenly left them and they slid in jagged fragments to the ground. Cars rose into the air and landed on their sides, their juices flowing from unseen wounds. The air was filled with triumphant shouts, as one by one lamp-posts and bollards were uprooted and piled on the tarmac, to form a barricade against the next van-load of policemen.

The van – known as a *panier à salade* on account of the wire mesh that covered its windows[2] – came cautiously round the

[2] The expression predates motorized transport, and was used to describe the two-wheeled horse-drawn carriages in which prisoners were transported, enclosed behind an iron grille. It is in such a vehicle that

corner from the Rue Descartes, jerked to a halt, and disgorged a score of frightened policemen. They were greeted by flying cobblestones and several of them fell. One rolled over on the ground clutching his face, from which the blood streamed through tightly clenched fingers. There was an exultant shout, the injured policeman was helped into the van, and the students ran off down a side-street, sneering at the *cochons* and throwing Parthian cobbles as they went.

That evening a friend came round: she had been on the barricades all day with a troupe of theatre people, under the captainship of Armand Gatti. She was very excited by the events, which Gatti, a follower of Antonin Artaud and the 'theatre of cruelty', had taught her to regard as the high point of situationist theatre – the artistic transfiguration of an absurdity that is the day-to-day meaning of bourgeois life. Great victories had been scored: policemen injured, cars set alight, slogans chanted, graffiti daubed. The bourgeoisie were on the run and soon the Old Fascist and his regime would be begging for mercy.

The Old Fascist was de Gaulle, whose *Mémoires de Guerre* I had been reading that day. The Memoirs begin with a striking sentence – 'Toute ma vie, je me suis fait une certaine idée de la France' – a sentence so alike in its rhythm and so contrary in its direction to that equally striking sentence that begins *A la recherche du temps perdu*: 'Longtemps, je me suis couché de bonne heure.' How amazing it had been to discover a politician who begins his self-vindication by *suggesting* something – and something so deeply hidden behind the bold mask of his words! I had been equally struck by the description of the state funeral for Valéry – de Gaulle's first public gesture on liberating Paris – since it, too, suggested priorities unimaginable in an English politician. The image of the cortège, as it made its way to the cathedral of Notre Dame, the proud general first among the mourners, and here and there a German sniper still looking down from the rooftops, had made a vivid impression on me. I irresistibly compared the two bird's-eye views of Paris: that of the sniper; and

cont.
Julien Sorel is taken, in *Le Rouge et le Noir*, to the place of execution. The original *panier à salade* is beautifully described by Balzac in the opening paragraphs of the third part of *Splendeurs et misères des courtisanes*.

my own on to the riots in the *Quartier Latin*. They were related as yes and no, the affirmation and denial of a national idea. According to the Gaullist vision, a nation is defined not by institutions or borders but by language, religion and high culture; in times of turmoil and conquest it is those spiritual things that must be protected and reaffirmed. The funeral for Valéry followed naturally from this way of seeing things. And I associated the France of de Gaulle with Valéry's *Cimetière marin* – that haunting invocation of the dead that conveyed to me, much more profoundly than any politician's words or gestures, the true meaning of a national idea.

Of course I was naive – as naive as my friend. But the ensuing argument is one to which I have often returned in my thoughts. What, I asked, do you propose to put in the place of this 'bourgeoisie' whom you so despise, and to whom you owe the freedom and prosperity that enable you to play on your toy barricades? What vision of France and its culture compels you? And are you prepared to die for your beliefs, or merely to put others at risk in order to display them? I was obnoxiously pompous: but for the first time in my life I felt a surge of political anger, finding myself on the other side of the barricades from all the people I knew.

She replied with a book: Foucault's *Les mots et les choses*, the bible of the *soixante-huitards*, the text that seemed to justify every form of transgression, by showing that obedience is merely defeat. It is an artful book, composed with a satanic mendacity, selectively appropriating facts in order to show that culture and knowledge are nothing but the 'discourses' of power. The book is not a work of philosophy but an exercise in rhetoric. Its goal is subversion, not truth, and it is careful to argue – by the old nominalist sleight of hand that was surely invented by the Father of Lies – that 'truth' requires inverted commas, that it changes from epoch to epoch, and is tied to the form of consciousness, the *episteme*, imposed by the class that profits from its propagation. The revolutionary spirit, which searches the world for things to hate, has found in Foucault a new literary formula. Look everywhere for power, he tells his readers, and you will find it. Where there is power there is oppression. And where there is oppression there is the right to destroy. In the street below my window was the translation of that message into deeds.

My friend is now a good bourgeoise like the rest of them. Armand Gatti is forgotten; and the works of Antonin Artaud have a quaint and *dépassé* air. The French intellectuals have turned their back on 1968, and the late Louis Pauwels, the greatest of their post-war novelists, has, in *Les Orphelins*, written the damning obituary of their adolescent rage. Foucault is dead from AIDS, contracted during well-funded tours as an intellectual celebrity. However, his books are on university reading lists all over Europe and America. His vision of European culture as the institutionalized form of oppressive power is taught everywhere as gospel, to students who have neither the culture nor the religion to resist it. Only in France is he widely regarded as a charlatan.

By 1971, when I moved from Cambridge to a permanent lectureship at Birkbeck College, London, I had become a conservative. So far as I could discover there was only one other conservative at Birkbeck, and that was Nunzia – Maria Annunziata – the Neapolitan lady who served meals in the Senior Common Room and who cocked a snook at the lecturers by plastering her counter with kitschy photos of the Pope.

One of those lecturers, towards whom Nunzia conceived a particular antipathy, was Eric Hobsbawm, the lionized historian of the Industrial Revolution, whose Marxist vision of our country is now the orthodoxy taught in British schools. Hobsbawm came to Britain as a refugee, bringing with him the Marxist commitment and Communist Party membership that he retained until he could retain it no longer – the Party, to his chagrin, having dissolved itself in embarrassment at the revelation of its crimes. No doubt in recognition of this heroic career, Hobsbawm was rewarded, at Mr Blair's behest, with the second highest award that the Queen can bestow – that of Companion of Honour. This little story is of enormous significance to a British conservative, for it is a symptom and a symbol of what has happened to our intellectual life since the sixties. We should ponder the extraordinary fact that Oxford University, which granted an honorary degree to Bill Clinton on the grounds that he had once hung around its precincts, refused the same honour to Margaret Thatcher, its most distinguished post-war graduate, and Britain's first woman Prime Minister. We should ponder some of the other recipients of honorary degrees from British academic institutions – Robert Mugabe, for example, or the late Mrs Ceausescu – or count (on the fingers of one hand) the number of conservatives who are elected to the British Academy.

Suffice it to say that I found myself, on arrival in Birkbeck College, at the heart of the left establishment that governed British scholarship. Birkbeck College had grown from the Mechanics Institution founded by George Birkbeck in 1823, and was devoted to the education of people in full-time employment. It was connected to the socialist ideals of the Workers' Education Association, and had links of a tenacious but undiscoverable kind to the Labour Party. My failure to conceal my conservative beliefs was both noticed and disapproved, and I began to think that I should look for another career.

Because of Birkbeck's mission as a centre of adult education, lectures began at 6 p.m. and the days were nominally free. I used my mornings to study for the Bar: my intention was to embark on a career in which realities enjoyed an advantage over utopias in the general struggle for human sympathy. In fact I never practised at the Bar, since I had a mortgage by then, and could not afford the unpaid year of pupillage without which barristers cannot take cases of their own. I therefore received from my studies only an intellectual benefit – but a benefit for which I have always been profoundly grateful. The common law of England is proof that there is a real distinction between legitimate and illegitimate power, that power can exist without oppression, and that authority is a living force in human conduct. English law, I discovered, is the answer to Foucault.

Inspired by my new studies I began to search for a conservative philosophy. In America this search could be conducted in a university. American departments of Political Science encourage their students to read Montesquieu, Burke, Tocqueville and the Founding Fathers. Leo Strauss, Eric Voegelin and others have grafted the metaphysical conservatism of Central Europe on to American roots, forming effective and durable schools of political thought. American intellectual life benefits from American patriotism, which has made it possible to defend American customs and institutions without fear of being laughed to scorn. It has benefited too from the Cold War, which sharpened native wits against the Marxist enemy in a way that they were never sharpened in Europe: the wholesale conversion of the social democratic Jewish intelligentsia of New York to the cause of neo-conservatism is a case in point. In seventies Britain, conservative philosophy was the preoccupation of a few half-mad recluses. Searching the library of my college I found Marx, Lenin and Mao, but no Strauss, Voegelin, Hayek or Friedman. I found every variety of socialist monthly, weekly or quarterly, but not a single journal that confessed to being conservative.

The view has for a long time prevailed in England that conservatism is simply no longer available – even if it ever has been really available to an intelligent person – as a social and political creed. Maybe, if you are an aristocrat or a child of wealthy and settled parents, you might *inherit* conservative beliefs, in the way that you might inherit a speech impediment. But you couldn't possibly *acquire* them – certainly not by any process of rational enquiry or serious thought. And yet there I was, in the early seventies, fresh from the shock of 1968, and from the countervailing shock of legal studies, with a fully articulated set of conservative beliefs. Where could I look for the people who shared them, for the thinkers who had spelled them out at proper length, for the social, economic and political theory that would give them force and authority sufficient to argue them in the forum of academic opinion?

To my rescue came Burke. Although not widely read at the time in our universities, he had not been dismissed as stupid, reactionary or absurd. He was simply irrelevant, of interest largely because he got everything wrong about the French Revolution and therefore could be studied as illustrating an episode in intellectual pathology. Students were still permitted to read him, usually in conjunction with the immeasurably less interesting Tom Paine, and from time to time you heard tell of a 'Burkean' philosophy, which was one strand within nineteenth-century British conservatism.

Burke was of additional interest to me on account of the intellectual path that he had trodden. His first work, like mine, was in aesthetics. And although I didn't find much of philosophical significance in his *Essay on the Sublime and the Beautiful*, I could see that, in the right cultural climate, it would convey a powerful sense of the meaning of aesthetic judgement and of its indispensable place in our lives. I suppose that, insofar as I had received any intimations of my future destiny as an intellectual pariah, it was through my early reactions to modern architecture and to the desecration of my childhood landscape by the 'horizontal vernacular'. I learned as a teenager that aesthetic judgement matters, that it is not merely a subjective opinion, unargued because unarguable, and of no significance to anyone besides oneself. I saw – though I did not have the philosophy to justify this – that aesthetic judgement lays a claim upon the world, that it issues from a deep social imperative, and that it matters to us in just the way that other people matter to us, when we strive to live with them in a community. And, so it seemed to me, the aesthetics of modernism, with its denial of the past, its vandalization of the landscape and townscape, and its attempt to purge the world of history, was also a denial of community, home and settlement. Modernism in architecture was an attempt to remake the world as though it contained nothing save atomic individuals, disinfected of the past, and living like ants within their metallic and functional shells.

Like Burke, therefore, I made the passage from aesthetics to conservative politics with no sense of intellectual incongruity, believing that, in each case, I was in search of a lost experience of home. And I suppose that underlying that sense of loss is the permanent belief that what has been lost can also be recaptured – not necessarily as it was when it first slipped from our grasp, but as it will be when consciously regained and remodelled, to reward us for all the toil of separation through which we are condemned by our original transgression. That belief is the romantic core of conservatism, as you find it – very differently expressed – in Burke and Hegel, in Coleridge, Ruskin, Dostoevsky and T. S. Eliot.

When I first read Burke's account of the French Revolution I was inclined to accept, since I knew no other, the liberal humanist view of the Revolution as a triumph of freedom over oppression, a liberation of a people from the yoke of absolute power. Although there were excesses – and no honest historian had ever denied this – the official humanist view was that they should be seen in retrospect as the birth-pangs of a new order, which would offer a model of popular sovereignty to the world. I therefore assumed that Burke's early doubts – expressed, remember, when the Revolution was in its very early infancy, when the King had not yet been executed nor the Terror begun – were simply alarmist reactions to an ill-understood event. What interested me in the *Reflections* was the positive political philosophy, distinguished from all the literature that was currently à la mode, by its absolute concretion, and its close reading of the human psyche in its ordinary and unexalted forms.

Burke was not writing about socialism, but about revolution. Nevertheless, he persuaded me that the utopian promises of socialism go hand in hand with a wholly abstract vision of the human mind – a geometrical version of our mental processes that has only the vaguest relation to the thoughts and feelings by which real human lives are conducted. He persuaded me that societies are not and cannot be organized according to a plan or a goal, that there is no direction to history, and no such thing as moral or spiritual progress. Most of all he emphasized that the new forms of politics, which hope to organize society around the rational pursuit of liberty, equality, fraternity or their modernist equivalents, are actually forms of militant irrationality. There is no way in which people can collectively pursue liberty, equality and fraternity, not only because those things are lamentably underdescribed and merely abstractly defined, but also because collective reason doesn't work that way.

People reason collectively towards a common goal only in times of emergency – when there is a threat to be vanquished, or a conquest to be achieved. Even then, they need organization, hierarchy and a structure of command if they are to pursue their goal effectively. Nevertheless, a form of collective rationality does emerge in these cases, and its popular name is war. Moreover – and here is the corollary that came home to me with a shock of recognition – any attempt to organize society according to this kind of rationality would involve exactly the same conditions: the declaration of war against some real or imagined enemy. Hence the strident and militant language of the socialist literature – the hate-filled, purpose-filled, bourgeois-baiting prose, one example of which had been offered to me in 1968 as the final vindication of the violence beneath my attic window, but other examples of which, starting with the *Communist Manifesto*, were the basic diet of political studies in my university. The literature of left-wing political science is a literature of conflict, in which the main variables are those identified by Lenin: 'Who? Whom?' The opening sentence of De Gaulle's memoirs is framed in the language of love, about an object of love – and I had spontaneously resonated to this in the years of the student 'struggle'. De Gaulle's allusion to Proust is to a masterly evocation of maternal love, and to a dim premonition of its loss.

Three other arguments of Burke's made a comparable impression. The first was the defence of authority and obedience. Far from being the evil and obnoxious thing that my contemporaries held it to be, authority was, for Burke, the root of political order. Society, he argued, is not held together by the abstract rights of the citizen, as the French Revolutionaries supposed. It is held together by authority – by which is meant the right to obedience, rather than the mere power to compel it. And obedience, in its turn, is the prime virtue of political beings, the disposition that makes it possible to govern them, and without which societies crumble into 'the dust and powder of individuality'. Those thoughts seemed as obvious to me as they were shocking to my contemporaries. In effect Burke was upholding the old view of man in society – as subject of a sovereign – against the new view of him – as citizen of a state. And what struck me vividly was that, in defending this old view, Burke demonstrated that it was a far more effective guarantee of the liberties of the individual than the new idea, which was founded in the promise of those very liberties, only abstractly, universally and therefore unreally defined. Real freedom, concrete freedom, the freedom that can actually be defined, claimed and granted, was not the opposite of obedience but its other side. The abstract, unreal freedom of the liberal intellect was really nothing more than childish disobedience, amplified into anarchy. Those ideas exhilarated me, since they made sense of what I had seen in 1968. But when I expressed them, in a book published in 1979 as *The Meaning of Conservatism*, I blighted what remained of my academic career.

The second argument of Burke's that impressed me was the subtle defence of tradition, prejudice and custom against the enlightened plans of the reformers. This defence engaged once again with my study of aesthetics. Already as a schoolboy I had had been struck by Eliot's essay 'Tradition and the Individual Talent', in which tradition is represented as a constantly evolving yet continuous thing, which is remade with every addition to it, and which adapts the past to the present and the present to the past. This conception, which seemed to make sense of Eliot's kind of modernism (a modernism that is the polar opposite of that which has prevailed in architecture), also rescued the study of the past, and made my own love of the classics in art, literature and music into a valid part of my psyche as a modern human being. Burke's defence of tradition seemed to translate this very concept into the world of politics, and to make respect for custom, establishment, and settled communal ways into a political virtue, rather than a sign, as my contemporaries mostly believed, of complacency.

Burke's provocative defence, in this connection, of 'prejudice' – by which he meant the set of beliefs and ideas that arise instinctively in social beings, and which reflect the root experiences of social life – was a revelation of something that until then I had entirely overlooked. Burke brought home to me that our most necessary beliefs may be both unjustified and unjustifiable from our own perspective, and that the attempt to justify them will lead merely to their loss. Replacing them with the abstract rational systems of the philosophers, we may think ourselves more rational and better equipped for life in the modern world. But in fact we are less well equipped, and our new beliefs are far less justified, for the very reason that they are justified by ourselves. The real justification for a prejudice is the one that justifies it *as* a prejudice, rather than as a rational conclusion of an argument. In other words it is a justification that cannot be conducted from our own perspective, but only from outside, as it were, as an anthropologist might justify the customs and rituals of an alien tribe.

An example will illustrate the point: the prejudices surrounding sexual relations. These vary from society to society; but until recently they have had a common feature, which is that people distinguish seemly from unseemly conduct, abhor explicit sexual display, and require modesty in women and chivalry in men, in the negotiations that precede sexual union. There are very good anthropological reasons for this, in terms of the long-term stability of sexual relations, and the commitment that is necessary if children are to be inducted into society. But these are not the reasons that motivate the traditional conduct of men and women. This conduct is guided by deep and immovable prejudice, in which outrage, shame and honour are the ultimate grounds. Sexual liberators have no difficulty in showing that those motives are irrational, in the sense of being founded on no reasoned justification available to the person whose motives they are. And they may propose sexual liberation as a rational alternative, a code of conduct that is rational from the first-person viewpoint, since it derives a complete code of practice from a transparently reasonable aim, which is sexual pleasure.

This substitution of reason for prejudice has indeed occurred. And the result is exactly as Burke would have anticipated. Not merely a breakdown in trust between the sexes, but a faltering in the reproductive process – a failing and enfeebled commitment of parents, not merely to each other, but also to their offspring. At the same time, individual feelings, which were shored up and fulfilled by the traditional prejudices, are left exposed and unprotected by the skeletal structures of rationality. Hence the extraordinary situation in America, where law suits have replaced common courtesy, where post-coital accusations of 'date-rape' take the place of pre-coital modesty, and where advances made by the unattractive are routinely penalized as 'sexual harassment'. This is an example of what happens when prejudice is wiped away in the name of reason, without regard for the real social function that prejudice alone can fulfil. Indeed, it was partly by reflecting on the disaster of sexual liberation, and the joyless world that it seems to have produced around us, that I came to see the truth of Burke's otherwise somewhat paradoxical idea.

The final argument that impressed me was Burke's response to the theory of the social contract. Although society can be seen as a contract, he argued, we must recognize that most parties to the contract are either dead or not yet born. The effect of the contemporary Rousseau-ist ideas of social contract was to place the present members of society in a position of dictatorial dominance over those who went before, and those who came after them. Hence these ideas led directly to the massive squandering of inherited resources at the Revolution, and to the cultural and ecological vandalism that Burke was perhaps the first to recognize as the principal danger of modern politics. In Burke's eyes the self-righteous contempt for ancestors that characterized the Revolutionaries was also a disinheriting of the unborn. Rightly understood, he argued, society is a partnership between the dead, the living and the unborn, and without what he called the 'hereditary principle', according to which rights could be inherited as well as acquired, both the dead and the unborn would be disenfranchised. Indeed, respect for the dead was, in Burke's view, the only real safeguard that the unborn could obtain, in a world that gave all its privileges to the living. His preferred vision of society was not as a contract, in fact, but as a trust, with the living members as trustees of an inheritance that they must strive to enhance and pass on.

In those deft, cool thoughts, Burke summarized all my instinctive doubts about the cry for liberation, all my hesitations about progress and about the unscrupulous belief in the future that has dominated and (in my view) perverted modern politics. In effect, Burke was joining in the old Platonic cry for a form of politics that would also be a form of nurture – 'care of the soul', as Plato put it, which would also be a care for absent generations. The graffiti paradoxes of the *soixante-huitards* were the very opposite of this: a kind of adolescent insouciance, a throwing away of all customs, institutions and achievements, for the sake of a momentary exultation that could have no lasting sense save anarchy. All that was implied in the 'C'est interdit d'interdire' sprayed on the wall below my garret.

Most of my friends at the time of my intellectual awakening were literary people with no interest in politics, still less in politics of the conservative kind. Among the exceptions were two academics – John Casey, who helped me to resume my studies, and Maurice Cowling, who became my colleague when I was elected to a fellowship at Peterhouse. I also had the good fortune to meet one or two Conservative politicians, the most notable and likeable of whom was Hugh Fraser, a Member of Parliament who was to stand against Mrs Thatcher as candidate for Party leader. I had come to know Hugh through his wife, Lady Antonia, whose combination of wit, elegance and learning placed her at the pinnacle of London society. And in my eyes it was a full and sufficient justification of London society that it could contain a woman like Antonia – a woman as admirable in her way as any I have known.

Someone once told me that Antonia had little time for my conservative beliefs. '*I believe* what *she enacts*,' was my reply. She did not *believe* in her way of life, since belief, for her, was an ineffectual smoke around the thing itself, a blemish far better dispensed with. Besides, she is Irish, daughter of a Labour politician: socialist in politics, liberal in morality, libertine in life and Catholic in religion – all of which helped her image as the representative of high culture in an age of decay, but none of which suggested English conservatism. For Antonia conservative beliefs were legacies, things that come down in the family like hideous portraits or Habsburg jaws, but which, like any inherited disability, should never be openly mentioned. To discover a convert, who adopted the old Tory doctrines not out of genetic necessity but because he thought them to be true, was, for her, like coming across someone who had hired a plastic surgeon to give him a Habsburg jaw. What in her husband was a matter of breeding and therefore unnoticeable was, in me, a self-inflicted wound, an embarrassing stigma from which one must avert one's gaze.

Hugh was in fact unusual for a Tory politician of the old patrician school, in that he awoke from time to time from the deep unconsciousness of his class and took stock of the surrounding disaster. It was in 1974, as we travelled together by train from his house in Scotland, that we decided to inject ideas into a Party that had hitherto been successful largely because it had none. Edward Heath had been driven from power by the miners' strike, and a Labour Government under Harold Wilson held on to a precarious majority in the Commons. The deviousness of Heath, the dreariness of Old Labour and the decline of English institutions encouraged in me the belief that conservatives needed to think more. This belief was not, I think, shared by Hugh. If he had an opinion on the matter, it was probably that conservatives needed to think less. Nevertheless, out of his abundant good nature he agreed to found a society, the purpose of which would be to discuss, at the highest level compatible with the presence of politicians, the doctrines of conservative philosophy. Thus was founded the Conservative Philosophy Group, whose first decision was to create a board of four members. John Casey and I were to search the intellectual world for conservatives; Hugh and Jonathan Aitken were to search the Conservative Party for members who could think.

Needless to say, none of us had much success. Nevertheless, the Conservative Philosophy Group existed for 20 or more years, addressed at first by some of the most serious post-war political thinkers – Hayek, Oakeshott, Friedman and Elie Kedouri – but gradually succumbing to inanition as the Party drifted in the stagnant days of John Major. Once or twice Mrs Thatcher looked in – an unwelcome intrusion, since politicians lose all self-respect in the presence of their leader, and seem quite unable to appreciate that the shabby academic who is speaking from the chair might have more to say to them than this person whose thoughts and whims and fancies they have studied obsessively all day. In any case, we had little influence on the high command of the Party, and none whatsoever on the academic world. Our meetings – which took place in Jonathan Aitken's house – were attended by backbenchers too sincere in their convictions to expect promotion, dons too contrary to learn from others, and – that most creative and under-acknowledged segment of our intellectual heritage – the hard core of drunken right-wing journalists, among whom the blind Peter Utley was king.

By the time our host was continuing his philosophical education in Belmarsh prison, the Conservative Philosophy Group was a memory. Still, I learned from the venture, and regret only that there is no record of the meetings, except for one episode, which dates from 11 July 1983, when I wrote what I could remember in my diary:

> Harold Macmillan came to address the Conservative Philosophy Group. To see him sunk in the chair, his hooded eyes unmovingly staring before him, his hands clasped over the bone handle of his walking stick, his shoulders tired and sloping – to see him thus, with Hugh Fraser mellifluously talking at him from the neighbouring chair, and the undrunk glass of champagne quietly bubbling beside him, you would have said that nothing of him existed beyond a corpse and a memory, and that this temporary exhumation was no more than one of those macabre jokes that Conservatives dream up whenever it occurs to them to posture as an intellectual force.
>
> However, when we had all sat down, expecting the worst, and Macmillan had surprised us by rising slowly and shakily to his feet, it immediately became clear that here was no ordinary human being, and that this 90-year-old body harboured the vigorous remainder of a dominant spirit. He began slowly, leaning forward on his stick, and seemingly

unaware of his surroundings. He said how moved and flattered he was that we had chosen to invite him, and how pleased he was that these gatherings existed, in which some of the great deficiency in conservative thinking could perhaps be made good.

'We have now won the election,' he continued, 'and I must tell you that it was like every other election in most respects. All elections have one thing in common which is that, in our opinion, they involve the resolution of the most critical question that the nation has ever faced. And then, when they are over, the illusion vanishes. For those who lost, it turns out that, after all, nothing very much was at stake, that the affair was no more than an interlude in government. For those who won, it demonstrates the good sense of the British people, who have shown where their natural loyalty lies.

'But in one respect this election was different from others that I have fought. It showed the change that has come about in politics, now that the media are an immovable part of it. Everything that was said was said to the nation as a whole, fed into every living room through mechanical appliances and according to a regulated schedule. An election is no longer the great occasion that it was, when you were there, before them, on the platform, speaking to the people from the living stage of politics, developing an argument as you might in the House of Commons. Now you say much less; but you say it to many more.'

Here he gradually stretched out his right hand, and it was as though the blood had slowly risen in his body to swell his arm, which lifted from his side and seemed to glow in the air with the life that was being restored to it.

'And it was different in another respect, although really it is the same respect. Nobody who fought in this election was inclined to believe his own manifesto. Certainly no Labour candidate: you *couldn't* believe it – it was a bundle of contradictions, and this was constantly apparent. Nobody could govern the country on the basis of such a manifesto, since it denied the two premises of English politics: national unity, and national defence. And then there was this other party, this new what's it called. Was that any better?

Nothing there except negatives. And how about the Conservative manifesto? What did it say? Just that we were going to continue in the same direction, doing what we had done, no plan or strategy for the future – nothing. Just: stay with us and we'll carry on! Nothing to believe there, nothing at all. Of course the Prime Minister is a remarkable woman. I am full of admiration for her resolve and her common sense . . .'

He went on to argue that the main parties could not look the principal problems in the face. Concern about unemployment, he said, is a middle-class fantasy.

'Look at the Labour Party's manifesto, complaining of poverty and starvation. Imagine preaching that on the doorstep of a council house, with its refrigerator and television and its two cars parked outside – it's just not on! People are offended by this language, since it places them in a past which they have either forgotten or never known. If they have a job they don't as a rule care about those who haven't. And if they haven't they don't care very much either. The problem of their life is not work but leisure – what are they going to do with their spare time; how are they to pass the time of day?

'We all know in fact that this is the real question that will confront us in the future. Increasing unemployment is inevitable. It is also desirable. For it stems from the fact that the machines are at last taking over. When I was in Japan, and saw the daily paper being produced in nine million copies, without a single workman having anything to do with the process, I felt that I was in the face of the future. If we do not go forward into that future – if we allow our unions and pressure groups to guarantee employment to their constituents, so as to retard the day when the machine relieves us of our burdens – then we shall lose our advantage over the countries of the Soviet Empire, and the political consequences will be disastrous.'

He went on to describe the aptitude of the old upper class for leisure, and the need to train the lower orders for the terrifying challenge of idleness – the challenge of the trout stream and the grouse moor. He argued also the case for the alliance and defence, and expressed his concern at the great pincer movement – the dream of the old Russian Empire, against which Dizzy had so successfully negotiated – that had now established itself in Afghanistan and Abyssinia.[3] He compared our situation to that which prevailed in 1935, not wanting to know the real danger that threatens us, wishing to 'face up to the enemy', but at the same time tempted to throw away our arms in the hope that, being defenceless, we could not possibly be attacked, since no one would find us threatening. He affectionately recalled the meetings 'which took place in this very room' (i.e. Jonathan Aitken's drawing room) between himself, Churchill and Brendan (by which I assume he meant Brendan Bracken, Churchill's PPS and Press Secretary), and in all this he spoke with such a vivid sense of the continuities of English politics, and such a charming recognition that his class had treated it as a private affair among school friends, that the room seemed filled with his spirit, and with familiar ghosts whom he addressed affectionately by their schoolboy names. Best of all was his conclusion, as he rose to a passionate crescendo, saying,

'and within these walls, among you, perhaps, the hope is growing; from such as yourself the person will emerge who will lead us to confront these tasks; for it is now that we conservatives must renew ourselves, find our roots in philosophy and speculative thought, and go forward, confronting the issues that our politicians, moved by their dead resentments, can neither face nor understand. And I hope, I have hope, that this will be so, that we shall lead again. It can be done. It will be done. But it is important to remember ...'

He paused. His hand, which had been waving about his head, fell to his side. His eyes remained fixed before him, small black points under their great hoods of white flesh, and he tottered slightly, supporting himself on his stick. His voice fell to a whisper.

'It is important to remember ... to remember ...'

[3] He was referring to the Soviet invasion of Afghanistan, and also to the Soviet-backed installation of Mengistu in Ethiopia, following British withdrawal from Aden and the KGB's success in Yemen.

His hand rose a little, shook, and then fell again.

'To remember . . . to remember . . . I have forgotten what I wanted to say.'

And he promptly sat down.

Those last words of Macmillan capture the essence of Conservative (with a capital C) philosophy. 'I have forgotten what I wanted to say,' is the true contribution of the Tory Party to the understanding of government in our time, and the full explanation of the Party's success. Ideas, in the Tory vision, are fleeting by-products of the social and political process, which are no sooner produced than forgotten. In this and other respects the Tory Party behaves as though Marx were its principal mentor: it treats philosophy as 'ideology', and economics as the motor of social life. This means that there is no such career in England as that of an intellectual Conservative. The Conservative Party takes exactly the same attitude to conservative beliefs as Lady Antonia Pinter (as she now is): they should be inherited and ignored, not acquired and defended. And never should they take the form of convictions.

I had an inkling of this in 1978 when, after four years of the Conservative Philosophy Group, and by now a barrister, I applied to join the Conservative Party's list of candidates – the first step towards representing the Party in a General Election. A veteran Member of Parliament, Dame Something Something, who conformed exactly to the old image of the blue-rinse maiden aunt, and who looked me up and down with angry sniffs as I answered her questions, demanded what I had done for the Party. Had I been a local councillor? Had I worked in my local office, canvassed at elections, attended functions, organized tea parties and speakers' events? Had I joined the Young Conservatives, spoken in Union debates, attended Party Conferences? And if none of those things, then what on earth *had* I done for the cause and in what conceivable respect did I regard myself as qualified?

I mentioned that I had founded the Conservative Philosophy Group. She made it clear that the conjunction of the two words 'conservative' and 'philosophy' was so absurd that she could only doubt the existence of such an organization. Under her withering stare I began to feel that I was as much a fake as she believed me to be. She asked me whether I wrote in the press, since that at least was useful, and I replied that I had written book reviews for the *Spectator*, so confirming her suspicion that if my name ever did appear in newspapers it would be in the wrong parts of them. I added that I had also written a book.

'A *book*? On what subject?'

I hesitated.

'Aesthetics.'

Her stare became suddenly vacant. She closed the file containing my application and turned to her colleague, a young MP who had remained silent throughout, occasionally sending out a pitying glance in my direction.

'I suppose he could apply for this new European Parliament thing, could he?'

I indicated that I did not believe in parliaments where there was no national loyalty. She laughed involuntarily at the quaintness of my words – the first sign that laughter lay within her behavioural repertoire. And then, after brief handshakes, I was dismissed.

I ceased to be an intellectual Conservative, and became a conservative intellectual instead. This was an even worse idea. Vociferous conservatives are accepted in politics, but not in the intellectual world. I suppose it was naive of me not to see this. I should have learned from Spinoza, who refused to publish his *Ethics*, and who chose for his device the single word *caute* – 'be cautious' – inscribed beneath a rose, the symbol of secrecy. Instead I decided to go public, with *The Meaning of Conservatism*, a somewhat Hegelian defence of Tory values in the face of their betrayal by the free marketeers. My credentials as an anachronism were thereby established, and when the Salisbury Group, a loose collection of reactionaries founded in memory of the great third Marquess of Salisbury, the Prime Minister who kept everything so well in place that nothing now is known about him, decided to found a journal and looked round for someone sufficiently anachronistic to serve as its editor, they alighted on me with something like the expressions attributed by Ronald Searle in the Molesworth books to Gabbitas and Thring, those ruthless hunters of recruits to the teaching profession.

The first difficulty was that of finding people to write in an explicitly conservative journal. I had friends in the academic world who were prepared in private to confess to conservative sympathies, but they were all acutely aware of the risks attached to 'coming out'. They had seen what a caning I had received for *The Meaning of Conservatism*, and few of them were far enough advanced in their academic careers to risk a similar treatment.

The second difficulty was that of establishing a readership. The money we had raised would cover the printing costs of three issues: after that the *Salisbury Review* would have to pay for itself, which would require 600 subscribers or more. I was confident that there were at least 600 intellectual conservatives in Britain, most of whom would welcome a journal dedicated to expressing, examining and exploring their endangered worldview. The problem was finding them.

The third difficulty was that of conservatism itself. I was often told by Maurice Cowling (a member – though in a spirit of irony – of the Salisbury Group) that I was deceiving myself if I thought that conservative politics could be given a philosophical backing sufficient to put it on a par with socialism, liberalism, nationalism and all the other isms that conservatism isn't. Conservatism, Maurice told me, is a political practice, the legacy of a long tradition of pragmatic decision-making and high-toned contempt for human folly. To try to encapsulate it in a philosophy was the kind of naive project that Americans might undertake. And that was one of the overwhelming reasons for not teaching, still less living, in America.

One of our earliest contributors was Ray Honeyford, the Bradford headmaster who argued for a policy of integration in our schools as the only way of averting ethnic conflict. Ray Honeyford was branded a racist, horribly pilloried (by some of my academic colleagues in the University of Bradford, among others) and eventually sacked, for saying what everyone now admits to be true. My attempts to defend him led to extensive libels of me and the *Review*. Other contributors were persecuted (and some were also sacked) for coming to Ray's defence. This episode was our first great success, and led to the 600 subscriptions that we needed.

Our next success came in 1985, when, at the annual congress of the British Association for the Advancement of Science, the *Review* was subjected to a show trial by the sociologists, and found guilty on the dual charge of 'scientific racism' and intellectual incompetence. Neither I nor any contributor to the

Review was invited to attend this show trial: and there was no way in which the charge could be disproved. Our contributors included Jews, Asians, Africans, Arabs, and Turks. But the advantage of the charge of *scientific* racism is that it can be proved without showing racial discrimination, and merely by examining words. It is a 'thought crime' in the sense made famous by Orwell. Thereafter the *Review* and its writers were ostracized in the academic world. The consequences of this for my career soon became apparent. Invited to give a paper to the Philosophy Society in the University of Glasgow I discovered, on arrival, that the Philosophy Department was mounting an official boycott of my talk, and had announced this fact to the world. I wandered around the campus for a while, watched a desultory procession of apparatchiks who were conferring an honorary degree on Robert Mugabe, and was eventually rescued by a fellow dissident, Flint Schier, who had arranged for the talk to go ahead as an 'unofficial seminar'.

I was used to such things in Eastern Europe, and in time got used to them in England too. On the whole, however, the Communist secret police treated one rather better than the reception parties organized by the Socialist Workers Party: there might be a slight roughing up and maybe a night in jail, but this would be relieved by intellectual discussion at a much higher level than could be obtained in our provincial universities. After a particularly frightening experience giving a lecture on 'toleration' at the University of York, and following a serious libel in the *Observer*, I began to wonder whether my position as a university professor was really tenable.

Eastern Europe was the occasion of another success. To my astonishment, a samizdat edition of the *Salisbury Review* began to appear in Prague in 1986. By then I had been expelled from Czechoslovakia, and was regularly followed in Poland. Things were not much better in Britain, where the *Review* might just as well have been a samizdat publication, so great was the venom directed towards those who wrote for it. So the news that the *Review* had achieved, under 'real socialism', an honour accorded, to my knowledge, to no other Western periodical, was especially gratifying. Examples were smuggled to us and their wafer-thin pages – the final carbon copies from sheaves of ten – had the spiritual quality of illuminated manuscripts. They were testimony to a belief in the written word that had been tried and proved through real suffering.

In 1987 the Police Museum in Prague – a propaganda institute to which teachers would take their quiet crocodiles of 'young pioneers' – composed a new exhibit devoted to the 'unofficial secret agent'. The central item was a maquette of a youngish man in Western clothes, with spy camera and binoculars. From his open briefcase there spilled – along with Plato and Aristotle – copies of the *Salisbury Review*. Some time later one of our regular contributors, Ján Čarnogursky, was arrested in Slovakia and charged with subversion of the state in collaboration with foreign powers. The indictment mentioned the *Salisbury Review* as clinching evidence. This was, I suppose, our greatest triumph: the first time that anybody with influence had conferred on us the status of an equal. Unfortunately, however, the trial never took place, with the Communists out of power and Ján on his way to becoming Prime Minister of Slovakia.

It was not only the issues of ethnic relations and national identity that had provoked the British intellectual establishment. The *Salisbury Review* was belligerently anti-communist, with a regular series of articles smuggled to us from underground writers in the Soviet bloc; it took a stand against CND and the Peace Movement; it drew attention to the plight of Christians in North Africa and the Middle East; it carried articles denouncing foreign aid; it was explicitly critical of feminism, modernism, postmodernism and deconstruction. Above all, it was anti-egalitarian, defending achievement against mediocrity and virtue against vice. Although all those positions are now widely accepted, we had the good fortune to express them at a time when each was actively censored by some group of sanctimonious half-wits. Hence we survived. One by one the conservatives came out and joined us, recognizing that it was worth sacrificing your chances of becoming a Fellow of the British Academy, a vice chancellor or an emeritus professor for the sheer relief of uttering the truth. With contributors ranging from Peter Bauer and A. L. Rowse to Václav Havel and P. D. James, we were able to deflect the charge of intellectual incompetence. Without claiming too much credit for this, I remain convinced that the *Salisbury Review* helped a new generation of conservative intellectuals to emerge. At last it was possible to be a conservative and also to the *left* of something, to say, 'Of course the *Salisbury Review* is beyond the pale; but ...'

Still, there was a price to pay. It became a matter of honour among English-speaking intellectuals to disassociate themselves from me, to write, if possible, damning and contemptuous reviews of my books, and to block my chances of promotion. Some of the criticisms were justified; once stigmatized as a conservative, however, there was nothing I could do to avoid them. However hard I tried, however much scholarship, thought and open-minded argument I put into what I wrote, it was routinely condemned as ignorant, sloppy, pernicious or just plain 'silly' – A. J. Ayer's verdict on *Sexual Desire*, a book I honestly believe to offer a cogent philosophical account of its subject matter, and an answer to the mendacious three-volume 'history' by Foucault.

One academic philosopher wrote to Longman's, who had published one of my books, saying that 'I may tell you with dismay that many colleagues here [i.e. in Oxford] feel that the Longman imprint – a respected one – has been tarnished by association with Scruton's work.' He went on to express the hope that 'the negative reactions generated by this particular publishing venture may make Longman think more carefully about its policy in the future'. Even more curious was the letter sent to my head of department by another colleague, who acted as external assessor for academic promotions. He would have had no difficulty in recommending me, he wrote, before my articles began to appear in *The Times*, and on the strength of my academic work. But those articles, with their unremitting conservative message, were the real proof of my intellectual powers, and the conclusive demonstration that I was unfit to hold a university chair.

In time I came to see that he was right. Someone who believes in real distinctions between people has no place in a humanities department, the main purpose of which is to deliver the ideology required by life in the postmodern world. What the *soixante-huitards* hoped to achieve by violence has been accomplished far more effectively by the peaceful self-censorship natural to the academic mind. The attacks that I suffered showed the health of the university organism, which surrounds each invading germ with antibodies, and expels it from the system. Perceiving the rightness and necessity of this I left the university and took up farming – or rather 'metafarming', a practice that I describe in *News from Somewhere*.

Nevertheless I remain what I have been since May 1968 – a conservative intellectual, who not only loves the high culture of Europe, but believes it to be a source of consolation and the repository of what we Europeans should know. It is, to put it bluntly, our best hope for the past. Such a hope animated de Gaulle; it enabled him to save his country from destruction not once but twice. And, by deflecting us from our self-centred projects, it offers a guarantee of national survival. That, to me, is the lesson of conservative politics, and it is one that will never be understood by those who place their hopes solely in the future, and without faith in the past.

The years of conflict have taught me that few will share my convictions, and that all attempts to conserve things come too late. But the philosopher who most clearly perceived this truth brought a message of peace: 'when philosophy paints its grey-in-grey, then is a form of life grown old. The Owl of Minerva spreads its wings only with the gathering of the dusk.' Hegel's words describe not the view from that attic window in the *Quartier Latin*, but the soul that absorbed it. It was not to change things, or to be part of things, or to be swept along by things, that I made my pilgrimage to Paris. It was to observe, to know, to understand. And so I acquired the consciousness of death and dying, without which the world cannot be *loved for what it is*. That, in essence, is what it means to be a conservative.

5

Stealing from Churches

Those who roam in search of beauty spend many hours in church. Few of them pray, fewer still cross themselves or kneel. Most breeze in on superstitionless feet, eyes peeled for pictures and minds stuffed with dates and names. Many of them are dressed in ways considered impious by the faithful – women with uncovered legs, men with open shirts flapping like curtains against their bellies. Some of them talk loudly during services, or march past holy icons indifferent to the people who kneel there. Others walk around the altar or take photographs with flash-light. All of them steal.

Of course, they don't steal the works of art, nor do they carry away the bones of the local martyr. Their thieving is of the spiritual kind. They take the fruit of pious giving, and empty it of religious sense. This theft of other people's holiness creates more damage than physical violence. For it compels a community to see itself from outside, as an object of anthropological curiosity. Those holy icons that returned the believer's gaze from a more heavenly region are suddenly demoted to the level of human inventions. Those once silent, God-filled spaces now sound with sacrilegious chatter, and what had been a place of recuperation, the interface between a community and its God, is translated to the realm of aesthetic values, so as to become unique, irreplaceable, and functionless. The tool that guaranteed a community's lastingness, becomes a useless symbol of the everlasting.

On graduating from Cambridge I was appointed lecteur in the Collège Universitaire at Pau, and lived for a year on the Côteaux de Jurançon, the incomparably beautiful foothills of the Pyrenees, which begin above the village of Jurançon across the river from

Pau, and roll for 30 miles until breaking in a white surf of scree against the mountains. On wave after wave of pasture the broad-roofed farmsteads bob like covered fishing boats. From my window in one of these farmsteads I looked down on terraced vineyards, which furrowed the hillside in their own little wavelets before disappearing over the horizon in a precipitous rush. Alas, not a single vine was growing: all had been left to die, poisoned by the gas extraction plant at Lacq, which sent clouds of toxic fumes across our hilltops. Lacq was a state enterprise, conducted by decrees from Parisian offices, and entirely immune to local protests. Nevertheless, the local villages and their populations were still intact, and I would visit them on my old Lambretta. I was not, in my own eyes, an aesthetic tourist, but an intellectual of the kind described by Isaac Babel, with spectacles on my nose and autumn in my heart.

In those days the churches were never locked. Their heavy doors under rude stone arches were creaking mouths, and opening them was an act of dialogue. As often as not the first thing you saw was an old widow kneeling at a prie-dieu, mumbling over her rosary. Her voice was the voice of the place – the voice of a love that refused to die with its object.

The rough Romanesque of the Béarn made little use of ornament, and the statues and altarpieces were naive, even kitsch. Nevertheless, those country churches were places of order and decorum; to breathe their bottled faith was to internalize an age-old stillness and completion, to stand for a moment inside a community and in reach of its past. They existed, as Proust wrote of the church of St Hilaire in Combray, in a four-dimensional space of their own. Standing in them, you also stood in Time. Villagers had for centuries been welcomed here by baptism, and had passed from here to their graves. In this sacred space people had raised their collective eyes to heaven. And those in trouble – the bereaved, the betrayed, the afflicted – had found their daily comfort in a sacrament that opened on eternity, and so made suffering holy and forgiveness sweet.

Within minutes I would lose all interest in the building and its aesthetic powers, and join the mumbling widows in their pew. And if – as sometimes happened – a priest entered from the sacristy, obedient to a calendar that mysteriously sanctified the hours, I would listen to the Latin words, and join in the Credo, whose plainsong opening phrase – 'Credo in unum Deum' – is surely one of the most succinct affirmations of faith in music. I was not a believer, but not a mocker either. Standing, kneeling, sitting and singing in obedience to imperatives that for me were options, I was for a moment a believer in belief, a fellow-traveller of pilgrims who would soon pass out of view.

One day I was in the company of a Parisian woman, a philosophy teacher, who confessed to loving these little churches as much as I did, and who drove from village to village in her car. I enjoyed her company, since she was able to explain the rituals that I did not understand, and to flesh out her narrative with anecdotes and local history.

We entered a church in a tiny hamlet. It was small, dark, deserted, with the dank soft smell of stone that has grown old in shadow. The light from the thin grisaille windows lay on the floor like blades of shining grass. My companion scouted the walls for monuments and tombstones, nosing into corners, and pausing by an altar where candles guttered in the breeze. There, on a little table that served the priest during his office, was a silver tray, bearing two exquisite bottles of silver-bound crystal – the cruets of the sacrament, from which, in the eyes of the believer, God Himself is poured.

'Qu'elles sont mignonnes!' she cried.

And she stood for a moment admiring them, as you would admire a piece of bathroom furniture.

Then, to my horror, she picked up the bottles and placed them, one on each side, in her jacket pockets.

'Pourquoi pas?' she responded to my muted protest. 'Ils ne les apprécient pas. Ils vont les remplacer avec quelques horreurs modernistes. On est même obligé de les chiper.'

And she led the way quickly to the open door.

I have many times thought of this crime, rehearsing the extent of my complicity, and the profound effect that it had, in reminding me of my own more invisible stealing. Stay away from holiness, was the lesson: stay away until you are sure it possesses you.

Much later, after a full apprenticeship in atheism and its discontents, I found myself drawn again into the ambit of the Catholic Church. The immediate cause was a woman, sister-in-law of the thief, who had been brought up in the Catholic Church not far from Jurançon. Danielle was beautiful, with a pure soul, a quick mind and artistic talent; she also kept her virtues hidden from the world. We had lived together on and off for several years, but shadows had fallen across our life – shadows for which I was much to blame – and marriage came about less as a final decision than as a remedy for all our mistakes. This, too, was a mistake, and I knew it. But a mistake blessed by the Church has a kind of sublimity. Indeed (such was my inner thought) it is not a mistake at all, since the vow would compel the commitment. This strange reasoning took increasing hold of me, as I attended the obligatory lessons with Father Napier of the Brompton Oratory, by way of preparing for the sacramental – and sacrificial – act.

The Oratory is one of the few holy places in London. It retains the permitted vestiges of the Latin mass and as a result has amplified its congregation of true believers with a reserve army of believers in belief. Next to the Italianate church where its priests sing in their gorgeous robes and a four-part choir responds, stands an altogether humbler building, the residence of the Oratorians, whose order requires them not only to maintain churches dedicated to the pomp and ceremony of the Church, but also to fast and pray in seclusion, in obedience to the vision of S. Filippo Neri, their activist founder and high priest of the Counter-Reformation. Neri made the term 'propaganda' part of the language, and the thing denoted by it part of life. But the home of his London followers, established in the last century by the great Cardinal Newman, has a serene, quotidian atmosphere; it is a place of quiet footsteps and mumbled greetings. Copper-plate engravings of forgotten saints gather dust in corners, and the smell of institutional cooking wafts down corridors where nothing moves save a shuffling old priest, a fluttering curtain, or an aproned housemaid too old and stiff to brush the high cobwebs away.

In the room set aside for instruction, Father Napier rehearsed the tenets of the Catholic faith. I assented to them all: not one of them created the slightest intellectual difficulty, save the major premise of God's existence. But this too could be held in place, I surmised, by the structure that had been built on it, and whose angles and junctures I knew from St Thomas Aquinas. A religion without orthodoxy is destined to be swept away by the first breath of doubt. When the doctrines are all in place, however, neatly interlocking, expressed and endorsed by ritual, then, I reasoned, none can be prised free from the edifice and exposed to questioning. The structure stands unshakeably, even though built upon nothing.

But then, seen in this way, religion is also a work of art, and its values are aesthetic values: beauty, wholeness, symmetry, harmony. My attitude to the Church whose rituals I was prepared to borrow was still not the attitude of a believer. I too was a thief, and the marriage that I stole one morning from the Oratory faced me thereafter with an immovable accusing stare. At last I disposed of it, and was duly punished. My years of guilt were clear proof of the Church's view of matrimony as an eternal and indissoluble tie. Subsequent attempts to obtain an annulment were rightly rebuffed and for two penitential decades I wandered among *jeunes filles en fleurs*, spoiling their bouquets.

In modern society there is a growing tendency to construe marriage as a kind of contract. This tendency is familiar to us from the sordid divorces of tycoons and pop stars, and is made explicit in the 'pre-nuptial agreement', under the terms of which an attractive woman sells her body at an inflated price, and a man secures his remaining assets from her future predations. Under such an agreement marriage becomes a preparation for divorce, a contract between two people for their short-term mutual exploitation.

This contractual view of marriage is deeply confused. Marriage is surrounded by moral, legal and religious prohibitions precisely because it is not a contract but a vow. Vows do not have terms, nor can they be legitimately broken. They are 'forever', and in making a vow you are placing yourself outside time and change, in a state of spiritual union, which can be translated into actions in the here and now, but which always lies in some way above and beyond the world of decaying things. That we can make vows is one part of the great miracle of human freedom; and when we cease to make them our lives are impoverished, since they involve no lasting commitment, no attempt to cross the frontier between self and other. Contracts have terms, and come to an end when the terms are fulfilled or when the parties agree to renounce them. They bind us to the temporal world, and have the transience of human appetite. To reduce marriage to a contract is to demote marriage to a tie of self-interest, to trivialize the erotic bond, and to jeopardize the emotions on which your children depend for their security.

I imagine the following response. The idea of marriage as a vow is simply one part of the great change in the concept of marriage that came with the Enlightenment, when people began to assume that marriages ought to be the free choice of the partners, motivated by romantic love. Set aside the literature of chivalry, and look at the reality of medieval society, and you will discover that, for many centuries prior to the modern age, marriages were based on economic or political calculation. Sentiment was no part of the deal, and the marriage was arranged, as a rule, by parents and relations, by the pressures of village society, or by the requirements of diplomacy. In a very real sense, therefore, marriages were traditionally contractual, means to ends, which had their equivalent in territory, power or cash.

That thought – familiar from the work of historians like Phillipe Ariès – deserves a sceptical rejoinder. The kind of marriage that we observe in the medieval village exists today in India. And although frequently motivated by economic or political interests, the Indian marriage cannot in any way be reduced to them. For the economic force of an arranged marriage depends on the fact that it is a *marriage* – an unbreakable tie between husband and wife, and therefore between their families, without which the long-term fusion of interests could not occur. It is only because marriage is based on a vow, and therefore in a conscious attempt to transcend contractual principles, that it has the economic force that historians have documented. The eruption of sentiment into the pre-nuptial process may be the peculiarly modern phenomenon that many historians claim it to be; but this sentiment was made possible only because marriage had already been raised to the level that could justify it – the level of a sacred tie sealed by unbreakable vows. And it is precisely because sentiment is in itself so fickle and prone to disease (the disease of sentimentality) that this transformation in the nuptial process led, in time, to its dissolution. It was then that marriage was replaced by a contract, and one suited to the lives of people used to pretending to the highest feelings, in order to gratify the lowest.

Hence divorce does not end a real marriage, which will remain sacred even to those who have drifted away from it, or who have tried to set its vows aside. For many years following my divorce I was conscious of floating in a world of chimerical affections, swept along by a mutable tide, and knowing that I was desecrating what had once been consecrated to a higher purpose. I was constantly aware of that other person, whom I no longer saw, but whose thoughts, feelings and reproaches were addressed to me in my own inner voice. I embarked on a kind of penitential routine, in the attempt to heal the part of me that had been torn free from the marriage and which continually bled. And when, to my surprise, I began to live and feel like a whole person once again, it was because I wanted at last to make an unbreakable vow – not to confirm an arrangement that already existed, but in order to begin life again. This vow was solemnized, however, not by the Roman Catholic, but by the Anglican Church. I was welcomed home at last by my tribal religion – the religion of the English, who don't believe a word of it.

My years as a voyeur of holiness brought me, nevertheless, into contact with true believers, and taught me that faith transfigures everything it touches, and raises the world to God. To believe as much is not yet to believe; but it is to know your insufficiency. And that knowledge has much in common with faith.

Two people stand out among the many who have illuminated for me the path to Rome – a path that I never took. One enjoyed wealth and social standing. The other lived at the bottom of society, impoverished, oppressed, but serene. The first was Monsignor Gilbey, who had been Catholic chaplain in Cambridge during my undergraduate days. Gilbey was descended on his mother's side from Spanish sherry merchants and on his father's from the Gilbeys who made their fortune from claret and their name from gin. Both his money and his faith were inherited, and both fed his posture of self-conscious anachronism. Following the reforms of Vatican II, he had successfully petitioned to be allowed to celebrate the Tridentine Latin Mass. He had refused to admit women undergraduates to Fisher House – the Roman Catholic Chaplaincy attached to Cambridge University – and as a result had been forced to resign. Meanwhile he had refurbished the chaplaincy in the style of a counter-reformation shrine, had searched assiduously for undergraduates whom he could attract into the faith, and had continued to live like a confessor to some Spanish monarch, while dressing in the old accoutrements of an

Anglican clergyman, with a wide-rimmed clerical hat, stockings held at the knee with gaiters, and a black frock coat over a silk waistcoat and purple shirt. He was an intimate of the old recusant nobility, had been brought up in a country house (Mark Hall in Essex, burned down in the last war by 'land girls', and now the site of a sprawling suburb), and went from Cambridge to haunt other such houses and the clubs of London. He even lived in a club – the Travellers' – where he had the confidence of the largely Catholic staff, most of them Spanish and Italian immigrants whose confessions he heard and whose penitence he later enjoyed when they waited at his own special table. To many who did not know him he was a snob, a bon viveur, and a corrupter of the youth, whose interest in young men was only nominally spiritual. To those who knew him he was a genuinely holy man, who attempted to synthesize the worldly competence of the gentleman, the sacrificial ardours of the saint, and the contemplative invulnerability of the monk in a single shining ideal, and to make that ideal into an example and a reality. Accused, like Socrates, of corrupting the youth, he might have replied, as Socrates did, that 'young men of the richer classes, who have the most leisure, come about me of their own accord; they like to hear the pretenders examined, and they often imitate me, and proceed to examine others'.[4]

Some of the young men who gathered around Monsignor Gilbey were converts, some were old members of the Catholic upper class, some were fellow-travellers charmed by his prelatic style. All of them admired the Catholic absolutes, which he imparted with such assuredness that his catechism, delivered in weekly lessons to a recent Cambridge undergraduate, was tape-recorded and printed verbatim as a book. *We Believe* is a succinct statement of the theological and moral doctrine of the Church, conveying timeless truth in serene and flowing prose. It has that unique combination of Chestertonian common sense, ardent faith and sparkling humour that characterized Gilbey's conversation, and is informed throughout by a sense of the beauty, as well as the truth, of the Catholic doctrine.

Gilbey spent much of his life in prayer, rising early to attend

[4] Plato, *Apology*, 23

mass at the Oratory, and spending hours on his knees in his own private chapel. Officially speaking this chapel did not exist, since it was situated in the Travellers Club, whose members would never have tolerated Popish hocus-pocus in the heart of their privileged territory. But the Club Secretary, Robin McDouall, was a member of the circle of slightly epicene clubmen who had formed the core of London's post-war élite. Gilbey also moved in that circle, as he moved in every circle where his peculiar message could be heard. McDouall understood that, while many people might *want* a private chapel in their club, Monsignor Gilbey *needed* one. For it was an important feature of the Travellers, and one much appreciated by its younger members, that it was Gilbey's home. His being there in the corner of the smoking room, peering over his reading glasses at every member who came or went, his eyes sparkling with the unfeigned enjoyment of life that, strange though it may seem, was his part of holiness, contributed to the club's distinctive atmosphere. Stepping in off Pall Mall was like falling out of modern London into a quiet bodega in pre-Republican Spain, where an old priest is taking sherry after blessing the marquis who lies dying upstairs.

Once Gilbey took me to visit his sanctuary: a converted boxroom in the tangled solar plexus of Sir Charles Barry's building. You approached it by a narrow back staircase, which pushed its way through a tangle of thrumming pipes, tubes and wires reminiscent of Fritz Lang's *Metropolis*. At a certain point you came across a cupboard door without a landing, and entering you found yourself transported into the world of Philip II of Spain. The room was hidden from public view and enjoyed a strange inward silence, disturbed only by the occasional clanking of an old-fashioned lift shaft. There was a tiny window, looking across a dark courtyard towards the back of the Athenaeum. Illumination came from dim electric lightbulbs under parchment shades. On the altar were candles in silver candlesticks, which Monsignor Gilbey lit with a box of matches kept in a polished silver case. A single row of chairs and prie-dieus – enough for the priest and his guests – occupied the centre of the cupboard. The rest of the space was taken up by a tall Charles II armchair with a prie-dieu in front of it. I recall a Madonna with flowing robes and downturned eyes, and a crucifix attached to the wall above the altar, bearing the long polished limbs of an El Greco-like Christ in ivory. Fragments of liturgical furniture had been assembled against the walls, with a stoup for holy water. All these odds and ends had been carefully fitted together in the tiny space to create the effect of an ancient and much-visited sanctuary, and although the Monsignor was careful not to burn incense lest his secret be known, there was nevertheless that indescribable smell that I knew from peasant churches – the smell of objects incessantly lapped by prayer.

And, of course, I asked myself how these things had got there: from what churches had they been stolen, and what communities had been brought down to earth to satisfy the Monsignor's need for everlastingness? Unlike those cruets, the memory of which still troubled me and which probably adorned some dressing table in the Paris suburbs, carefully filled each week with crème hydratante by Lancôme, these objects had come to rest in another holy place, unaltered, and yet un-altared, deprived of the communities whose spirit they had breathed. Was this stealing? And even if not, was it rightly done?

Those questions were answered for me only much later, after the Monsignor's death, when I happened to speak to one of his flock about 'Jock's music room', as Gilbey called it – Jock being the old Scottish bedmaker who had occupied the cupboard before him, and who had used it to listen to his collection of music-hall classics. I learned that Gilbey had obtained permission from Cardinal Heenan not only to say the Tridentine Mass, but also to reserve the Blessed Sacrament in this very cupboard. He had furnished the place with family heirlooms, some rescued from Mark Hall. And the cupboard was a fully functioning chapel, where Gilbey would, once a week, serve mass at the altar to a packed congregation of 12.

Gilbey left his ecclesiastical fittings and vestments to the Oratory, and after his death the chapel was dismantled and its contents transferred. Supporting the starched linen cloth that composed the altar was an old chest of drawers from the nursery at Mark Hall, the drawers of which were filled with the stuffed animals, notably elephants, with which the Monsignor had played as a child. Like every aspect of Gilbey's life, the chapel had been both an invocation of eternity and a link to the vanished home that he had loved. He had never lost his innocence, and carried into the adult world that sense of being wholly protected which is the privilege of childhood. His love of ritual was the other side of his intense devotion to the past – the past of England, the past of the Catholic Church, and his own past, which had been filled with so much innocent joy. Through him I came to see that conservatism of Gilbey's kind is quite unlike the fashionable social doctrines of our day, all of which are founded, in the end, on anger or resentment. Conservatism is founded on love: love of what has been good to you, and forgiveness of what has not.

On 1 August 1985, I had dinner with Alfred Gilbey in the Oxford and Cambridge Club (the kitchens in the Travellers' being closed for the summer holiday). Here is what I wrote in my diary:

> How strange the vision of his face as he talks, his eyes fast shut and ringed with folded flesh, his mouth closed and half smiling, his speech barely audible, as though addressed to another, invisible and immaterial presence. His soft slabs of cheek are encased by two symmetrical squares of wrinkles, which seem like deep-cut mouldings around monumental panels of marble. And the voice so rapid and so quiet, glancing off the surface of a thousand subjects, each of which seems to reach out and touch it, only to be left trembling and unfulfilled. He referred to a recent letter of the Catholic Bishops of England and Wales to the Pope in Rome, lamenting the decline in their congregations, and calling for a teaching and a practice that would be more 'relevant' to the needs of today.
>
> 'What an absurd demand – to be relevant! Was Christ relevant? To be relevant means to accept the standard of the world in which you are, and therefore to cease to aspire beyond it. Relevance is not merely an un-Christian but an anti-Christian ambition.'
>
> It is hard to fault that argument; but also difficult to welcome its corollary, which is the vision of a Church enduring forever, but acknowledged only by a few old priests living in spiritual catacombs of their own devising, celebrating the rituals of a Church so truly universal that it has no living members. But that was another of his sayings, that all the best people are dead. Alfred went on to add that Christian charity is now entirely misunderstood, as a kind of collective effort to improve the world.

'We are not asked to undo the work of creation or to rectify the Fall. The duty of a Christian is not to leave this world a better place. His duty is to leave this world a better man.'

He was dismissive of academic historians, saying that 'any historian who makes history readable is suspect to those who can't'. And he had some harsh words to say concerning the modern approach to education, as an 'education for life'; such clichés awaken the old recusant instinct, which tells him that people might be entirely mistaken, *especially* in those beliefs that they take to be self-evident. 'True education,' he retorted, 'is not for life, but for death.' His aphoristic way of talking gains much from his soft, liquid voice, barely audible yet resounding nevertheless in the moral echo-chamber that invisibly surrounds him. He recounted anecdotes of his friend Archbishop David Mathew, who had described Pius XI as a 'great believer in *moderate* rewards', of his Cambridge days and of his long-standing connection with Trinity. He recalled an after-dinner silence in the combination room:

A to B: How is your wife?

Long pause.

B (slowly turning, with raised eyebrows): Compared to whom?

This dialogue neatly encapsulates the relation between the sexes, as Alfred conceives it.

He also told with great feeling an apocryphal story concerning the composition of Leonardo's *Last Supper*, which, in this version of events, the artist composed over many decades, constantly searching the streets and alley-ways of Milan for the ideal types upon whom to model the twelve apostles, and having begun with the beautiful and innocent face of a young man whose expression seemed to capture all the grace, dignity and tender compassion of Jesus. After years of labour the apostles had all been assembled, representing in their carefully differentiated expressions the fine gradations of hope, resolution, weak-ness and despair. Only one remained and that was Judas, whose baseness no citizen of Milan seemed to wear on his face, and to whom Leonardo began to despair of giving the absolute lifelikeness that was vital to his conception. At last, in a mean alleyway, a dark figure, engaged in some whispered transaction, caught the painter's eye. Recognizing in those fear-filled, treacherous glances the lineaments of Judas, Leonardo enticed him to the *cenaculo* with a gift of silver.

The figure, shifty, suspicious and huddled into himself, is pushed into a corner and told to sit. Looking up at last, and recognizing the painter and the tools of his trade, he says, 'You have painted me before.'

'Have I?' asks the startled painter. 'When?'

'Oh, a long time ago.'

'And for what purpose?'

Judas turns to the nearly completed fresco that is taking shape above them.

'There I am,' he says, and points to Christ.

The story is characteristic. Although Alfred's anecdotes range far and wide, and contain a large streak of satire and even flippancy, there is a single point of reference in all of them, and that is not Catholicism or the Church or Christian civilization or any socially constructed thing, but Christ himself, in all his mystical completeness and simplicity.

This intense personal relation to the Redeemer rescued Monsignor Gilbey from worldliness, made him stand out like a visiting angel wherever he appeared, and in a strange way justified his impeccable turnout and polished manners. The maxim that 'Cleanliness is next to godliness' is often ridiculed, since it suggests the religion of the nursery, by which Nanny calls God to her aid. But the maxim is ridiculed only by those who have not seen what cleanliness and godliness have in common – namely, the maintenance of the human body as the soul's earthly vessel and the sensory image of God. Hence it is not only in Protestant countries that the maxim is repeated; nor is it confined to Christian communities. The Muslims will tell you that *an-nazaafa min al-imaan* – cleanliness is like faith.

Monsignor Gilbey was not so much a snob as a believer in hierarchy. He was fond of quoting Ulysses' great speech from *Troilus and Cressida*, in which Shakespeare gives voice to his own highly conservative vision:

Take but degree away, untune that string,
And, hark! What discord follows: each thing meets
In mere oppugnancy . . .
. . . The general's disdained
By him one step below, he by the next,
That next by him beneath; so every step,
Exampled by the first place that is sick
Of his superior, grows to an envious fever
Of pale and bloodless emulation.

We need hierarchy in our customs, Gilbey believed, because we need order in our souls. And even if human hierarchies are artificial things, tainted by the fallen condition of those who built them, it is better to accept them than to fall prey to the 'envious fever of pale and bloodless emulation', which some call the pursuit of equality and others the Devil's work.

Gilbey would often talk with regret of the changes wrought in the Church by Vatican II, but never did he give voice to an uncharitable thought towards those who had instigated them, nor did he challenge the Church's authority. On the contrary: he believed the Church to be the continuity of the Incarnation, subject to earthly fluctuations and weaknesses like any other incarnate person. In an egalitarian age the Church too will be egalitarian, and even if this is in some measure a departure from the Holy Spirit's aims for her, it does not detract from her authority, which is God-given and absolute. He as a priest had a duty to obey, and it was another facet of his charmed existence that he could obey without changing the smallest detail of his intensely ritualized life.

And even if you take his sartorial perfectionism, his clubbability, his Beerbohmian zest for social nuances, his lifelong addiction to hunting with hounds, his antiquarianism and his love of the old England of country house and Trollopian intrigue – even if you take all this and, discounting his constant visits among the poor, the sick and the dying, and the universal reach of his friendship, make it add up in some way to snobbery, then that only shows that snobbery can be close to sanctity. This strange thought occurs to me as a way of understanding the intense spirituality of which his social manner was, in the last analysis, a sign. Gilbey's nurturing of hierarchies resembled that of Proust; it was an alchemical process, whereby the base metal of human appetite was changed into the gold of style. Or, to alter the simile, it was like a stained-glass window, which fractures the light of life into its component colours, and stains each fragment with some entrancing story.

Something like that is true even of snobbery in its lower forms, as Proust brilliantly shows. Mme Verdurin's snobbery is a kind of narrative, told by the snob herself, in which her own life is raised to a higher level, and in which the effort of being distinguished is rewarded with some intangible version of the fairy-tale prince. And this habit of story-telling resembles that infinitely more graceful habit which was Gilbey's, and which gave heart to his religion. In his social manner he showed that faith is an invitation to re-work the human body as a sacred vessel, to transubstantiate ourselves in thought, from appetite to will, and from flesh to spirit.

It was not Monsignor Gilbey who showed me what this narrative of transubstantiation really means, however. Gilbey resembled Proust's Swann: moving in many spheres, but carefully holding each apart from its neighbour, lest they contaminate each other with alien forms of life. And in each of his spheres he was, like Swann, utterly attentive, utterly sensitive to the needs, the aspirations and the norms that prevailed there. Gilbey found much comfort in Christ's words, 'in my Father's house there are many mansions'; for clearly he would be at home only where the furnishings, the catering and the company matched those of the Travellers. He is unlikely to meet, in that section of the celestial city to which he aspired, the other holy person in my life, although she, like Alfred Gilbey, owed her holiness to a personal connection with Christ.

Barbara lived with her mother in a back street on the outskirts of Gdańsk. When I met her she was 26 years old, though still a student in the Catholic University, the only independent university in the Communist bloc, situated on the outskirts of the crumbling town of Lublin in South East Poland.

I had organized a short summer school at Każimierż Dolny, where the Catholic University had a hostel, and had brought with me students and a colleague from Oxford. Such gatherings were difficult for me because I was being followed. But they were also exciting, since they were an opportunity to speak freely about the matters that most concerned me, to young people who were naturally disposed to sympathize with what I said. In Poland, an occupied country with a censored press, there was, comparatively speaking, complete freedom of speech, and the Catholic University of Lublin was the only university I knew where a right-winger could speak openly in defence of his views. In British universities right-wingers risked intimidation from students and ostracism from colleagues. In Poland they were an accepted part of academic life. And, in the company of their Polish peers, British students would change almost overnight, responding not merely to the evident oppression and poverty, but to the gentle, courteous and pious ways of their new companions. Yet more agreeable than bringing modern ideas and scholarship to the Poles was the sight of the old tried ways of Europe, thriving in the face of oppression, and awakening in the young British visitor the deep-down awareness of the Christian way of life. The Oxford students would come to Poland with left-liberal politics, agnostic beliefs, pleasure-loving ways and a habit of sneering at things old and venerable. All of them would leave in a thoughtful frame of mind, sceptical of political utopias, respectful of religion and with a new appreciation of the orderly soul and its destiny.

I differed from the students only in my starting point. I too was moved, refreshed and also troubled by those orderly souls that I encountered – whether in the monastery where I sometimes stayed in Lublin, or in the student hostel at Każimierż Dolny. Most orderly of all was Barbara, and her beautiful lop-sided face with its high Slavonic cheekbones, dark eyes and left-handed smile gave the impression, when she looked at me – which she did often – that she opened a door into my soul and stood quietly inside it. She was a messenger from another realm – an angel in the original meaning of the term; and she entered my life like an annunciation.

Barbara – Basia (pronounced Basha) in the diminutive – was the oldest of the students and also their leader, since she was reading for a higher degree. Officially her subject was philosophy – but I could not make head or tail of it. The professor of philosophy at Lublin, Father Krąpiec (pronounced Krompiets), had devised one of those arcane syntheses of Thomism and phenomenology that enable its adepts to speak incessantly about Being, Becoming, and Eternity while drawing ever larger circles on a blackboard, to the credulous admiration of students who might otherwise have wondered what purpose philosophy might serve. The English students who came to Każimierż had been taught analytical philosophy, from which they had retained only one certain axiom, which is that philosophy serves no purpose whatsoever. It is difficult, in retrospect, to determine which school of thought is to be preferred, as an influence on young minds. Nevertheless, the fact remained that Basia's intellectual interests were almost entirely opaque to me. She had an acute mind, and later we used to argue about Wittgenstein in a way that always taught me something. But it was not her mind that intrigued me nor even her body, beautiful though it was. I was drawn to Basia by her soul.

The word 'soul' is now rarely used by those academics who call themselves philosophers, most of whom see it as heralding some kind of threat to their materialist assumptions, not to speak of their way of life. But it is a useful, indeed a necessary word, since it reminds us of what we are for each other. And what we are for each other is a large part of what we are. The soul is what one person elicits in another, when he sees the other as a free, self-conscious, self-governed and answerable being. This is the true mystery of the Annunciation, as Simone Martini painted it: a simple woman surprised by an angel, who addresses her I to I.

On my second day in Każimierż I met Basia's eyes as I spoke from the podium, and saw that she was judging, debating, assessing and forgiving me. Her queer smile, static and pinched on one side and soft, almost maternal, on the other, conveyed an impression of inner absorption and indifference to the world. This impression was enhanced by her deep brown, wide-set eyes, by the clear unpainted flesh of her cheeks and by her hair, cut short against sea-shell ears. This was not a face that had been shaped by lust or greed or social climbing. Nor, for all its youthfulness, was it addicted to the things of youth. It had an inner serenity which was both childlike in its innocence, and also a title to adulthood, like a religious vow.

Of course Basia was a creature of flesh and blood. A spark had been ignited between us, and it could be fanned at any moment to a flame. But her look, which candidly displayed this possibility, also retreated from it. When the lecture was over she rose quickly and went outside.

The hostel was a kind of log cabin in the woods, reached by a winding road from which you could see the two Renaissance churches of Każimierż, rising amid trees over the old town square. The woods had the uncared-for air of Communist Europe – belonging to no one, closed to everyone, trampled by anyone, a place with no relation to mankind. Trees, shrubs, ferns, wildflowers, animals – all were as if nameless, neither wild nor tame, neither owned nor unowned, neither part of the human world nor wholly apart from it. The red squirrels in the branches quivered in a peculiar limbo, as though waiting for some sign that would not come; their existence had been half forbidden, half permitted, and they trembled on the edge of things. The people whom I met in places like this knew me by the code name 'Squirrel' – *Wiewiórka* – a tribute to my red hair. I too existed on the edge of things, my name in abeyance, my normal unheroic life concealed.

But it was no underground activist, no banned writer, no samizdat publisher, no chivalrous knight of a forbidden order who waited for me in the woods at Każimierż. It was Basia, who stepped quietly across my path and looked with a disarming seriousness into my eyes.

'You have no ring on finger,' she said. 'But in West is freedom, and rings make chains. So I ask a question.'

I took her hand, which was small, like a child's.

'Someone waits for you? You get down from that airplane and maybe a face with smiles and a flower comes out of a crowd?'

'No flower,' I responded, truthfully.

'So, just a face.' She detached her hand. 'This is pity because already you are a little bit in my heart.'

I received this news in unastonished silence. All at once and with no two ways about it, I was being told to put my life in order. I reviewed the chaos that had dogged me from year to year since my divorce, and to which I had never yet confessed.

'Well yes,' she said, 'you say nothing. It is not for a woman to tell feelings – woman must hide otherwise she is cheap. But you come here for truth I think. So it is much worse than I tell. I love you. I want to be yours. And it is impossible. This is God's work for me. To – how do you say – come over my love?'

'Overcome.'

'Yes, overcome,' she said with a self-deprecating laugh.

I rehearsed the reasons for thinking that no other course was possible. They were like the pages of a book that had become unbound, fallen into a chaos of non sequiturs. Somehow I hoped that she would take them, assemble them in another order, and show me that the book of my life made sense. But she merely nodded, watching me with a placid smile. I even referred to my marriage, to the divorce and the pain that had followed – though I did not say, as I should have said, that the marriage was stolen from her church. And this leaf too remained where I had placed it, accidentally on top of the pile.

But then Basia was young, and her first need was to confess. I learned that the order in her soul was not innate but acquired, and acquired by swimming constantly against the current of sensual desire. She had visited England as an au pair to a Pakistani family, had been seduced by the husband, and had come back to Poland with his baby inside her. She had lived thereafter in the full consciousness of her body, knowing that it must be ruled and guided. She confessed to her unchastities with chaste and reverent words. And she brought home to me, then and subsequently, what is perhaps the most important truth conveyed by religion, and one that Monsignor Gilbey, incidentally, had built into the foundations of his life – the truth that sex is either consecration or desecration, with no neutral territory between, and that nothing matters more than the customs, ceremonies and rites with which we lift the body above its material need and reshape it as soul. In so far as this thought survives in our modernist culture, it is in some garbled version of the panegyrics of D. H. Lawrence. Basia phrased it in the pure, simple, liturgical language of her church, and showed through her emotion that she had re-made herself, so as one day to give herself entirely. Perhaps she should have been a nun; but it was too late for that. Now her first thought was to encounter the temptation that I presented, not to flee from it, but to vanquish it. For the crazy idea had also come into her head that she could help me to salvation.

'Surely there is no hope of that,' I said.

'Yes, I had this thought once – that there is no hope, that this salvation is a nonsense. And almost I committed a suicide. I was such a small shrinked person. But He did not accept. He hunted me, He found me, He was there in dark corner where I go to hide. And now you see, He gives me you for a rescue.'

This rescue took on a strange significance over the months that followed: it was to be a rescue not of her only, but of me too. Together we were to go in search of peace, and we would find it, since God wanted only this for us. Basia's letters told an extraordinary story of her continual conversation with God. Every little detail of her life entered this conversation and was raised by it to a higher level, irradiated there by the light of her faith. She described her life as though it were a private song of praise: whether queuing for food, singing to her daughter, praying in church, studying logic, reading the poets, arguing, carousing or dancing with her friends, wandering in the deserted calm of the Polish countryside, learning the names of birds and flowers, she rejoiced. And she took me always with her in her thoughts, testing me against these things, and asking God to approve both me and her and to show us that we, like the world, were blessed.

After a while I could read Polish well enough for her to write to me in her native language, in which she expressed herself with great economy and liveliness, so that all the characters in her surroundings became real to me, and part of my experience. She observed her world with the eye of religion, seeing in everything the sign of God's creative power and the call to free obedience. Hers was a simple, humble, priest-haunted life, and yet it was lived more intensely and more completely than mine. It was wholly natural to her to believe that fulfilment and renunciation coincide, and that a carnal love could be transcended, as the priestess Diotima revealed to Socrates, so as to rescue both lover and beloved from the dross of this world.

For this reason our few brief meetings were troubled and painful. Without chastity there was no sense to our relationship. But chastity was hard, like an examination for which we were always insufficiently prepared. It was thanks to her that we got through these times undamaged, she constantly aiming her thoughts and emotions not beyond this world, but to the divine light that inhabits it. To her there was no mystery in the world, except the *mysterium iniquitatis*, as she quaintly described it. Her pure heart saw clearly into everything, and her vision was clouded only when tempted to sin.

Everything that occurred in those last years of communism had a peculiar urgency. The communists had justified themselves as the servants of history, the midwives who would ease the birth of a new order that was in any case inevitable. In every place where they had achieved power they had released what was lowest in human nature, rejoicing in destruction and despising every loyalty that was not motivated by cynical calculation. In every communist country you were presented with a vision of chaos. It was as though a great tide flowed through the sewers, into which the people were being thrust by the armed insentient guardians of an order whose main aim was to make people unnecessary, an order in which, as Marx and Engels rightly prophesied, 'the government of men would give way to the administration of things'.

In these circumstances you became acutely aware of the fact that law, government and justice are temporary arrangements, achieved only by individual sacrifice and destined to be swept away by the self-renewing chaos that the communists had dignified by the name of Progress, but which was revealed in all its nothingness as sin. In those orderly souls who stood upright in the flow of lies you saw how civilizations survive. They were like organisms growing in a polluted habitat, retaining in embryo all the beauty and completion to which they never cease to tend. And their effort was of a piece with that labour of the soul described to Socrates by Diotima, and which marked Basia's every gesture towards me: the effort of erotic love. The erotic and the personal belong together: they are temples built above the roar of animal life, into which we scramble in desperation from the flood. Here we find refuge, are idealized and made whole. But only by our own work are these temples constructed, and when the work is neglected, chaos supervenes. In those communist backwaters the contests between person and animal, eros and sex, law and calculation, religion and appetite, were felt as one single contest, and every word, every gesture fed the aims of one or other protagonist in a fight to the death.

Once I went to see Basia in Gdańsk. Her mother and daughter were away, and we had a day together undisturbed. It happened to be the anniversary of her grandfather's death, and because he had meant much to her, she had planned to tend his grave. We walked from her ugly street to a park, a place with the ashen quality of the woods near Każimierż. Martial law was no longer in force; nevertheless, the people were tense, angry, and many had found refuge in drunkenness. We picked one man up from the street where he had fallen and stowed him on a bench beside the park. Turning as we entered the tattered copse, we saw him rise to his feet and fall full length again in the roadway.

As we walked, Basia spoke easily and quietly of communism, which she saw as the Devil's work – a swindle, born of the father of lies, but no different in essence from all other attempts, both great and small, both public and private, to live a lie. She was not an activist, since this too, she believed, could lead a person into lies, by placing a cause and a project more prominently in the scheme of things than personal feeling. She recited Norwid's 'Ode to Tenderness' (*czułość*), and spoke eloquently of Kant's categorical imperative, by which decent atheists try to live. Kant's Practical Reason, she said, is a God-shaped hole in the heart of his philosophy. There can be no motive for pursuing truth in this abstract empty praise of it: truth must be incarnate in a person, and that person is Christ, who calls us to obedience through love. These thoughts were delivered, not as a sermon, but as the fruit of her experience, and of the daily attempt, to which her every gesture bore witness, to be something higher and purer than she might have been were she to compromise with the surrounding nothingness.

Perhaps it is true that we make God in our own image, I thought; but still, the image redeems us, since it makes us objects of a higher love. Working to create that image, we re-create ourselves. Nietzsche's *Übermensch*, the higher man who would replace the old ideals of Christian morality (the slave-morality, as he called it), was, for Basia, mere blasphemy. We can become higher than our nature, she said, only by directing our eyes to the man who redeemed us, and who called us to imitate his life. Take away redemption and we are lower than the brutes. But this, she added, can be known only through love, and not through Reason.

We had reached the gate of the cemetery, where Basia bought flowers from an old woman who ran a stall there, and where she asked me to wait, since she wanted to be alone with her grandfather. I sat by the crumbling stucco wall, watching the people come and go with their flowers.

All over communist Europe the cemeteries had been vandalized, since the communists had destroyed the institutions, customs and offices that might have protected them. What place, after all, had the dead, in the great project conceived in the brain of Lenin? In this, as in so many things, Poland was the exception. Indeed, Polish cemeteries were the only places in the landscape that were properly settled and properly owned.

The people seemed cheerful, busying themselves with the needs of their dead as though attending to children. In a religious community people can accept the death of their loved ones because they can continue to care for them. Private grief is relieved through public mourning, and the daily routines of piety domesticate the dead and bring them back to us. 'All the best people are dead,' said Monsignor Gilbey. The remark would have come as no surprise to Basia. And I reflected on the extraordinary girl who had opened this door on my life, and who stood in a light whose source was hidden from me, but which conveyed an almost tangible forgiveness.

A face appeared that did not belong in this place of reconciliation. It was that of the gritty-featured young man with jug-handle ears whom I had noticed at the airport, and who had attracted my attention by doing his utmost not to attract my attention. He walked quickly through the gate and into the cemetery, looking straight ahead like a parading soldier. Basia reappeared and I mentioned that he was following me.

'He is your alter ego,' she said.

'But perhaps I shall cause you troubles.'

'*Those* troubles are not real troubles,' she replied. 'Besides, you are not such dangerous man. For me yes. For them no.'

We discussed the situation in Poland. Father Popiełuszko had recently been murdered by the secret police, and Basia, like most Poles, saw him as a saint and a martyr. Nevertheless, she believed that the queues, shortages, privations, and the indignities of daily life under communism were so many opportunities for inner freedom. It was necessary to resist, of course; but the real fight was within you, to overcome the spirit of selfish calculation. The important thing, she said, was not to improve the world, but to improve yourself. That Basia, living in poverty in her communist prison, should repeat the words of Monsignor Gilbey in his London club, testified to the reality of the Church, as a unified spiritual entity, a corporate person whose members are, in St Paul's words, 'members in Christ'.

Thinking on this I discovered an intellectual question that has since occupied many of my waking hours. You could not understand either Alfred or Basia if you disbelieved in corporate persons. Both lived in constant and fruitful communication with the person they called Holy Mother Church, whom they believed to be animated by the Holy Spirit, and whom they loved with a fervour that surpassed their most ardent earthly attachment. And in Basia's case this love fortified her against a political system that denied the corporate person, for just the reason that it denied the individual, namely because it hated freedom, judgement and accountability in all their God-given forms. The Communist Party, which controlled everything, could be blamed for nothing. It was impossible to sue it in a court of law; it had neither legal personality nor moral responsibility; it held its assets in secret and was never called upon to account for them, even to its members. Not only did the Party refuse to be a person: it stormed through society in the desolate post-war years extinguishing the light of personality wherever the flame still flickered. Schools, universities, unions, clubs, orchestras – all were either closed down or conscripted. Charities were outlawed, and autonomous institutions taken over, their assets confiscated and their leadership often jailed. The Catholic Church in Poland and the Catholic University of Lublin were the sole exceptions: elsewhere even the churches had been penetrated, their priesthood terrorized, and their assets seized.

The absence of corporate personality is one explanation for the haunting moral void of the communist countries: human society had been atomized, and its members surrounded by impregnable walls of suspicion which only membership, of the kind invoked by St Paul, could have overcome. And since membership was outlawed, suspicion reigned supreme. It dawned on me that conservatism is rooted in the belief that corporate persons are real, that we owe them a debt of allegiance, and that they contain the order, the rule-guidedness and the accountability before a higher judge that governed both Alfred's punctilious routines and Basia's tender glances.

Basia entered no further into my life, but stood at the door she had opened, keeping silent vigil. I wrote to confess that I had stolen my marriage from her Church – so causing her pain and prayer in equal proportions, as she came to terms with the fact that the obstacles to marrying me were not just human but divine. But she continued to stand where God, she thought, had placed her, a benevolent presence whose care I could never reward. For Basia there was no such thing as a wasted life, since life was only a prelude. Her patient waiting for me ceased to be a thing of earth and time and retreated into eternity, like a mother withdrawing from her grown-up child, the better to watch over him.

I tried to make sense of her in secular, even dismissive ways. What to me seemed like holiness might appear, from another perspective that for the sake of experiment I would strive to adopt, as suffocating piety. Her purity could be rephrased in Freudian terms as a kind of aggression. I could even imagine that this girl, who put aside all interest and calculation, was really prey to the most cunning form of calculation, and that I myself was the target. And I recalled the remark of La Rochefoucauld, that interest takes many forms, including that of disinterest. For there was something that I did not like about this unruffled, observing, forgiving angel, who stood so immovably on the threshold of my inner self.

And then, a year later, I discovered the concept that I needed to describe her, and it showed to me how immeasurably superior she was to me, in thought and word and deed, and how much she had been prepared, was still prepared, to suffer. It was an ordinary winter's day in Lebanon. Shells were falling everywhere in the Christian enclave around Beirut, which still held firm, however, against the Syrian army. Elsewhere, in the Shouf, in the Beqa'a, in the south and north of the country, the Christian communities had been driven from their homes, their churches destroyed, their holy icons smashed or stolen.

That morning I went to see Father Labaky, the Maronite priest who had tried in vain to awaken the conscience of the West to the plight of the Lebanese Christians.[5] I had asked to meet Father Saba Dagher, the Melkite priest from Maghdousheh, a village in the south of the country built around the sanctuary of Notre Dame de Mantara, which had reputedly been visited by the Holy Virgin during her wanderings while pregnant with Christ. A beautiful Byzantine liturgy had been preserved in Maghdousheh, with ceremonies and processions that filled the whole town and countryside with a jubilant Christian witness. Father Dagher had

[5] See Mansour Labaky, *Kfar Sama: A Village in Lebanon*, Ignatius Press, San Francisco, 1984

devoted his life to this holy place, to the congregation he had been called to instruct and protect, and to the Shi'ite community who shared their village.

He was a frail, shattered man with a grey beard and trembling hands, who was too troubled to converse directly but who read from a prepared text. His story was one that I had heard in many versions. The Amal militia – ostensibly Shi'ite, and therefore in principle friendly – had arrived in Maghdousheh, offering to protect the town from the roving gangs of Palestinians who were destroying the Lebanese countryside. The Palestinians promptly entered without a fight, and installed their artillery between the houses. Amal then opened fire from the surrounding fields and reduced Maghdousheh to rubble. For two weeks Father Dagher had been obliged to stay in a house only one minute from his home, crouching in the cellar. When the Palestinians quietly left one night, again without a fight, Amal replaced them and began to shoot the villagers, both young and old, in reprisal 'for having allowed the Palestinians to enter'. Those who were not murdered were driven from their homes, or taken hostage.

Father Dagher was ill, having become deaf from the bombardments. He was put in an ambulance belonging to Hezbollah, to be driven to the 'Islamic Committee' centre; but the ambulance crashed, and he was able to escape with a fellow passenger across the fields. Now he was condemned to death by the 'Islamo-Progressist' forces, for having worked for good relations between Christians and Shi'ites.

The tears ran slowly down Father Dagher's cheeks as he told his story. He recalled the sacking and burning of the houses, the villagers fleeing into barren hills with no one to protect them, the shrine of Our Lady, one of the holiest and most ancient in Christendom, desecrated, its icons and vestments pillaged or burned. But what grieved him most was that his work of reconciliation had come to nothing. It was for this that Maghdousheh had been singled out for destruction and he it was who was blamed for it.

I asked him at last why the Christians had done so much for the Shi'ites, if this was their only reward.

'C'était notre apostolat,' he said simply.

And in that one word I saw why Basia still stood so calmly in her chosen place, and why Monsignor Gilbey worked so tirelessly to maintain the social distinctions which Heaven too respected. I saw too why Father Popiełuszko was murdered and why the world can sink away from God and still belong to Him. Rightly or wrongly, Basia had seen me as her apostolate: in caring for me she was following Him. And to follow Him is holiness. (I thought of the peculiar way in which she referred to Him, with the capital letter always audible – *On*, in Polish, in whose steps she trod.) Perhaps the best summary of Basia's church, as I finally understood it, was given not by a Catholic but by a Protestant, one who had lived through the previous time of desolation in Central Europe:

> God is offended by nothing and bears everything, even crucifixion; he loves humanity boundlessly and helps in the manner of a disarmed man: he teaches, leads, praises, gives examples, chides and warns. How does he practise this method? He sends good people into the world, who are a model to those around them . . .[6]

The apostolic church is a church of the heart. When you steal from it you steal the heart. Hence the theft is easy; and amends are long and hard.

[6] Emanuel Rádl, *Utecha z filosofie*, Prague, 1946, p. 23

6
Growing up with Sam

I was six years old when Sam came into my life. We were halfway home from school, my two sisters and I, and had reached the main road below the railway cutting. We would have to follow this road for half a mile before turning left into Hammersley Lane, where we lived in a pebbledashed semi behind a patch of cinders. Hammersley Lane passed beneath a blue-brick viaduct where you could regain the path by the railway. And here we would dawdle, picking blackberries and damsons from the high hedges, and running up the embankment to watch the trains as they fought their way through envelopes of steam. Alas, however, our mother was coming towards us from the turning, with that tense look on her face that bespoke some unavoidable errand.

'I've been waiting for you for hours,' she said.

We made no answer, assuming that she never required one.

'I've got some exciting news.'

It was a peculiar characteristic of our mother that her words never coincided with her facial expressions. To emphasize the exciting nature of what she was about to say she gave us an anxious frown, as though wondering whether we could handle it.

'Really exciting, though,' she insisted, turning slowly for home.

She walked a few steps, sadly shaking her head. It couldn't be that she had murdered Dad at last, since we had seen him only half an hour before in our school, where he taught. There being no other excitement that occurred to us, we followed in silence.

'You see,' she said after a while, 'we've got a dog.'

'A dog!' we cried in unison. 'How big is he? What colour? How old? What's he called? Where is he?'

Soon we were running, our mother calling out to us to slow

down as we rounded the corner into Hammersley Lane. We burst through the back door into the house, ran from room to room, opened cupboards and looked under chairs, but we found no dog. Only the same old shabby house with its three-piece Parker Knoll suite, its machine-made Axminster carpets and its smell of dried peas and washing powder.

Our mother arrived to a chorus of disappointment.

'You should have waited for me,' she said. 'He's still in his box.'

'What box? Where? He can't be! It's cruel! Show us! Where did he come from? Show us the box!'

The box was in the garden shed, a wooden crate with bars on top. A small black and white mongrel lay curled beneath the bars, cocking one ear and staring bright-eyed at our mother.

'What's he called? What's his name?'

'I haven't thought of one yet. Maybe you should choose.'

The name rushed to my lips: an inspiration that was to resound through my life thereafter.

'Sam,' I said. 'That's what he's called. Sam.'

'Sam, yes, Sam! Good old Sam! Where did he come from? Where will he sleep? Good boy Sam!'

Sam didn't object when we lifted him from his box, but he continued to look fixedly at our mother as though she alone had any meaning for him. And she returned his look with the kind of tender expression that she was too embarrassed to bestow on any human. Thereafter our mother was first in Sam's affections, and although he made a place, in time, for me, it was abundantly clear that I could never really substitute for the person who had rescued him from the RSPCA, and given him his first tin of gelid dogfood. From the moment I set eyes on Sam, however, I was determined to win his heart; for he had won mine.

There is no explanation for this love. Sam was without obvious merit as a dog, being of no determinate breed, with short ugly legs like a bulldog, a nondescript body concealed by wiry hair, and a lopsided tail that waved loosely as though not properly attached to his always filthy buttocks. Only his face was endearing, with large ears, bright black eyes and a moist black nose at the end of his spaniel-like muzzle. He was playful at first, but soon narrowed his repertoire of amusements to catching and lifting stones. Eventually only one game had any interest for him, which was to pick up the largest stone he could find and display it in his jaws until some human being applauded. Then he would drop the stone with a 'that's nothing!' look and wander off in search of a bigger one. In the end this game acquired an identity-forming character: it was the ritual through which Sam laid claim to his nature. By showing his stones he was showing his Samhood, his essence as a Sam. After a while I upgraded him from Samuel to Samson in my thinking, and was as proud of his feats of futile jaw-work as he was himself.

I quickly established a right of ownership, volunteering to walk Sam each morning before school and again on my return; preparing his meals of boiled giblets and gravy; attending to his ailments, and cleaning up when the house training failed. Often he would sit beside me, so that I could scratch his armpits, marking my fingers with his rancid doggy smell. I was the only one in the household who liked the smell, and sometimes I would lie down next to him on the carpet to enjoy it. I felt close to him then, lost in the perception that defined his canine world.

John Locke distinguished primary qualities like shape, which are intrinsic properties of the things that possess them, from secondary qualities like redness, which belong to the way things appear. Secondary qualities include colours and also, according to Locke, sounds, smells and tastes. Lying next to Sam on our hair-infested carpet I was presented with the refutation of Locke. Smells are not secondary qualities at all. They are objects. Sam's smell was caused by him but not predicated of him as his blackness and his whiteness were. This smell was present in the room, recognizable, imbued with the very same Samhood as the ritual levitation of the stone. And by smelling it I was led more completely into Sam's world than by any visual perception. For Sam's was an olfactory world, in which smells stood alertly to attention, each with a life of its own, each solid, independent, awaiting discovery.

Sounds are like smells: not qualities but objects, events in space that take no room in it. Years later I came to reflect on this, and on the strange world into which we are led by serious music. Sounds, listened to for their own sake and without reference to a cause, create a space of their own, and fill that space with movement. Schelling described architecture as 'frozen music', and was much applauded for the metaphor. But it would be more true to say that music is 'fluent architecture'. Recall the beckoning A minor melody on the bassoon that opens *The Rite of Spring*, the horn interrupting with a curious C sharp, while clarinet and bass clarinet pick up the movement in a chromatic version of A flat major. Soon the cor anglais is singing out a birdlike melody, in a pentatonic scale on F sharp. Each voice is alive with its own movement, yet somehow standing in a space of its own. Nature comes alive like a forest in spring, and you wander from pillar to pillar as in a great cathedral:

> *La nature est un temple où de vivants piliers*
> *Laissent parfois sortir des confuses paroles ...*

Sam was led by the nose as I was later by the ears. When we walked together we were not walking in the same place – nor even in the same world. Sam was exploring a labyrinth of odours, which were the *vivants piliers* of Baudelaire's sonnet, living caryatids beneath a twinkling canopy of smells. The curious twists and turns of his body as he wrapped himself round one stink, or took exception to another, were like the gestures of a dancer, outlining the contours of another space than the one he moved in. At every point on his walk Sam would discern long vistas of scent, leading away from me into enchanted regions, and each successive smellscape would call to him with siren voices. Only by keeping a tight grip on the lead could I prevent him from fleeing towards these glimpses of paradise, and if ever I pitied his anguish and let him run loose in some open space I instantly regretted it. Often I was late for school on account of running from field to field in the wake of Sam, and never would he acknowledge me when at last I caught up with him and clipped on the lead.

Not only was Sam a rather stupid dog, who would follow scents into bewildering regions and retain in his smell-bank no memory of the path back home; he was also a very randy dog. When the scent of a bitch in season wafted past our garden, he would slip away in pursuit of its source, whatever the time of day and however closely he was guarded. Bedtime would come and still no sign of Sam. I would lie awake into the early hours, imagining his body lying shot in a farmyard or squashed on the road. His was the only body I had hugged with true and conscious emotion, and I had felt the little heartbeat under the ribcage like a signal from the world beyond. As my parents went to bed I would cry out to them, asking whether Sam had come home. And the answer would be no. Usually we would find him on the doorstep in the morning, shivering from cold, covered in the vile stuffs in which he had rolled. Once he went AWOL for three days, during which I decided that I must free myself from this penitential attachment. When on the third morning I discovered him lying exhausted in the porch, I stepped over his body as though it were a piece of débris, leaving the door ajar. He went in without a glance at me, and I ran back, pained to the quick.

'Can't you even say hello?' I shouted.

Ignoring the commotion he climbed into his bed. I knew then that while Sam lived I would never be free from this bondage. I put down a bowl of food; he looked in my direction, acknowledging my devotion with a vague wag of the tail. He ate the food in one gulp and promptly curled up to sleep.

It was when I was about 10 years old that there began to gather over our family the cloud that was to darken our remaining days together. Coming home from school with a curse on his face my father would sit in silence in the living room, a pile of exercise books beside him, a pencil between his teeth. Sometimes he would pick up one of the books and scratch in it angrily. More often he would stare before him, turning feverish eyes and bitter sighs on the ghosts that haunted the household. Rather than attend the meal that we shared and which, on his seething instructions, we were to describe only as tea and never as supper, dinner, high tea or any other such upper-class abomination, he would remain by the enamel coke-stove in the sitting room, waiting for our mother to bring his plate and a mug of tea. She received no thanks for this, not even a look, though sometimes he would make a sideways snarl in her direction before seizing the plate and throwing it to the floor. Often she would beg us to perform the duty in her stead, and we would tremblingly accede to her request, always ensuring that my younger sister, towards whom he retained a thread of tenderness – a tenderness inexplicable to us for, after all, she was implicated in all our crimes – should step forward with the plate. And he would take it from her quietly, and place it without a word on the carpet.

His silences would sometimes last for days, though they were not really silences, since he was wound like a spring, ready to jump, strike or scream, and the malign energy that filled the living room made us prickle with horror as we tiptoed past. Our mother's timid nature, which forbade overt affection, forbade anger too. She had no defences against this cruel ritual, and could only look on in helpless dismay as her children began to avoid the home. In truth, although we loved her dearly, we had each grown a carapace against this love, knowing how much it would expose us to his anger.

Only one of us escaped from the shadow of my father's bitterness, and that was Sam. My father would kick him from time to time, but a kick, for Sam, was a kick, to be answered with a yelp and a scamper. As far as Sam was concerned my father was not an individual but an ambient mood, and the distinction between a kick of irritation and a kick that issued from the deepest gulf of existential despair was not a distinction that he was inclined to credit. His serenity during the worst days of terror made him a refuge; he was the only living creature in the household who did not respond with fear and anxiety when you looked him in the eyes.

The years between 8 and 12 are surely among the most difficult years of our life. Puberty points the way, however obscurely, to a place beyond the family. In its very despair lie the seeds of hope. To have lost the joys of childhood, without yet acquiring that premonition of adult pain, is to enter a limbo of uncertainty. Friends come and go, holidays and hobbies dapple the soulscape like fleeting sunlight in a summer wind, and the hunger for affection is cut off at every point by the fear of judgement. So it was for me and my sisters, at least, and our situation was all the more troubling on account of the knowledge that we had been definitively judged and condemned. Moreover, because we belonged to a generation and a class that had forbidden itself the luxury of self-exposure, so as to sit in silence with our griefs and horrors, only attempting from time to time a wan and sickened smile, we could not comfort one another, but merely felt the stirrings of a hopeless mutual compassion. And gradually, each in our several ways, we made plans to run away, to save ourselves, even if it meant abandoning our siblings to their fate.

I turned to Sam, as many children of that age will turn to favourite animals, in search of a love without judgement. The pleasure that I read in his features when I stepped through the door was my pleasure; the joy with which he received his supper was my joy, and it was with my own sense of adventure that he set out on his walks. In everything that we did together he mirrored my emotions, and never did the opaque screen of disapproval stand between us, bearing the message of an adverse point of view. Love for Sam involved no move towards the Other, no risky venture outside the Self to the place where freedom is real, rewarding and dangerous. By investing so much love in Sam I was refusing to grow up. He could be cuddled without embarrassment, since embarrassment was an emotion that he could not feel and which therefore had no place in our relations. He could be praised for his futile stonework and reproached for his nocturnal escapades, without raising the question whether the one was worthwhile or the other truly demeaning. Since all that he did was innocent, we lived together in a world voided of both good and evil, a world in which the true task of love – which is to know oneself as other, by knowing another as oneself – had been postponed.

Love for a pet animal is deeply defective, acceptable in a child, but questionable in an adult, unless confined to some quiet domestic corner where it threatens nothing in the web of human society. To say as much is to assume that there is something special and important about love between human beings. It is to imply that our love for each other exists on a higher moral plane than our love for our pets, and rises to this higher plane precisely because it is an exercise of judgement. This is a truth beautifully dramatized by Jane Austen; and it is a truth universally acknowledged, if only by instinct. In this matter, however, instinct is easily overruled by wishful thinking, by the needs of solitude, and by that great human vice which is the avoidance of love.

One day, when my elder sister had already left for college and I too, being 16, was plotting my escape, our mother came in to the back room, where I was sitting with a book. She had been crying, and her large, quiet, regular face had a crumpled look, like an unmade bed. For a long time we had talked to each other only obliquely. It was as though the angry silence in the front room had swollen, filling the house like a monstrous fungus, pressing us into walls and corners, extinguishing our breath. At the same time we had ceased to know each other. Our lives were secret, furtive, carried on elsewhere. Our mother's peculiar English timidity, her repeated failure to call attention to herself or to acknowledge her suffering, seemed in any case to forbid discussion. We were not to remind her of the truths that she avoided, and who were we, in any case, to acknowledge them as truths? I looked away from my mother's face, and felt a surge of resentment that I should be put upon by this helpless stranger.

She went to her habitual chair with the worn fabric of pink and blue flowers. Her sewing was on one side table, her book on the other. She picked up neither, but sat with her hands pressed together in her lap, frowning at the carpet, silently moving her lips as though in prayer. The proposition that she eventually uttered was so outrageous that I decided at first to ignore it. I ostentatiously turned the pages of my book, as she began again.

'It would be easy, honestly. I could go back to work at the estate agent's. We could rent a place in Wycombe, a nice little cottage in a back street. Just the two of us. We could be happy.'

I could think of no worse fate than to be trapped with a helpless middle-aged woman, in a state which, for want of the capacity to envision it, she recklessly described as 'happiness'. It seemed scarcely to affect the case that the woman in question was my mother.

'Don't be ridiculous,' I said, not meeting her look.

She made no reply. And a few minutes later she crept noiselessly round my chair and went upstairs, where I heard her shuffling in the bedroom. My father's cough tore the silence like a burst of machine-gun fire, the slippered footsteps froze, and a rushing movement erupted from the front room into the hallway. With a blood-curdling yell and a violent slamming of the door he left for the pub. My mother came down again, poked her head into the back-room, met my unyielding stare, and withdrew in consternation. It was the last bid for freedom that she made. A short while later she was diagnosed with breast cancer, and gave up her hopes.

The only response then authorized by the doctors was the mutilating operation of mastectomy, and this she underwent in our local hospital, where we would go to stand dumbfounded and guilt-ridden before her weeping form. Such a calamity had not been foreseen in my father's calculations, and for a while he set aside his campaign against an unjust world in order to look on his family with a certain compassionate distaste. While she was detained in hospital we decorated her bedroom, choosing pastel shades that seemed to convey just the right tone of spring-like optimism, and hanging reproductions of Monet, Pissarro and Cézanne. We polished the floor, cleaned the rugs, and bought a white meshwork bedspread that my father could ill afford to crown the bed he seldom visited, preferring the bed vacated by my elder sister on leaving for college. For the first time we were making a place for my mother, and making it together. For those brief weeks of her absence she was, for the only time I remember, a legitimate occupant of the house that was theoretically hers.

Only Sam felt otherwise. The sense of catastrophe had been conveyed to him at once when the hospital rang to summon her. He watched her confusion, saw with astonishment my father's awakened face, and followed with his eyes as she staggered to her armchair in tears. He traipsed behind her from room to room as she packed her clothes, and watched from the window as she climbed beside my father into the taxi. With downcast head and drooping tail he retired to his bed in the kitchen, and lay there whimpering, refusing all food. I was able to coax him out for a walk, since he would never spoil the nest, not because it was his nest, but because it was hers.

Our mother was absent for nearly a month. During this time Sam hardly ate, became weak and unsteady, approaching me only to place his head in my lap and look up with eyes that expressed his hopeless sorrow. He lifted no stones, pursued no scents, and walked only far enough to relieve himself against a lamp-post, his head hanging low and his tail drooping between his legs. My own life was changing now: I had friends with whom I played music; I was studying hard for the Cambridge scholarship exam; a vision of the future was unfolding in my mind, and I drew a curtain across the enclave where my mother lay, refusing to feel what I some day must. Sam's slavish devotion distressed me: couldn't he understand that it was all for the best, that we had covered up the awkwardness with emulsion paint and Impressionist kitsch? Didn't he realize that the problem was, like so many others that confront the adolescent mind, a question of aesthetics, a challenge to make things fit?

All my casuistry was lost on Sam and for a while I thought he might die – thought it, and hardly regretted it. This creature in whom I had failed to instil the love that I had sought, who remained obstinately attached to a helpless woman who had done nothing to earn his affection, had now chosen to join himself as an additional problem to our burden of domestic misery. I thought of the tons of liver and giblets I had served him, the hours I had devoted to walking him, the anxious nights when I had lain awake, praying for his return, and all of it seemed wasted, a vast expense of labour and emotion at a time when there had been little of either to spare. I projected on to Sam all the anger against myself that had been prompted by our mother's illness: anger for not doing, not wanting, not feeling as I should.

The day came when she was released from hospital, to stay for a few days with her mother, who lived at the end of our road. Sam came with us to see her, shuffling morosely beside me and indifferent to the smells of the street. But when we opened the garden gate he ran with a jolt into another smell, the smell that he had lost all hope of re-encountering, the smell that had once rescued him from the RSPCA and put down before him that first grim bowl of dogfood. He rushed forward, choking on the lead. She was weak and I dared not let him jump at her. As he strained towards her on the lead there emerged from his strangled throat a long agonized hiss, as though his soul were escaping along his tongue. And she put out her hand to him and smiled, calling his name. There occurred between them a reunion that had no equivalent in my emotions. It was as though both were being reborn, returning from their separate deaths to an illuminated place of pure affection, where nothing mattered save their mutual need. Observing them, transfigured in their quintessential uselessness, I realized that they belonged together, in a dream that could never be mine. All day Sam scampered around the garden, wagging his tail, watering plants and chairs, running back to her from each adventure, and listening to her softly spoken and inconsequential words. And because he knew nothing of her illness or of the terrible future that it foretold, she took from him the only comfort available: the comfort of disbelief. From that moment until her death my mother surrounded her illness with a cloud of unknowing, and whenever she was troubled by the thought of future suffering, it was to Sam that she turned. Even if he had once been mine, he was mine no longer: they retired to her corner of the house, where she sniffed her dreams and he dreamed her scent. My father's thunderous anger returned, the house darkened, and soon they were isolated in their conspicuous harmlessness like the woman and child in Giorgione's *Tempest.*

Nothing distinguishes us from the animals more clearly than death. Animals flee from danger, and face it with fear. They are conscious of loss when a companion dies. But the thought that 'this is my death', and 'henceforth I am no more' is beyond their mental powers. They face death, when it comes, with no fear of extinction, and no knowledge of defeat. And if we love them we help them to die, even arranging their death, putting them out of their misery when they are too much in ours. To do this to a person would be murder; we are condemned by consciousness to be conscious of death, to bear our fated suffering, and to offer at the last some proof that the soul can triumph as the body dissolves.

When Sam's turn came I was briefly at home, preparing to leave for university, ill at ease in this house from which I had fled nine months before in fear and anger. I had been greeted by silence, my father's bitter and contemptuous, my mother's melancholy, anxious, tinged by a forbidden love. Sam had crawled from his bed to greet me, but had promptly sunk to the floor. She tearfully explained that he had been ailing; the cysts that covered his body were becoming septic, lumps had appeared here and there under his skin, he was walking with difficulty and his breathing was laboured. In short, he was too vivid an illustration of the fate that awaited her to be easily borne, and it was time for him to go. She could not bring herself to do it; so Sam was returned to me at last. I was to accompany him on his final journey, to stroke him and console him as the vet plunged his sharp needle into the heart I had never quite won.

A hardened cyst had formed over Sam's rib-cage, and the needle couldn't pierce it. The vet – who was young and nervous – pushed too hard on the syringe so that it broke, and one of the shards cut his finger. He ran around the surgery in a panic, fearing that the lethal drug had entered his vein. Sam looked at me and whimpered. His eyes were clouding over, I spoke his name and with a sigh he fell over onto his side. I stroked his head for the last time, before turning to the vet and helping him to wash out his finger. I was annoyed that he charged for an injection that had never occurred. But I paid and, with one last glance at the body that was about to be sent off with the rest of the day's cull of dogs, cats, rabbits and hamsters to the incinerator in Reading, I left for home and for Cambridge.

Four years later, as I sat with my mother during her final illness, oppressed by her wilful refusal, notwithstanding incapacity, discomfort and pain that no dog would be permitted to suffer, to believe that she might die, oppressed too by the censorship that her *gran rifiuto* imposed on all my thoughts and emotions, guilty beyond the point where guilt can even be confessed at my inability to discover in myself one single fragment of the warmth that was due to her but which she would hardly have acknowledged in any case, weary with the endless task of nursing her while pretending that I was doing no such thing, fearing the tread in the hallway as my father paraded his silent bitterness from the front door to the kitchen and back again in an unceasing rehearsal for the scaffold, I recalled the ease with which I had dispatched poor Sam across the Styx, and the immediate conviction, as I saw him etherized upon the table, that he would never return to haunt me or to accuse me of a failure that I could no longer redeem. And I looked at my mother's wasted form and knew that it would be otherwise with her, that, for the very same reason that I could not now (though heaven knows I thought of it) fill the syringe by the bed with a double dose of morphine and put her out of my misery for good, that this misery was there to be endured by both of us and that the guilt of it and the grief of it would remain to torment me forever, which they did.

I learned to live even with that emotional burden. Grief and guilt prowled constantly around me, awaiting their chance; but in time my heart grew a cyst as tough as that which had shielded the heart of Sam. By degrees I began to live a normal life, and by the time Sam returned to me, a quarter of a century later, I was in most observable respects indistinguishable from a human being. I was even, in my own way, happy. Marriage and divorce were both long behind me, along with persecutions incurred in other and more careless ways. I had taken up hunting and, being in need of a horse, would each Thursday leaf through *Horse and Hound*, the back pages of which contain advertisements for hunters. I came across an advertisement for a horse that seemed exactly right and very reasonably priced:

> Midnight Monarch. 16.2 hands, Brown gelding, seven-year-old, three-quarter bred, safe, reliable, easy to catch, clip, shoe; bomb-proof, £2,000 o.n.o.

I drove 30 miles to his stable. His owners were pony-paddock people: man, wife and daughter who lived in a suburban bungalow, and had a horse or two in a wooden shack beneath the motorway. Of the assorted animals who had been imprisoned there Midnight Monarch alone was presentable: a tall, shapely, bright-eyed creature who came towards me as I stood by his box and immediately began rummaging in my pockets. 'Brown', like 'Grey', 'Coloured' and 'Skewbald', is a technical term, meaning, in this case, jet black, though with a brownish sheen that enhanced his air of eager involvement.

The owners, I learned, were selling up and moving; the last thing they wanted was to part with the horse, whom they had bred themselves and raised by bottle-feeding after his dam died giving birth to him. Midnight Monarch was his official name, and his ancestors included some reputable horses of whose virtues, it was assumed, I did not need to be reminded. But his real name, they told me, was Sam.

No sooner had the name sounded in my ears than Sam the horse leaned his head across the stable door, seized my jacket in his teeth and gave a hearty tug. Then, letting go, he thrust his muzzle into my face and sniffed deeply, leaving my nose wet with his saliva.

'That's his way,' his owner said, and went on to explain that during his first years Sam had known no other company but people and had never really learned to distinguish between a person and a horse. In fact he was a family pet. All my enquiries about his qualities were hastily brushed aside; it was not Sam who was in question but me. Would I be giving him a good home? Would he have company? How often would I be there? Would I not overwork him? Would I see to it that he didn't eat the spring grass, in case he got colic? Yes, yes, of course he jumps, but the point is, you need to get him fit first, so as not to put a strain on the tendons. He thrives on oats, and likes a bran mash from time to time. If we sold him to you, could we visit him? Just to see if he's all right? Also he needs carrots or apples if you've got them. And once a week a pint of beer.

Sam had all the vices you would expect from a horse who had been – to use the language of *Great Expectations* – 'brought up by hand'. Crib-biting, wind-sucking, weaving and barging had been irremediably installed by his loving owners. He had also been hobdayed – subjected to the operation named after the famous Victorian vet who invented it. This operation, performed on horses that easily run out of breath, opens the windpipe and allows enough air for a sustained gallop. Hobdaying destroys the larynx, changing the neigh to a desolate exhalation, a faint mooing sound which is useless for inter-equine communication and which therefore removes all possibility of a horse posing as a true alpha male or even (in Sam's case) an alpha gelding. Still, for £1,800 Sam was mine and the owners, reluctantly handing him over, assured me that I had by far the better part of the deal. As I put him in the trailer the daughter cried, and once a week thereafter her mother would telephone to enquire whether Sam was well and if not whether she could come over and see to him.

Our feelings towards animals are inevitably tempered by their capacity to reciprocate. And because favourite horses don't really miss the people who have spoiled them, Sam's former mistress in time lost all sense that she had any special claim on him and invested her emotions elsewhere. I, meanwhile, had formed a strong attachment to this peculiar horse, whose vices did not detract from, but on the contrary enhanced his charm. Unlike Sam the dog, whose mediocre intellect had risen no higher than the lowliest of canine accomplishments, Sam the horse soon showed himself to be as bright as a horse can be. In *The Man Without Qualities* Robert Musil ridicules one of his characters for describing a horse as a genius. It was not long, however, before I discovered that Sam is exactly that. Horses have small brains and a narrow repertoire of responses: features that have proved greatly to their advantage as a species, since they lack the ability to think their way out of being ridden. Had people not learned to ride horses, neither human nor horse would have survived – so it has been argued by Stephen Budiansky in his persuasive account of the bond between our species.[7] And in everything that pertains to instinct, and which therefore can be trained to a human use, Sam has proved entirely normal. But around the edges of his

[7] Stephen Budiansky, *The Nature of Horses*, London, 1997

instinctual brain there lies a strange halo of originality, a layer of consciousness quite beyond the normal equine repertoire. This halo endows him with an almost human approach to problem-solving, and a touching, if sometimes cantankerous, concern for his conspecifics.

I discovered this immediately after I had shut Sam into his new accommodation. Returning after a minute or two to rejoice in my purchase I found an empty stable, the bolt undone and the door pushed aside. Sam was in the feed room, where he had lifted the lid from one of the bins and buried his head in a pile of pony nuts. He allowed me to lead him by the mane back to his box, exemplifying a wondrous docility which has always earned forgiveness, whatever fault might have disturbed the stable routine. Some time later, I chanced to lean the broom against Sam's stable door (secured now with a bottom bolt that he could not reach), while tending to another horse, whose feed bucket I had left in the corridor. I turned to discover that Sam had picked up the broom in his teeth and was using it to slide the bucket towards his door. I watched in astonishment as he manoeuvred the prize within reach of his teeth and then, casting aside the broom, picked up the bucket and heaved it into his stable. I allowed him this reward, only wondering whether the feat deserved an article in some scientific journal. According to Köhler the use of tools marks the intellectual barrier between the primates and all other species; and if Köhler's view has been refuted it is surely not by a horse.

Once, several years later, when Sam's antics were so familiar that only some new departure would have attracted my admiration, I awoke in the middle of the night to hear a commotion in the stable building. I quickly dressed and went down to investigate. I discovered that Sam had dragged all the feed bins into the corridor, and thrown their lids to the floor. He was going from one stable to the next, sliding the bolts with his teeth so that his companions could come out and join the feast. When I turned on the light he looked round at me, blinked a little, and then went back calmly to his box. I was surprised only that he didn't shut the door after him.

This sensitivity to his conspecifics extended – extends, I should say, for Sam is still with us – to humans. Perhaps because he was bottle-fed and coddled as a foal he approaches you in the same way as he might a horse, thrusting his muzzle into your face and sniffing copiously as he did when first we met. He scratches your shoulders with his teeth, in the hope of reciprocal attentions, and follows meekly when you pass him in the field. And while most horses regard the weight on their back while hunting as a burden to be discharged at the first opportunity, Sam – should you lose your stirrups – will scoop you up with his neck and slow down until you are back in the saddle.

Needless to say my attitude to animals had changed substantially in the years since Sam the First. Hunting introduces you to another kind of canine, one every bit as attached to the human world and dependent upon human interest, but immersed nevertheless in the collective life of the species. And the joy of hunting consists largely in an act of surrender to your own species life, sensing the primeval exhilaration of the animal beneath you as it runs with the herd, and the exultant cries of the hounds, animated by the collective soul of the pack. Hunting helped to rescue me from an unhappiness that had lasted for the two decades since my divorce, and by reuniting me with my own species life it also opened the way to love.

Here again Sam showed his singular merits. I met Sophie at a Saturday meet of the Beaufort hounds, she on a dark bay mare called Petra, I on Sam. We sat on our horses side by side in silence as the hounds drew a large covert. This silence was a sign of our mutual interest, and Sam responded in his own way. Usually he puts back his ears if a horse gets too close to him, anxious to preserve the distance that will guarantee safety; on this occasion, however, he stood quietly beside Petra, and then followed her as the hunt moved off. The next Saturday he caught sight of her across a field of 200 horses, seized the bit and cantered across to where she stood, fulfilling simultaneously his desire and mine. Petra has no remarkable features and Sam's eagerness to find her again after that one encounter showed an awareness that she was henceforth to be included in our plans. Petra had no such awareness, and came to reciprocate Sam's attachment only much later, after our marriage, which was also theirs.

As to his equestrian qualities, it should be said that Sam is not the kind of horse that would win prizes. His mouth is hard as an old boot, and once the hunt has begun it is impossible to stop him. But then again, his intelligence is such that you do not need to, since he stops himself, never running into the back of the horse in front, and always keeping an eye on the field master, the 'alpha stallion' of the hunting herd. When he sees a jump he takes the bit between his teeth and yanks the reins from your hands, determined to jump at his own pace and in his own style, which involves cantering forward and throwing himself over, with a huge mooing exhalation through his wounded larynx, and a proud lift of the head as he lands.

Coming home from the hunt one day I opened the horsebox to find that Sam was unable to move. After much coaxing he staggered down the ramp into his stable and stood motionless, his head hanging down and his sides heaving. Vets, who charge for every visit, every needle and every plaster, arrive within minutes of your phone call, whatever the time of day. Within half an hour we knew that Sam had pneumonia, and would probably die. However, he was insured for veterinary fees, and we decided to try the cure – antibiotics, and saline solution fed into his veins from a bottle that was tied to the rafter above his head. As the solution percolated into him, he would gradually revive, his ears rising from his neck, his eyes clearing, and his head slowly emerging from beneath his knees. At a certain point the old Sam would suddenly start forward, to begin crib-biting and wind-sucking, pushing his muzzle into whatever moved, and generally making such a commotion as to bring down the bottle on his head and wrench the tube from the vein where it had been implanted. And then he would wind down like the doll Olympia until his body was motionless, his legs locked to the floor, his head drooping and his eye clouded over. We would re-attach the saline solution and again he would revive, with exactly the same result. Watching this repeated cycle of events I came to understand what is meant by character in a horse.

Aristotle argues that happiness requires good habits, and habits must be acquired early if they are to be acquired at all. Virtues are not mere habits, since they involve rational choice and the attempt to do right. But, like vices, they are acquired by habit. A vice is not like a facial tic or a stoop, since it is a way of intending things – intending against reason, so to speak, and planning to thwart our better plans. Virtues, too, are expressed in intentional action. The courageous man is not the one who runs angry and oblivious into battle: for rashness is as much a vice as cowardice, and one that jeopardizes every rational enterprise. Courage is the settled disposition to do what is right, whether or not anger or fear counsel some other course of action. It involves the whole self, and is shaped by the rational choices that it also shapes. No person's courage is exactly like another's and each forms a strand in the thing called character, which is the very moral heart and selfhood of the person, the object of love and hate, of friendship and enmity.

Nothing like that is true or could be true of a horse. Sam is undeniably a creature of habit, and his habits – some of them commonplace, some of them striking and unusual – shape his character. But they do not compose a moral heart, a selfhood, a centre of free choice and responsible action. They are habits of the body, which come with a penumbra of mind. That was why he recalled the clockwork doll in Hoffmann's tale (so brilliantly set to music by Offenbach). The character, now dormant, now muscling its way forward for attention, consists of habits without intention, quirks of the body that are run down by sickness and wound up by health. Of course these quirks also have a tincture of mind; but this mental side is like the colour added to a monochrome photograph, and represents no additional centre of agency, no network of ambitions, responsibilities and choices – in short no self.

This observation goes, I believe, to the heart of our relationship with animals. I have always loved Sam, and will often share my wine with him, he being partial to the yeastier kinds of Sauvignon. St Thomas Aquinas says in the *Summa Theologica* that it is nonsense to speak of friendship for wine or a horse. There are times when I believe that Aquinas is dismissing my two most reliable companions. What he means, however, is plain. Friendship is a moral relation, which occurs only between beings who are free; love is a destiny, and it can touch all warm-blooded things. For this very reason it is necessary to discipline love: to avoid the self-centred forms of it, and the pretend loves that have no cost attached to them. Sentimentality is that peculiarly human vice which consists in directing your emotions towards your own emotions, so as to be the subject of a story told by yourself. Pets do not judge us and therefore stimulate this vice, which has a nasty habit of entering the blood stream, producing its own hardened cyst around the heart.

I cannot love Sam the horse as a person, nor can I link myself to the self in him. At best there is a side-by-sideness to our relationship, a cheerful sharing of situations that have a significance in his mind unrelated to their significance in mine. His claims on me are not the claims of a moral being. It is no injustice to confine him to his stables, nor can he disarm me with a plea for his rights. Hence, faced with his illness, I found myself in a moral dilemma – a dilemma that would have been extremely serious had he not been insured. He recovered from pneumonia, but only after we had laid out £3,000 in veterinary expenses. Was that a justifiable use of scarce resources? And if the resources had been my own, should I not have gone out and looked for a person in need before squandering so much on a horse?

Those moral questions have been projected into unusual prominence by the controversy over Sam's favourite occupation. The Government's inquiry into hunting with dogs showed how weak is the argument against hunting from considerations of animal welfare and how strong the argument, on the other side, from liberty.[8] But hunting raises the question of permissible against impermissible pleasures. Those who hunt do so because they enjoy the sport. Enjoyment is not an evil in itself, but to enjoy an activity at the expense of an innocent animal, knowing full well that the animal is suffering, is immoral: so say the opponents of hunting. Even if it is true that hunt followers take no pleasure *in* the suffering of their quarry, their pleasure is bought *at the expense of* suffering, and this is wrong.

The argument is serious and challenging, especially if expressed (as it rarely is) by someone who knows what hunting actually involves. However, a moral argument must be consistent if it is to be sincere. The pleasure taken by cat-lovers in their pets (who cause 200 million painful deaths each year in Britain alone) is also a pleasure bought 'at the expense of' animal suffering. The RSPCA, which moralizes volubly against hunting, shooting and fishing, keeps quiet about cat-keeping, for fear of offending its principal donors. To my mind this is clear proof that the moral judgements so fervently expressed are not in fact sincerely held.

8 This is not the place to rehearse the argument, but those interested can read R. Scruton, 'Ethics and welfare: the case of hunting', *Philosophy*, 77 (2002), 543–64.

We have entered the realm of sentimentality – the realm of cost-free emotions, in which moral judgement too is without a cost, since it can be made and escaped from at will.

Since I enjoy hunting, and enjoy it as a form of companionship between species, expressed in a momentary eruption of all-suffusing love for a horse, I have had to search my own conscience in the matter. Monsignor Gilbey, for whom hunting with hounds was a lifelong passion, believed that the problem was simply resolved by faith, which requires us to have the correct relation to creatures below us in the natural hierarchy, just as we must have the correct relation to those above. In hunting we express our God-given sovereignty over the animals, while experiencing wonder at God's creation, an acceptance of death and joy in our own incarnation.

That reasoning flows from the meticulous logic of a position that few people now can share. However, I came to the conclusion early on that hunting should be justified in another way, as a managed adaptation of a natural form of predation, which the quarry avoids by instinct. What is happening is, from the quarry's point of view, a routine challenge to which it rises without undue strain. Hunt followers strive not to prolong any suffering that might occur, but to minimize it. Just how much suffering is involved in the final running down and capture of the quarry is a matter of dispute. But it is surely less than that caused by trapping or wounding with a shotgun, both of which involve, moreover, playing tricks on an animal that it has neither the capacity to avoid nor the ability to understand. If moral condemnation there must be, should it not be directed at shooting, as mean a trick as can be played on a defenceless creature?

Those who follow the hunt are enjoying and participating in a natural event, one that is repeated every day in the wild, and which has to be repeated if species are to remain strong, healthy and in ecological balance. This is the foundation of the hunt follower's enjoyment, and this enjoyment coexists without strain with an alert sympathy for the quarry and the desire both to protect it from abuse and to minimize its suffering.

To live with an animal as I have lived with Sam the horse is to begin to grasp the distinction – so clear and beautiful to the religious way of thinking – between mind and soul or (to use

Aristotle's terms) between *psuche* and *nous*. Sam has the first but, even in his most brilliant bursts of inspiration, he shows no sign of the second. Many people now find it difficult to credit this distinction. After all, human beings are animals, composed of nerves and sinews, cardiovascular systems and digestive tracts. We hang from the tree of evolution on the same branch as the chimpanzee and the bonobo and not far from those of the elephant, the zebra and the mouse. We are governed by the laws of biology and even our thoughts and emotions are the result of electrochemical processes in the brain. Such, at any rate, is the conception fostered by popular science, and tub-thumped into us by Richard Dawkins. What room is there in this picture for the soul – the divine spark that supposedly distinguishes humanity from the rest of creation and that bears within itself the meaning of our life on earth? Can we not give a complete account of the human condition in biological terms, without referring to the elusive soul-stuff within? And if that is possible, what grounds have we for thinking that the soul exists, still less that it is the inner essence, the originating cause and the final end of our existence?

Suppose you were to look at a painting – say Manet's *Bar at the Folies Bergères* in the Courtauld Gallery – and ask yourself how it is composed. From the point of view of chemical science, it is a canvas, on which pigments are distributed. From the point of view of the art-lover it is an image of a woman, on whose face the last pale twilight of innocence is fading. You could draw a graph across the picture, and indicate exactly what pigment is to be found at every pair of coordinates. This description would not mention the woman, still less her fading innocence or her blank but haunting gaze. Yet it could be a complete description. Somebody who daubed a canvas in the way mapped by the graph would produce an exact copy of Manet's picture. He would do this even if he had not noticed the woman and even if he were entirely blind to pictorial images. From the scientific point of view, therefore, the woman is nothing over and above the pigments in which she is seen.

But this woman exists in a space of her own. We see the back of her head, reflected in the mirror, some ten feet behind her. Of course, there is no part of this canvas that is ten feet behind any other part. The space within the picture is not mapped by our imaginary graph, even if it will be automatically reconstituted when we follow the graph's instructions. Moreover, no smear of chrome white can possibly have a fading innocence, nor can patches of cerulean and Prussian blue look at us inquiringly or await our interest. But all those things can be seen in the painting, and someone who doesn't see them doesn't understand what he is looking at.

In short, the picture can be described in two contrasting ways, and the descriptions are incommensurable. This resembles the case of the human soul. We can imagine a complete account of the human being as a biological organism, from which nothing observable has been left out. Any creature with just this biological constitution will behave as I do, and lead the life that is distinctive of our kind. So why add a further story about the soul? Why not draw the obvious conclusion, that because nothing needs to be added to the biology, the biology is all that there is?

That would be like saying that, since no woman is mentioned in the scientific description of Manet's canvas, there is no woman in the picture. We can tell two stories about Manet's canvas, both complete. One explains it, the other tells us what it means. Likewise we can tell two stories about the human organism, one explaining its physical appearance and behaviour, the other telling us what it means to us. Many concepts that feature in this second story have no application in the first. For example, we describe people as responsible and free. We praise them, blame them and see worth and meaning in the things that they do. We criticize, argue, persuade. A complex language has emerged through which we relate to each other, and this language bypasses reference to the organism in something like the way our description of the woman in Manet's picture ignores the physical constitution of the canvas.

As in the case of the picture, the two descriptions that we give of the human being are incommensurable. There is no place in the language of biology for the concepts of freedom and responsibility. Biology can describe grimaces and facial contortions, but it lacks the concept of a smile – 'for smiles from Reason flow, and are of love the food', as Milton finely put it. The concepts that we spontaneously use to describe the human being do not explain – they interpret. And the interpretation that we favour describes a reasonable creature, accountable to his kind.

Crucial to this interpretation is the concept of self. Other animals are conscious, have thoughts, desires and emotions. But only we are self-conscious, able to address each other from 'I' to 'I', and to know ourselves in the first person, as subjects in a world of objects. As Kant plausibly argued, self-consciousness and freedom are two sides of a coin. It is I, not my body, who chooses, and it is I who am praised or blamed, not my limbs, my feelings or my movements. There is a mystery here: how can I be both a free subject and a determined object, both the 'I' that decides and the body that carries the decision through? Kant argued that the understanding stops at the threshold of this mystery, and I suspect that he was right. It is precisely this mystery that religions try to normalize, with the story of the soul.

The story varies from epoch to epoch and creed to creed. But it is never more simply put than in the language of the Koran, in which one word – *nafs* – means both 'self' and 'soul'. This soul is raised in me: only by learning the ways of accountability do I rise to the condition of a free being, who realizes his freedom in his deeds. Hence the soul can be corrupted. There is such a thing as the Devil's work, which consists in undermining the self, tempting people to see themselves as objects, leading them to identify completely with their biological condition, to squander their selfhood in orgies of concupiscence, and to refuse all accountability for what they are and do. This moral truth is conveyed with admirable simplicity in the great Sura of the Sun, Koran 91, which invokes the wonders of creation: sun and moon, day and night, heaven and earth, and finally 'a soul, and what formed her, to which He revealed both right and wrong'. The Sura goes on to tell us that the one who safeguards the soul's purity will prosper, while he who corrupts it is destroyed. It requires no metaphysics to understand the words *wa nafsin* ... ('And a soul ...') They are spoken in me and to me. The verse refers to the self that harbours knowledge of right and wrong, and it is just this that is the source of meaning in me.

One function of religion is to present the fundamental truths of our condition in lively images and improving stories: to make available to the imagination facts that people may find extremely difficult to understand when presented to the intellect. Reflecting on this the great twelfth-century Andalusian jurist and philosopher, Ibn Rushd, known in the Latin world as Averroës, argued that propositions can be assented to in three different ways. Some people arrive at their beliefs by rational demonstration, others by dialectical discussion, others still by rhetoric. Rhetoric can lead us astray; nevertheless revelation (*shar*ʿ) enters the souls of ordinary people by rhetorical devices – images, stories, analogies that help people to grasp and adhere to truths whose full meaning only those skilled in deduction can understand. We are, as he put it, *mutafaadil* in our assent – meaning distinguished, but equally and politely acceptable to each other. The revelation granted in the Koran helps the ordinary person to understand his own nature, as a soul living in judgement under the eyes of a benevolent God, even if words like 'soul', 'judgement' and 'God' are to be understood in their true meaning only through the science of demonstration, which is philosophy. Ibn Rushd went further, and argued that it would be wrong to introduce ordinary people to the philosophical interpretation of those terms: people would lose sight of their literal meaning, while failing to understand the intellectual arguments in which the terms are grounded. They would learn doubt, without finding the intellectual path from doubt to faith.

Ibn Rushd was surely right in this. It is no disrespect to the mass of mankind to say that they do not have the capacity to give a philosophical justification of fundamental truths. Nor is it disrespect to add that they nevertheless need to grasp those truths and to build them into their lives, if they are to live as they should. In particular people need to understand that they live on a different plane from the other animals, and that if they refuse this truth they will fall into discontent and self-alienation (as indeed they have done).

Christians, Jews, Hindus and Buddhists have distinct ways of capturing and revealing the soul idea, but the fundamental observation is shared. Human beings stand out from the rest of creation. They are subjects in a world of objects, and as a result they judge and are judged. Hence they can be redeemed and corrupted. This work of redemption and corruption is never-ending. We do not need a metaphysical doctrine of the soul to make sense of this: as we learn from the Koran, the reflexive pronoun is enough. Faith adds just one crucial detail: namely, that the reflexive pronoun is used also by God.

Of course, seeing the matter in this way, we do nothing to

justify the belief in immortality. Nevertheless, we can begin to make that belief intelligible. Although the woman in Manet's picture is nothing over and above the pigments in which we see her, you do not destroy her by destroying the pigments. If Manet's work were perfectly copied and then burned, we would confront a new canvas, but the *same woman*. The person seen in the new painting would be identical with the person seen in the old. This is a strange kind of identity, and not without paradox.[9] But it provides a model for theologians, should they wish to explain the identity between the person that I encounter in you, and the person who exists eternally in God's perception. Immortality, seen in that way, is not a prospect to look forward to, but a light in which we stand.

It was another Sam who brought those truths home to me – and did so by bringing me home. The good fortune that brought Petra to live with Sam the second brought Sam the third into the world. Quite early in her pregnancy Sophie was told that she was carrying a boy, and there was never a question in our minds about his name. And it was during the birth of Sam that, after decades of arrested development, I grew up.

Our hospital was built as a private house in the nineteenth century, and stands on the outskirts of Malmesbury, a proud mansion of Cotswold stone. You enter the building through a mock Tudor arch of stone, by lifting a cast-iron latch in an oak-panelled door. This door creaks like the door of a church, and opens on to a quiet vestibule, from which you proceed past a roomful of cheerful old ladies to a wide newelled staircase and thence to the maternity ward on the upper floor. The rooms of the old house have been divided, but each has its share of neo-Gothic mouldings, a stone arch or two, and corbel tables carved with oak leaves. Unlike the sterile surroundings of the modern hospital, these details carry a message of affirmation. As with so much that our ancestors carved in stone, they are a bid for immortality, a statement that we like it here and are glad to have been born.

From the window you see meadows in which cows are grazing; clumps of willow, ash and hawthorn; a stone cottage or two;

9 Those interested might consult the fascinating essay on 'Intentional identity' by P. T. Geach, reprinted in his *Logic Matters*.

wooden fences and blackthorn hedges. On one side there is a neat kitchen garden with flowering marrows, sweetcorn and beans, on the other a paddock with two horses and a donkey. All this refreshes the spirit and raises the morale – not only of the mother, but also of the nurses, who move around these airy rooms as though at home there, bringing linen from panelled cupboards in armfuls and making their patients feel like guests.

Within an hour of our arrival, however, pain pressed its claw on Sophie's face, convulsions wracked her body, and this woman whose goodness had shone into my heart like morning sunlight was now eclipsed by suffering. That suffering was caused by our child, fighting for the exit and not caring whom he killed along the way – just as Sam the Second had fought for that exit and killed his suffering dam. Malmesbury hospital pays for its beauty by its lack of staff. It has no anaesthetist, no surgeon and a local GP as its visiting doctor. For the relief of the mother only the old arts of midwifery are supplied: the chin-up cheerful chatter of the seen-it-all nurse. Hour after hour Sam tortured his mother, once showing his head, but then sinking back to beat in fury on some merely imaginary exit.

The pain that precedes birth is the image of our final agony: a life-and-death struggle, in which the organism stands on the brink of collapse. From time to time I would retreat to the hospital bathroom, hoping to re-emerge with the strength that she needed. And there the image of my mother came back to me, she who had suffered just this dreadful thing at my hands, worse when I had run away from home and left her grieving, worse again when I sat by her dying form like Stephen Dedalus and would not speak. What I had reproached in my mother as timidity I remembered now as gentleness; what I had deplored as puritanism I recalled as moral sense; what I had feared as anxiety I knew to be love – love baffled by my selfishness, love that would not intrude since it cherished my freedom and wanted only what was best for me. The sun of womanly feeling that had shone on me from Sophie had shone, though with a pallid light, from her. And the tears that I shed for Sophie were also tears for the mother whom I was learning now to mourn. My repentance came too late; yet something of her remained, and after a time her voice came through to me, and its stillness, its diffidence, its unwillingness to cause trouble or to stake a claim I understood at last as the signs of her unselfish interest. She was asking that I build for Sam the home that she, through no fault of her own, had struggled in vain to provide during the dark days of Sam the First. When, after 18 hours of labour, Sam the Third lay in the arms of his mother, Sophie looked at me with the same quiet smile that I now remembered from childhood, the smile that only a mother can give.

To grow up aged 54 is not a great achievement. But it is better than not growing up at all. No non-human animal can grow up. The foal drops from its mother and is at once on its feet, endowed with all that it needs for survival. The child is born helpless, and remains helpless from year to year. This fact – known to biologists as 'neoteny' – has been remarked on since the beginning of human history, and by no one more clearly than Aristotle, who noticed the crucial point: that the feature that distinguishes us from all other natural objects is simply not there when we are born, or there only *in potentia*. We are essentially rational beings, with all that this implies by way of self-consciousness, responsibility, moral agency and soul; and yet we are not rational at birth. We acquire our soul by a slow process in which we are entirely dependent on others. Without help from those who have already achieved it, rationality is something that we might never gain. Of all God's creatures we, who are the most capable, are the most helpless, the most likely to fail – as individuals and even as a species – to become what we essentially are.

Neoteny explains the fragility and incompleteness of the human child: it explains the burden of responsibility, and also the quiet joy that fills a father's life thereafter – the joy that comes from giving the power that is yours to the child that is hers. In the first hours of Sam's life I recalled the art critic Peter Fuller, killed in a car crash at the age of 42, who had tried to build from the Darwinian theory of neoteny a comprehensive vision of culture. Peter had been heavily influenced by the child psychologist D. W. Winnicot, from whom he took the view of childhood as a relation simultaneously of absolute independence and absolute dependence. A child comes into its mother's life as something entirely other, an organism unaware of anything but its own urgent appetites. But it also issues from its mother, and remains bound to her for year after year. At first, according to Peter's view of things, the child inhabits a fantasy world, in which its own desire is the magic force that moves and governs everything. Then it learns that it is not its own desire, but the desire of another, that gives and withholds the breast. Reality dawns through the mist of fantasy. The process of weaning is repeated at every level of consciousness, as the child learns that he must offer love if he is to receive it, and that his self-centred desire is not, after all, the motor of the universe.

Holding little Sam while his mother slept I remembered how fiercely I had disagreed with Peter, whose death nine years before had deprived me of a perceptive opponent and a most cherished friend. The theories of Winnicot and Melanie Klein struck me as presumptuous metaphors, attempts to read back into the child the adult that had yet to be made, and might never be made if the wrong influences were brought to bear on him and the wrong theories believed. Peter was obstinate, however, for he had invested in the psychoanalytic theory of the human condition all his sense of the human tragedy. It was this, he believed, that accounted for his own suffering while growing up, and which also freed him from that suffering when, finally, he turned round and saw the impotent Father face to face.

Peter's first love, intellectually speaking, was not Freud but Marx, from whom he took the vision of 'unalienated man', of man 'restored to himself' in a community without bondage or mediation – a community, as Freud might say, without the Father. But Peter had grown to immaturity as I did, by discovering high culture at school. And he had grown up as I did, by producing a son of his own. Lawrence Fuller's birth had acted on Peter like a religious conversion: it summoned him to prove that father and son can be bound together, not by edicts, but by love. And I wished I could talk again to Peter – so as to point to this calm little face before me and to say, no, it is not an animal, not a bundle of selfish appetites, but the beginnings of a person, and one that is already growing up.

Peter's most distinctive feature was his voice: slow, level, almost toneless – like a child's theatrical imitation of his father. Into this flat voice, which seemed to issue from somewhere behind the place where he stood, Peter would inject all kinds of resonances and inflections, which ruffled its surface without altering its steady drone. When first I met him in 1989 I described him thus:

'Peter is like something that has been dredged up from the bottom of a pond – flabby, white and eyeless. His flesh and his voice equally without colour, his body soft and limp. And yet, as soon as he begins to touch on some serious topic – art, religion, psychoanalysis, philosophy – a strange subterranean agitation begins to visit him, and gradually not only he, but the whole surrounding world is transformed, his inner battle with the Father becomes a universal cause, dividing the world into light and dark, illuminating with a keen intelligence all that is friendly, and casting deep shadows over all that is not. You want, then, to be part of his battle, even if only because of the immense moral seriousness with which it is waged.'

That moral seriousness drew me to Peter during our too few years of friendship, and I looked forward to our meetings as a child looks forward to holidays. Peter's greatest desire was to be loved, and especially by those he respected. In order to obtain love he would often embark on the fiercest criticism of the one from whom he sought it, hoping to be corrected, hoping that the other would care. But not any correction would satisfy him. His personality was inseparable from the stream of ideas that coursed perpetually through him, and in relating to others he invited them to plunge into that stream and swim with him side by side. Seldom have I met a person who was simultaneously so courageous in announcing his beliefs, and so vulnerable in defending them. As his belligerence softened, his vulnerability became more pronounced and his writings acquired a Hardyesque melancholy. Long after he had overcome the trauma of his father's vindictive absolutes, Peter would search the world for the signs that his existence was permitted, and his will endorsed. Art and culture had an overwhelming significance for him, because they contained the permission that he sought: he had been foretold in poetry and painting, and foretold in words of acceptance.

I thought of him as I looked down on Sam, not only because of Peter's crazy theories of childhood, but also because of the way in which his childhood had stayed with him and weighed on him. The conflict between Peter and his father was re-enacted at every turn, forcing him to see all opposition as a test of his own authenticity. As a result he had been marginalized by the art establishment, which can tolerate criticism only when played as a game. Peter was a living proof of Wilde's maxim that, in matters of the first importance, it is style, not sincerity, that counts. Style, too, is part of growing up. My mother had wished me to have it, and for that reason had called me Vernon. But she hadn't the faintest idea how to proceed beyond that point, and such style as I acquired came only later, when Roger had ceased his belligerence and settled into a Hamlet-like routine of poignant loneliness. Peter had never acquired style, but only enemies, among people wounded to the quick by his well-meaning description of their failings.

To be fully grown up is to recognize the costs of being free, one of which was paid by Peter, when he discovered that all avenues to advancement were closed to him, his status as the most insightful and influential critic of his generation notwithstanding. Thinking of Peter I resolved never to transfer the costs of fatherhood to Sam, as Dr Fuller had transferred them to Peter, and Jack Scruton to me. For that was what my mother asked of me.

Sam the baby responded by calmly accepting – what most people accept only in middle age – the fact of having been born. He did not cry, he returned all smiles and gurgles, he slept through the night and everyone loved him. But just as the pleasures of fatherhood begin at once, so too do the pains, as you realize that your past has no importance, besides the future of your child. Sam the baby had his own way of showing this. He crawled around the house, which I had so proudly furnished and so meticulously arranged, and which Sophie had hardly dared to disturb since her first intrusion, with the clear design of destroying it. I had spent my life exporting entropy to the borders of my universe and projecting it thence into space. And entropy was now returning, in the form of life that I had shaped, to spell out before my flabbergasted eyes its proof of the Second Law of Thermodynamics. All books within reach were taken from their shelves and spread across the floor. All papers were swept from the desk and tablecloths pulled from the tables. Knobs were turned, switches flicked and buttons pressed, arbitrarily stopping and starting everything from computers to the mains transformer, and from the hair-drier to the Magimix. Sam made a sharp distinction between liquids that could be poured on the carpet and those better reserved for the table, the first being gooey, insoluble and likely to harden within minutes, the second watery, abundant and brightly coloured, able to run quickly onto the floor and to penetrate, where possible, to the ceiling below, there to expand in an indelible and multi-coloured stain. He had a genius for discovering items that needed to be found at the last minute, and which for that reason had been carefully put away in boxes, drawers and cupboards. Collar studs, cuff links, stock pins; black ties, dress shoes; cycle lamps, rucksacks, torches, maps, diaries – everything that needed to be exactly where it had always been, to be snatched in those moments when the difference between catching and missing a train might be less than a minute, and concerning which calm assurance had for decades prevailed over ignominious panic – all such objects would disappear for days on end, to reappear at last in a packet of cereal, under the lid of the butter dish, or at the bottom of the laundry basket amid unmatched socks and sodden teddy bears. During my years as a bachelor I could sweep the whole house with my eyes and report 'Alles in Ordnung'; now I was fighting day and night to create islands of order in an expanding sea of chaos. As for my soul, however, chaos had been conquered by order, and my very exasperation, as I struggled from island to island about the house, was proof of a new contentment with my lot, since it was a lot that I shared.

In one matter, it should be said, Sam strove for order, just as soon as he was able to stand on his feet, and this was the matter of building. He watched with fascination the men who were working on our extension, and very soon decided, although he could not yet express himself in words, that his help was indispensable. Furnishing himself with a trowel, and scooping dollops of fresh mortar from the communal wheelbarrow, he would follow along behind the bricklayer, adjusting positions, aligning edges and adding more brickwork of his own. For hours on end he would pursue this task, his little face puckered and frowning, his hands red with the cold, his body bent over with the effort of patting down mortar and lifting in bricks. He was apprenticing himself to his future manhood, and claiming our place as his home.

To watch a child grow up is to become detached from yourself and attached to another, whose total dependence compels independence in you. You are the guardian, the commander, the protector and enforcer on this child's behalf, and your principal duty is to prevent his destruction by the world. Evils that had previously been merely hypothetical now loom forward in their actuality, and it is no longer possible to look on the corruption and stupidity of the world as though you could set it at a distance and go back to your books.

What then is the solution? Animals too can be spoiled, as when a horse goes unpunished for its vices. But the spoiling of a child is the spoiling of a soul – such is thought presented so vividly in the Sura of the Sun. It is a crime against the moral order, and one of which our society is guilty in a hundred ways: through its failure to punish faults, through its proliferation of temptations, through its refusal to educate in the name of 'child-centred' learning, through its determination to sexualize children from the earliest age and to put lust above love in their hearts, so destroying their hearts in any case. There is no weapon in the armoury of nothingness more lethal than TV. Now entirely managed by its own spoiled children the television has one purpose and one effect – which is to ephemeralize our affections by putting momentary fantasy in the place of lasting interest, idle curiosity in the place of knowledge and voyeuristic appetite in the place of feeling. Television presents all that it touches in the guise of fleeting images, which must be ever louder, ever cruder, ever more eye-catching and vulgar, if the craving of its victims is to be assuaged. The simple answer is to forbid it, and it was my father's answer. He was forced to accept a telly in the house, since my maternal grandmother made a gift of one so that we could watch the coronation of Elizabeth II in 1952. But he saw no reason at all to turn it on. If the screen were glowing as he passed on his silent vigil he would turn it off without a word. Not being a product of television, he had retained the capacity to ignore it. Today we live in another world – a world of fantasy, delusion and unfreedom, in which the effort of rational choice is in many areas beyond our powers. Growing up with Sam I have come to see this and, having spoiled Sam the First, done little to improve Sam the Second, and generally – like many childless people – devoted more time to evading responsibilities than to fulfilling them, have decided to reward my mother's otherwise patient love for me by protecting Sam the Third.

It is not that television is forbidden: we simply don't have one, just as some people don't have a car or a dog. Of course, Sam is allowed to watch the box elsewhere. But returning home, he enters a place of talk and games and books. He is granted a vision of normality in a grossly abnormal world. And this search for normality is surely the true purpose of education. Sam is destined to be a person, a free being with reason, knowledge, imagination and moral sense. He will need the freedom of thought that comes from mental discipline. He will need the moral virtues that make human beings lovable. He will need a knowledge of his community and its past, without which he will find no place in the world. He will need foreign languages – not 'so as to fight the battles of life with the waiters in foreign hotels', as Matthew Arnold put it, but so as to understand the universal human condition beneath the superficial differences of speech. And he will need imagination, the precious gift that re-enchants our disenchanted world. Thinking of all this, we found no difficulty in endorsing the traditional curriculum, and meanwhile the children's literature (Grimm, Andersen, the Alice books, and Pooh) which has the reproduction of innocence as its secret purpose.

It is only since becoming part of a family that I have become fully aware of the depth and seriousness of the opposition between the family and the State. The family has become a subversive institution – almost an underground conspiracy – which is at war with the State-sponsored culture. Hence the family has been rigorously excluded from the official curriculum. Mothers appear from time to time in schoolbooks, but they are conspicuously single. Fathers have become unmentionable, as trousers were to our Victorian ancestors. The state-imposed lessons in sex education seem to be designed precisely to sever the link between sex and the family, by showing the family to be an 'option' rather than a norm. These lessons will ensure that the next generation will not form families, since it will have destroyed in itself everything that leads one sex to idealize the other, and so to channel its erotic feelings into marriage.

Sophie and I belong to a growing class of dissidents, at war with the official culture and prepared to challenge it. This official culture is founded on the premise that human material is infinitely plastic, and can be moulded by the State into any shape required. This is one of the first of the official doctrines that you learn, as a parent, to doubt. We compared Sam with other boys, and could not help remarking how similar they are in one fundamental respect, which is that they all want to be men. Moreover, they all associate manliness with action, with using tools, with making something out of nothing, and with power and the machines that produce it. Sam spends his days on the building site quietly playing at manhood. Although he is unlikely to emulate either Mill or Mozart, his eager, co-operative nature, his determination to be useful and his narrow but real curiosity about the world of masculine labour is proof of the only normality that really counts.

In the world described by Jane Austen, men and women enjoyed separate spheres of action, the first public, the second private, the first involving influence without intimacy, the second intimacy that was also a form of far-reaching, though publicly hidden, influence. Dress, manners, education, recreation and language all reinforced this division, with marriage as the great life choice in which it culminated, and whose purpose it was. Although there may be no going back to the society described by Jane Austen, we do our children a disservice if we fail to acknowledge that their sexual nature sets them from the beginning on different paths. It seems to me that we should learn not to deny sex, but to idealize it – to set before our children an image of the good man and the good woman, and to teach them to imitate what can be loved and admired.

Idealization is natural to human beings; for it is the process whereby they try to make themselves lovable, and to live in the only security that our life provides. In our marriage vows Sophie and I were making the same attempt. We knew the fickle lot of the human animal; we knew that married life would be fraught with temptation. But we knew also that those things are not the only reality. We become fully human when we aim to be more than human; it is by living in the light of an ideal that we live with our imperfections. That is the deep reason why a vow can never be reduced to a contract: the vow is a pledge to the ideal light in you; a contract is signed by your self-interested shadow.

Happiness comes through ideals, and it is only by idealizing each other that people can really fall in love. The strange superstition has arisen in the Western world that we can start all over again, remaking human nature, human society and the possibilities of happiness, as though the knowledge and experience of our ancestors were now entirely irrelevant. But on what fund of knowledge are we to draw when framing our alternative? The utopias have proved to be illusions, and the most evident result of our 'liberation' from traditional constraints has been widespread discontent with the human condition. It seems to me, therefore, that you should prepare your children to be happy in the way that you are happy. Treat them exactly as you would if your own ideals were generally shared. After all, your ideals, like your children, define you: between them, they are all that you have.

7
Sleeping Cities

During the 1980s I often travelled to Eastern Europe, hoping to make some small contribution to the anti-communist cause. My main points of call were cities, and my errands took me equally to their ancient hearts and their dismal peripheries. Of old Warsaw little remained apart from the centre, which had been burned by the Nazis and then painstakingly restored as a Renaissance city fortress. Prague and Budapest, however, had come through the war more or less unscathed. Subsequent building had been restricted to outlying socialist housing projects, with the occasional faceless block in the city centre, devoted to some inscrutable Party function and surrounded by armed guards.

A red star had been affixed to the dome of the beautiful Hungarian Parliament – a neo-Gothic castle inspired by Westminster – signifying that it was now an annex of the functionalist block next door, headquarters of the Communist Party. The same red star had been scattered over the roofs and pinnacles of Prague, giving to the dilapidated palaces a sad and temporary air, like ornaments from last year's Christmas. The façades of public buildings were defaced with slogans: 'Fight for Peace', 'Forward in Brotherhood with the Soviet Union', 'The Programme of the Party is the Programme of the People', and similar inanities, which caught the attention only because they coincided, more or less, with the jargon and the sentiments of the textbooks studied in British departments of sociology.

Almost every street would contain long platforms, raised on wooden stakes above the pavement to protect pedestrians from the slow, steady rain of stucco that fell from the untended walls. Since all buildings were publicly owned, no building was cared for, and visitors to Prague were granted the spectacle of a baroque city – a city of surfaces – the hollow core of which showed through its crumbling skin. Despite this, and also because of it, Prague seemed utterly removed from the real world, a relic of vanished life, frozen in its final posture. Arriving there was like entering the room of someone who has died, and whose belongings lie untouched and decaying where he left them.

This experience was especially vivid if you took the bus from the airport to the quarter then named Leninova, and changed to the tram that clattered down the cobbled hillside into town. By this route you entered Prague through Malá Strana, the 'Little Side', which grew up in the sixteenth and seventeenth centuries beneath the castle of Hradčany, hemmed in between the hill and the river. Domes and campaniles crowd into the bowl of the Little Side, and behind them a peaceful orchard stretches on the hillside towards the twin-towered monastery of Strahov. Each building embraces its neighbour, gable touching gable, curlicue wrapped in curlicue, roof sloping into roof. Cornices and string courses shoot sideways, rush together like laughing streams, and lose themselves in foreign windowsills. Turrets and pediments poke above the clutter, and here and there the crumbling wall of a palace abruptly severs the street. The cone-capped towers of gates and bridges, the spikes of onion domes, the gesticulating statues on the parapets, barely arrested in the architectural whirlwind, like flimsy ballerinas on a surging sea of stucco – this superfluity of form and detail was thrown into drastic relief by the dirt and decay. Things seemed to remain standing only by a miracle, each building propped against its neighbour, reduced to a flaking shell. One breath and the whole contraption would collapse, and nothing of Prague would remain but a cloud of dust.

Spiritually speaking, something like this had already happened. In the streets the people seemed to notice nothing and to smile at no one. But they walked towards the place where a queue was forming with the same unhurried and obstinate pace, grasping bags of frayed plastic like children gripping toys. The shop window would contain dusty piles of tinned and bottled vegetables, a few slogans, perhaps a sculpted sausage or an artist's impression of a cheese. The people stared at these things from fixed and expressionless eyes. These unwanted goods were decoys, designed to drive away all curiosity. The real merchandise had arrived that morning in the early hours – a van-load of chicken wings, Cuban oranges, Hungarian sausage. In such a scene you saw the state-controlled scarcity, whereby the instinct of rebellion was neutralized and the people regimented into queues. You also saw the ruling principle of communist Czechoslovakia: the deception that deceives no one; the lie that no one believes.

Nowhere was this principle more in evidence than in the window of the 'Agitation Centre', last remaining outpost (apart from Western universities) of the 'agitprop' set in motion by the Bolsheviks. Behind glass that had never been cleaned, in a window that had never been dusted, a sloping board of posters would proclaim the socialist cause: Nazi-faced American GIs thrust their bayonets into Vietnamese babies, fat capitalists with bulging cigars stood on the heads of helpless workers, and huge missiles, decorated with the stars and stripes, flew in regimented flocks over the cowering cities of Europe. Dusty photographs showed weary communist potentates in grey alpaca suits, signing with fat old hands the bits of paper set before them on modernist desks, while Marx and Lenin stared across their porcine bodies into the future. Notices would be pinned to a screen of cork behind the window: more slogans, written in a shaky old hand, composed in the same impersonal syntax, and with the same impenetrable vagueness: 'Forward with the Party to a Socialist Future!!' 'Long live our Friendship with the Soviet People!!' Strange that some frail old person should have taken the trouble to copy out those empty words, to etch them round with quotation marks, and to place them in this dusty shrine.

It was on my third or fourth visit, when I knew the language well enough to read what I saw, that the pathos of the Agitation Centre came fully home to me: the pathos of an 'agitation' that has dwindled to a palsy. The message of the Centre was that things here cannot change, that you are not to hope or plan or strive, that everything has been fixed eternally, and that nothing remains for each successive generation but to append its signature to the fixed and senseless decree. Looking through that dirty window, I saw fear in a handful of dust.

Ten years later I visited that Agitation Centre and went inside for the first time. It was now the local headquarters of the Občanské Hnutí – the Citizen's Movement – which had driven the communists from power. In charge of the office was Petr Pithart, whom I had visited in secret ten years earlier, and who was soon to be Prime Minister of his country.

Before those great events, which so few of us foresaw, the cities of Eastern Europe lay like unopened coffins in the vault of time. Few people in the West gave much thought to their future, and – except for the brief awakening of Solidarity – no sound emerged from them save an indistinct and discontented murmur. To the visitor, these densely inhabited places lacked everything that make cities live. For one thing, there were no markets, and not only because there was nothing to sell. Where buying and selling are forbidden, the economy goes underground. The black market is the spectre of a commerce that has died. It haunts the city, poisoning all natural dealings between living people. The visitor to the sleeping cities of Eastern Europe quickly came to see that true cities depend on the free co-operation of those who buy and sell. Markets are not luxuries, but a necessary part of the urban project.

The absence of a free economy goes hand in hand with an absence of migrants – or at any rate of voluntary migrants. Markets are the most natural form of co-operation between strangers. They are therefore cosmopolitan. In a market the foreigner is the equal of the native. Hence cities were centres of immigration, places where peasants came to sell their labour, where merchants sold products brought from distant lands, where financiers with relations in every port would set up shop and bargain. Those, like the Jews, who had no other territory could nevertheless be at home in cities. From the great energy of human exchange the culture of the city arose – that distinctive, all-embracing festival, in which racial and religious differences dissolve. Only vestiges of this culture remained in communist Europe, kept alive as a symbol of progress, but scorned in the official ideology. 'Cosmopolitan' was, for the communists, a term of abuse like 'bourgeois'; the culture of the town was to be 'proletarian', a mish-mash of coarse humour and anti-capitalist rage.

A more important thing was also missing. People come together in cities not merely to exchange goods and labour, but to protect themselves from enemies. The walled towns of Europe are testimony to the danger in which our ancestors lived, and to the surest means of self-protection, which is the city itself. The communist city was not a place of safety but a panopticon, irradiated by unseen eyes. You were not protected from danger in the town, but additionally exposed to it. Most townspeople, if they could afford it, escaped to the country at weekends, if only to rest their spirits from the x-rays that poured unceasingly through every public and private space.

And of course, there was no real night life in a communist city. A few bars stayed open, but they were shifty, muffled places, where unexplained figures sat alone in corners, and where every gathering was observed by those with power to arrest you. The Communist Party had its own variant of Christ's saying: where two or three are gathered together in any name but mine, there I shall be in the midst of them. In such circumstances, even a private dinner party was a risk. There were theatres and concerts; but people rushed home from them without lingering in the streets, and making no effort to prolong any snatches of conviviality. My own evening entertainments were not entertainments at all, but hushed gatherings in private apartments, where people entered quietly and at carefully staggered intervals. Leaving such a gathering, going into the extraordinary stillness of a town where street lighting was sparse, where cars were an object of suspicion, and where few people ventured after dark, was like stepping into a darkened theatre after the players and the audience have gone home, when only the ghost of a drama remained on stage.

In some respects, however, the communist system preserved the memory of an older and deeper experience of the city. This was in fact most apparent at night-time, when you walked through darkened streets, hearing no sound except your own footstep on the cobbles, and sometimes another, fainter footstep, which stopped and started when you did. You knew then that you were walking through a sleeping city. The capitalist city never sleeps as Prague slept in its mortuary silence. All night long in London or New York the noise, the light and the commotion continue; for the modern capitalist city has taken leave of its residents, and functions like a machine. In fact it has taken leave of its senses, since that is what the residents are. The modern city has been programmed to work, to speak, to sing and to riot on its own, almost without human company; to enter such a city is to be taken up by it, to be swept along into a rhythm that is more relentless than a monologue and more exhausting than a dance.

Whenever I was sure that I was not being followed, I would stand in the squares and streets of Prague and listen to the quiet noises of a city sleeping: the turning of a key in the latch; a window opening; the flapping of curtains in a sudden breeze. These are noises that you can no longer hear in London or New York – the noises made by strangers as they settle down, divided by thin partitions, and melt into a common sleep. Those people sleeping side by side in that ancient city probably never spoke to one another by day, or did so only in the cautious and shifty way that the Party required of them. At night, however, in the side-by-sideness of sleep, they seemed unconsciously to acknowledge their need of one another, and to repair in secret ways the social bond that the communist machine would tear apart each day.

And this led me to another aspect of that old urban experience: the social mixture that comes about when people are confined together within city walls. Many of the residents of Prague had been born there, most of them under Nazi or communist rule, and few of them with the right or the means to move. The communist habit of transporting inconvenient populations went hand-in-hand with a desire to prevent the migration of those who seemed to be living where the plan required. The residents of Prague were therefore genuine locals, fixed, whatever their occupation, in places allocated by the municipal machine. There were no ghettoes, and – apart from the vulgar suburbs set aside for the Party apparatchiks – no real distinctions between rich and poor. Bureaucratic inertia, combined with a vestige of egalitarian morality, ensured that a single staircase in a dilapidated palace might be shared by a police official, a well-known dissident, a plumber, a dustman and a once-famous artist whose works could no longer be sold or shown. The philosopher Radim Palouš, veteran of the underground seminars, who had lost his university position after the Soviet invasion, still lived in the medieval house above the mill-race in Kampa – surely the most picturesque urban location in Europe. Although his apartment was surveyed day and night, he sat there among books and *Jugendstil* furniture like an old cobbler among shoes left by customers who were long in their graves, ignoring the disaster beyond the walls. His neighbours were ordinary people; he too had become an ordinary person.

Indeed, the all-encompassing ordinariness was like a shared feeling of loyalty, a common sense of being tied to the city, as Londoners felt tied during the Blitz.

I was reminded of the Blitz on my very first visit, when I went to address a private seminar. After walking deserted streets, I found myself in the empty stairwell of an old apartment block, where dirty marble steps stretched upwards into the darkness. Everywhere the same expectant quiet hung in the air, as when an air raid has been announced, and the town hides from its imminent destruction. I groped my way to the third floor, found the number I was looking for, and pressed the bell. The small sound amplified the silence. But it was a listening silence; I imagined ears pressed to every latch on the stairwell. I was about to reach for the bell again, when shuffling footsteps sounded on the other side of the door. I was ushered in with whispers and, to my astonishment, found myself in a room full of people, wrapped in the same noiseless expectancy. I understood that there really was going to be an air raid, and that the air raid was me. In that room were the battered remnants of Prague's intelligentsia: old professors in their shabby waistcoats; long-haired poets; fresh-faced students who had been denied admission to university for their parents' political 'crimes'; priests and religious in plain clothes; a would-be rabbi; even a psychoanalyst. They all belonged, I discovered, to the same profession: that of stoker. Some stoked boilers in hospitals, others in apartment blocks; one stoked at a railway station, another in a school. Some stoked where there were no boilers to stoke, and these imaginary boilers came to be, for me, a fitting symbol of the communist economy. On that memorable evening, however, one thought dominated all others: here, for the first time, I was lecturing to a working-class audience, an audience of workers united by their chains.

There were other and more brutal sides to the communist housing policy. The residents of Prague were tied down in their city, offered menial employment and left more or less to their own devices. Elsewhere – in Prostějov, for example, or the once beautiful Slovakian town of Považska Bystrice – the old town centres were bulldozed, and the population stacked up in blocks on the perimeter: for the Party was anxious to destroy the past and the loyalties that grew in it. Populations were also forcibly displaced. The Moravian town of Olomouc (the Austrian

Olmütz, centre of culture where Mahler conducted at the tiny opera house) had been allocated to gypsies from Slovakia. Swept up from their ancient roads and lay-bys, these half-nomadic, half-agrarian people were pushed into the crumbling old buildings that comprised the once noble centre of this once noble town. They could find nothing to do there – or at any rate, nothing compatible with their old way of life – and as a result decayed as visibly as their surroundings. Nor would they relinquish their old ways. From the third floor of an eighteenth-century palace I was once greeted by a neigh, as a horse, seeing me pass in the deserted street, stuck his head through the window and cried out for rescue – though whether he could ever get down a staircase which, in my experience, no horse could have got up, I doubted.

This attempt at forcible integration did not work. In Prague, however, where the native population had been imprisoned in its city, so that city and citizen should decay together, lapsing into the state of resentful acquiescence that the Party required, there grew, beneath the stagnant surface, little pockets of civic feeling, and it was in these pockets that the dissidents lived and thrived.

In Prague, as in Warsaw, you also found another survival of the medieval city. These towns were once holy places; their churches and monasteries each had its own private sanctity, its own story of faith and martyrdom, and its own patron saint. Even the most sceptical would visit some sacred place in times of trouble, and find consolation in prayer. The Prague Church of St James was a place of pilgrimage for the opposition. Under a particular pew, known to insiders, the samizdat bulletin of the underground church – *Informace o cirkví* (Information about the Church) – was hidden in a bag attached to the underside of the bench. Before and after each interrogation young people would attend mass at the church of St Joseph in the Little Side. These churches, like the church of Father Popiełuszko outside Warsaw, were the scenes of miracles – not those spectacular events in which statues weep blood or cripples walk, but the intimate miracles of the conscience, in which courage suddenly appears in the faint-hearted, and a desire for sacrifice in the spirit of a would-be pop star.

Of course, these remnants of civic feeling were fed by the imagination. Cynics might dismiss them as illusions. But the work of the imagination is necessary to us, and we owe to it all that is most precious in human life – including love itself. And the imagination thrives in adversity. Deprived of any field of action, it creates for itself a world in which virtue is rewarded and vice held at bay, a world that exactly corresponds to the faith that built the city of Prague, and whose traces remained in the hollow carcasses of buildings torn from their history and left to rot in the common graveyard.

And then everything changed. The light of the modern world burst on these sleeping cities and awoke them from their dreams. Never again will those intimations be afforded of the old, quiet, rooted urban togetherness. Prague, Warsaw and Budapest are now modern cities, enjoying the abundance, the excitement and the smiling co-operation between strangers that are the gifts of freedom.

With freedom comes speed. Cosmopolitan cities must match the pace of the world that includes them and which they in turn include. Fast-food restaurants, porn shops, travel agents and multinational chain stores stimulate the lust for new experience, while also ensuring that never again will experience be truly new; flocks of chirping tourists settle and start up again like migrating starlings; expensive cars stand bumper to bumper in the street, poisoning the narrow alleyways; the churches, once tranquil islands in a sea of fear, have become busy open thoroughfares where foreign voices sound; trivial pop music is heard in every bar, filling the corners where, not so long ago, young idealists whispered of forbidden things – of Kafka and Rilke, of Mahler and Schoenberg, of Musil and Roth and 'The World of Yesterday' that Stefan Zweig so movingly lamented.

That world has vanished. Communism preserved it as a dream; capitalism processed and packaged its waking fragments. Nothing is available now, save mass-produced replicas. Prague too is a replica – a Disneyland version, a stage-set for *Die Meistersinger*. The market has come to Prague – not as a centripetal but as a centrifugal force. It has blown the town apart, clearing the centre of its old and settled residents, and ghettoizing the poor. Those who can afford it are moving to the suburbs. The poorer people of Živkov, where only ten years ago doctors and tram drivers lived side by side, have been abandoned by their middle-class neighbours, and look on helplessly as Ukrainian mafiosi, illegal immigrants from the Balkans, and international smuggling rings take up residence on their once silent stairwells, to settle old scores with guns. The hypermarkets and shopping malls are descending from the stratosphere into the fields around the city, while the little shops that served the stokers whom I knew (many of whom now hurry from one official building to another in chauffeur-driven cars) are closing down. We are witnessing a quaint variation of a global theme: the theme of 'Edge City', as Joel Garreau describes it. Prague is not yet Detroit. After all, it has a living and beautiful centre. But its life is no longer a local product. The new life of Prague has flooded in from the global market, colonizing this unowned space with a stubborn determination equal to that of the refugees in Živkov.

That is how it seems, at least, to the visitor. But I remember these alleyways and palaces, these echoing stairwells and mansard studios, when they were not unowned at all. True, they belonged to no living human being – for the communists had abolished private property. They belonged to the city itself, the city that had died when the communists took charge of it. And at night, as the citizens slept, the ghost of Prague would return to them, to tell of a community living in peace, working, resting and praying as one. The tale remained in their waking thoughts, not as a hope, still less as an aim, but as a reminder of what might have been, had history been kinder. And the ghost of the city lingered on, until that day when peace was restored, and prayer forgotten. And with a faint cry heard only by the poets, it vanished forever.

8
Opera and I

For many years our family house contained neither gramophone nor musical instrument, and the radio was tuned constantly to the Home Service, switching to the Light Programme only on Saturday afternoons, when my father would listen to the football match. He had been loyal to Manchester United since childhood, and whenever his team made some damn-fool mistake Jack Scruton would lean forward in his chair, his body shaking with emotion, his right fist repeatedly slapping into the palm of his left hand. During those 'wireless' years nobody in our household sang, and it was understood that only cissies went to concerts. All sounds in our house were spoken sounds, and even these were brought into question during the long days of vindictive silence.

When I was 13, however, just before I discovered books, I discovered music. It happened that my father inherited the old upright piano on which his favourite sister had earned her LRAM before dying of TB at the age of 18. It was a treasured possession, not for the music, to which my father had been largely indifferent, but for the still remembered joy of its purchase, for the brief ray of hope that had shone from his sister's face into the gloom of that back-street parlour, and for the evenings of working-class togetherness around the piano, from which memory had deleted all the violence and the pain. The piano arrived one day on a Pickford's lorry, and was carried into our poky sitting room. To my astonishment my mother sat down and began to play: the slow movement of Beethoven's *Pathétique* Sonata, which she had learned as a child, and of which she recalled only the melody and the alto accompaniment. It was the most beautiful sound I had ever heard, and because my mother played it shyly and sadly I knew at once that music was both the cause of sadness and its cure.

I resolved to learn, begged for lessons, and was granted the right to visit Miss Benstead, a neat, fussy spinster, whose one chance of marriage had been forbidden by the domineering mother with whom she lived. Miss Benstead taught by the rules, and in those days the rules were weighty with knowledge. Not only did I have to learn my pieces; I was made to analyse them too. Within a year or so she had taught me to provide alto, tenor and bass to a given melody, had made me aware of the triads and their functions, had compelled me to read about the history of music and in general so copiously justified her sad existence as to earn my undying gratitude. However, I was not grateful in the least, and look back now in shame on the torments inflicted on that lonely, innocent and well-meaning woman, when Roger forced her to struggle through Bartók, poured scorn on Gilbert and Sullivan and sneered at her favourite Grieg, while Vernon looked on secretly and smiled.

About the same time as I began lessons with Miss Benstead my mother spent her savings on a gramophone, with 78s of *Eine Kleine Nachtmusik*, the *Hebrides Overture*, and the overture to *The Thieving Magpie*. I recall the poignant odour of those records as we took them from their sleeves, the exciting explosion as the needle hit the groove, and the vigorous old-fashioned performances that sounded through the crackle like a storm through the patter on a window-pane. After a year or so of piano lessons I began to frequent High Wycombe town library. The music shelves had been expertly stocked in the days before the gramophone, when piano playing was an accomplishment as common as graffiti-spraying today. I would bring home armfuls of music, forcing myself to bash through the classics and to imagine the notes that I couldn't play.

One day a distant cousin of my mother's visited. She was introduced to us as Auntie Betty, and we were told that she was known in the family for her piano playing. My mother's 'family' consisted of middle-aged ladies and secretive couples. They lived obscure lives in unvisited suburbs, had produced no children and were known for no exploit worth recording. Betty's piano playing was the only fact attached to her name, and her visit was a surprise and also a violation, since my mother's 'family' – to which she was attached only by the slenderest threads of affection – voted Conservative and were for that reason not allowed in the house. Auntie Betty was a simple soul, a middle-aged spinster, who came on a day when my father was absent, carrying presents for the children and fussing over everything and everyone with an eager desire to be liked. She saw open on the piano the score of Mozart's Sonata in C, and asked me to play it. I stumbled through the first movement, and she was fulsome in her praise: not for my playing but for the far more impressive feat of being able to read music, something she had never achieved.

'Won't you play something, Auntie Betty?' we asked.

She looked at us shyly, and protested that she was only an amateur and merely tried to copy others. She gave in to our requests at last and said she would play something she had heard yesterday on the wireless. She sat down, thought a moment, and played without a mistake Chopin's C sharp minor Nocturne. We listened in stunned silence. This was my first encounter with a real musician – someone for whom music is so instinctive a gift that it lodges itself effortlessly in the ear, the brain and the fingertips. I saw at once that it was not Betty who was the amateur, but I, who stood outside the world of music, cut off by a screen of written notes.

Some time before Auntie Betty's visit, and under Miss Benstead's instruction, I began to read about the great composers. In this way I discovered opera – *The Marriage of Figaro*, to be precise. I cannot remember the title of the book, but it told me that there was no aria more full of pathos than 'Dove sono'; that Mozart had never written a sweeter melody than 'Voi che sapete', and that the overture was a sublime piece of symphonic writing that entirely captured the spirit of the opera. Words like 'pathos' and 'sublime' had an unearthly resonance, and although I did not know what they could mean in such a context, I used them myself in enthusiastic praise of this unheard music. Soon I had become an expert on *The Marriage of Figaro*, and was prepared to defend its merits against *Oklahoma!*, *Guys and Dolls* and even *The Black and White Minstrel Show*. This early expression of conservative sentiment led to the stern judgement that the gramophone should not be played when Dad was at home. This in turn increased my eagerness to hear the masterpiece that I had championed, and eventually my mother devised a scheme to assist me.

She recalled another relative – a distant cousin called Uncle Tink, who lived in London and who was reputed to like music. At least, a pile of records and a gramophone were associated with Uncle Tink in my mother's memory, and she distinctly remembered him playing one day a symphony by Beethoven. After an exchange of letters Uncle Tink agreed to take me, on my fourteenth birthday, to a performance of *Figaro*.

A frail man with a military moustache and a dapper appearance, Uncle Tink (who was a tax inspector by profession) lived with his childless wife in a respectable mansion block on Shaftesbury Avenue. His liking for music extended no further than the Beethoven and Tchaikovsky symphonies, and his favourite evening occupation was to sit with a glass of sherry and a copy of *The Times*, filling in the crossword. The idea of taking an uncouth child to the opera clearly appalled him, and no sooner had we taken our places in the balcony circle than he dozed off, leaving unanswered my eager questions about the length of the overture, which aria came before which, and when was 'Dove sono'. It had been an exciting day, with much travelling, and the wonderful gaiety of the overture so transported me that I was quickly exhausted. As Cherubino began to sing the aria which I was sure must be 'Voi che sapete', my eyes involuntarily closed, and my head fell heavily against Uncle Tink's shoulder. Starting awake to find me half asleep beside him Uncle Tink saw his advantage and whisked me away. It was five years before I was able to sit through a full performance of Mozart's masterpiece.

It was 30 years, however, before I came to understand its greatness. By then I had gone through a long apprenticeship in the Wagner music dramas; I had come to love the early moderns – Berg, Janáček and Britten especially; and I had allowed a weakness for Verdi (as I foolishly saw it) to grow. But even the greatest of those composers, I felt, had not matched the achievement of *Figaro* – a cogent drama, a comedy full of sadness, a portrait of society in which every class is equally individualized and equally real, and all this conveyed through the music. And who, besides Wagner, had rivalled Mozart in uniting the musical structure with the dramatic argument, so that each is compelled by the other and shaped by its demands?

Figaro therefore remained with me as a kind of artistic ideal – a paradigm of the unity between music and drama. Operas with irrelevant ballets, marches past, gratuitous arias for famous tenors, or snatches of dialogue in which the music stands still and the action moves on without it – these have always annoyed me. However great the music, and however interesting the drama, such features exhibit, to me, an insuperable artistic failing. I have never ceased to lament the fact that *The Magic Flute* is a Singspiel and not an opera; *Fidelio* is all but spoiled for me by its spoken dialogue; and the works of Donizetti, with their extravagant arias framed by mediocre recitative, leave me cold. And yes, I even came to agree, in time, with Ivor Deas's reservations about *Don Giovanni*.

This is wrong, I know, and while artistic puritanism pulls one way, emotion pulls another. I am drawn to those wonderful works – from Monteverdi's *Orfeo* to *Aïda* and *The Bartered Bride* – in which the drama is treated as a series of episodes, and the music as an intense exploration of situations and states of mind. The free handling of the narrative enables composers like Monteverdi and Lully to lift an emotion clear of the surrounding drama, and to give it a lyrical power that the drama itself cannot supply. Nevertheless I still return to the Wagnerian ideal of the integrated music drama – the *Gesamtkunstwerk* – and am convinced that it was Mozart, not Wagner, who first achieved it.

That is one reason why I seldom visit opera houses – one reason, that is, in addition to the huge expense. For the chances are that what you see on the stage will have nothing to do with what you hear from the pit. The habit has grown of ignoring not merely the stage directions given by the composer, but also the spirit of the music, the sense of the words, and even the nature of the drama. A nineteenth-century opera may be set in Hitler's Germany, so that the producer can reveal that he is, contrary to rumour, sound on the Nazi question. Or it may be transported, like Wagner's *Ring*, to the world of industrial capitalism, so that the producer can show that he too has read Feuerbach, Marx and Bernard Shaw.

It is odd that this habit of disobedience should have come into existence now, when so much energy has been devoted to the goal of authentic musical performance. So far as the music goes, we believe, the performer is the servant of the composer, with a duty to produce the sounds, the tones, the mood and the movement that the composer desired. Wagner performances, therefore, are musically as authentic as possible, following meticulously the instructions in the score. After all, Wagner went to the trouble of inventing his own musical instrument – the Wagner tuba – in order to obtain exactly the sound that he wanted, and who would think of replacing that instrument with a saxophone, say, or a military euphonium? Yet Wagner productions are invariably travesties – not productions, in fact, but 'interpretations', with the ego of the producer placed squarely between the work and the audience, so turning every seat in the opera house into one with an obstructed view.

There are special reasons, of course, for the mutilation of Wagner. For Wagner's dramas concern sacred things, and sacred things are intolerable to those who no longer believe in them: an urge to desecrate replaces the desire to worship and – just as in periods of religious iconoclasm, such as that which destroyed the interiors of our English churches – the finest and most beautiful symbols are torn down and trampled on, lest they retain their power over the human soul. That is why Siegfried is wearing schoolboy shorts and carrying a satchel; it is why Wotan is encumbered with a suitcase, a bicycle, a teddy bear or a mobile telephone. These are moralizing gestures on the producer's part: warnings against corruption and deliberate gestures of mockery towards gods that have died. Moreover, it was Wagner who made the greatest claim for opera as the equivalent for the modern world of the Greek tragic stage: a festival experience in which the spirit of religion lives as it can no longer live (according to Wagner) except in art. In opera we do not find drama alone; we rediscover, through the orchestra, the ancient experience of the chorus, the voice of the community in which all our emotions, all our hopes and fears, all our unacknowledged destinies, are pooled and redeemed. By mutilating the drama you neutralize the chorus, so that its voice becomes strange, cavernous and remote, addressing us from regions that we cannot visit, as though crying to us from across the Styx.

Although Wagner is the principal victim of the new iconoclasm, he is not the only one. Producers emerge from their apprenticeship in Wagner-smashing with the urge to smash on. They have discovered the unique opportunity that opera provides – namely, a silent audience, whose ears are in the grip of the music, and who can be invited to confuse the genius of the composer with that of the ignoramus who dances above him on the stage. Never is the modernist treatment more painful or destructive than when applied, as it is now invariably applied, to Debussy's *Pelléas et Mélisande*, the high point of French symbolist art, and the most graceful, shimmering cobweb of musical impressions that has ever been woven around a story. Maeterlinck's original play consists of lifeless platitudes uttered by paper-thin characters who know nothing of each other and even less of themselves. But it proves, in Debussy's hands, to be the perfect vehicle for musical evocation, in which all that is missing from Maeterlinck's sketchy symbols is provided by the music. The dialogue marks out areas of consciousness, and the music brilliantly colours them in.

The story is set in a mythic nowhere, on that timeless edge between hunting and farming that provides the setting for Wagner's *Ring*. The characters have nothing to do except ponder the surrounding symbols: the dark forest, the glimpses of the sea beneath them; the sun, moon and stars indifferently circling a trapped and futile love. These symbols provide the frame: the meaning lies in the tissue of orchestral sound, in which all is atmosphere and evocation, rising to moments of lyrical beauty that have no peer in modern music. *Pelléas* opens a window in the cluttered wall of modern life, through which we look back for the last time across the landscape of Romanticism. The immaculate music expresses a tenderness that wishes neither to defy the world nor to belong to it, but which rustles in the whole-tone harmonies like a dryad in the trees. *Pelléas* stands at the summit of modern French art. It offers a vision, a civilization-long memory, caught in the distorting lens of modern symbolism, of the cult of transience. From the erotic glimmer of a Watteau picnic, to the melancholy sighs of Paul Verlaine and the morose inwardness of Proust, the distinctive enigma of uncommitted passion has shaped the soul of France, and *Pelléas* is the highest expression of this enigma. Debussy's opera is therefore one of the iconic works through which European civilization can come to understand itself. Like *Paradise Lost*, *Faust*, *The Prelude*, *Middlemarch* and *Tristan und Isolde*, it should be held aloft with utter reverence, lest even the smallest drop of its concentrated meaning be spilled.

Peter Sellars decided to set this drama of evocation and non-event on Malibu beach – the setting furthest imaginable in atmosphere and lifestyle from that intended by the composer (whose setting comprehends all the inimitable sadness and aristocratic absurdism of French nineteenth-century literature, from the *Mémoires d'outre-tombe* to *Axel*, and from *Le Rouge et le Noir* to *Le grand Meaulnes*). In a recent production for ENO, Richard Jones, fresh from mutilating Wagner's *Ring*, decided to go one stage further along the path of desecration, and to replace every symbol with its opposite and every Gothic allusion with the random débris of modern life. No castle; not a scrap of vegetation to remind you of the dark forest and its constant rebirth; only a council house with three bedrooms containing the cast washed up on hospital beds. No tower with Mélisande's tresses falling onto the face of Pelléas, but only a room in which Pelléas inexplicably tries to nail his beloved to the wall by her hair.

I suppose you could see some sense in it, had the producer taken the same liberties with the text as he takes with the stage directions. But when the work opens in a bedroom corridor, with Golaud stumbling from room to room in search of his hounds, and proceeds in this way in blatant self-contradiction right up to the death of Mélisande, there comes a point where you have to close your eyes if you are to appreciate the aptness and beauty of Debussy's music. Better, on the whole, never to have opened them.

The mutilation of the operatic stage has been one of the most significant triumphs of the 'culture of repudiation': the culture of Mephistopheles, which finds its meaning in denial. I remain convinced, despite all the alienation, nihilism and existential despair that have come to perch in the rafters, that high culture is a monument to ideals, part of the attempt – always necessary, and never successful – to make us at home in the world and to affirm our moral right to it. Myths, stories, dramas, music, painting – all have lent themselves to the proof that life is worthwhile, that we are something more than animals, and that our suffering is not the meaningless thing that it might sometimes seem to be, but one stage on the path to redemption. High culture has in this respect been the handmaiden of religion, and because he saw this and made the insight explicit in his music dramas, Wagner has been the principal target of the vandals. Their philosophy stems from a nihilism born of distrust, from a desire to 'ruin the sacred truths' that ask for their credence. It seems to me that they are in the business of destroying consolation, not because they have anything to put in the place of it, but because the consolations of other people are a reproach to their own moral emptiness.

Thank God, therefore, for recordings, which make it possible to imagine opera in all its glory – the glory of the religious festival that Wagner intended. And thank God for vocal scores, which enable you to produce the work yourself, and to conjure the action from the keyboard. For many periods of my life I have preferred playing through the Wagner scores to listening to recordings. The exercise has convinced me that it is possible to achieve the unity between action and music that Wagner advocated, and to vindicate the Wagnerian vision of opera as the highest form of art.

As a teenager I toyed with the idea of composing an opera based on Gogol's *Christmas Eve*. I envisaged a beautiful prelude, with gossamer strings and harp depicting the tranquil winter moon over the Steppes, and then a sudden crash of timpani as the Devil dances in from the wings with the moon in his hands. I even sat in the little cabin of the petrol station where I was working as an attendant, with a great sheet of music paper on the table before me. In the course of a week I managed two bars. In later life I encountered Tchaikovsky's *Little Shoes* (*Tcherevichky*), a charming adaptation of Gogol's story, which, had I come across it as a teenager, might have brought home to me the full extent of my musical presumption. By that time, however, the desire to write an opera had lain dormant for 30 years, and was ready to reawaken. I had become fascinated by the peculiar constraints governing the libretto, if it is to guide the music along the groove of a drama, and I was tempted to try my hand. I wanted to compose a libretto as succinct as Boïto's *Otello*, and as subtle as Hofmannsthal's *Der Rosenkavalier*. My first attempt ran to 70 sides of rhyming couplets, in which the characters explain themselves at such tedious length that the music could have nothing more to say. My next attempt was somewhat shorter, but so full of dramatic ironies that it had to be sealed away in a short story (subsequently published as 'The Seminar' in *A Dove Descending and Other Stories*). Eventually I came up with the idea for a one-act chamber opera – *The Minister* – set in the England of the sixties, and telling the tale of a politician who exchanges love for power.

Opera is an art form in which it is still possible to introduce magic, without the result appearing contrived or didactic. This is perhaps because music already passes with such ease across the barrier between the actual and the possible: what might have been is always present in the present tense of music. Hence we have a long tradition of magic opera – from the god-haunted dramas of Monteverdi, Cavalli and the French court composers, through *Semele*, *The Magic Flute*, *Der Freischütz*, *The Flying Dutchman*, *Parsifal* and *Die Frau ohne Schatten*, down to *The Turn of the Screw* and *Curlew River*. In all those works the drama, guided by the music, moves effortlessly between the material and the spiritual worlds.

I conceived *The Minister* as a magic opera in this tradition, and, in a gesture of supreme impertinence, decided to follow the great and inimitable example set by Britten in *Curlew River*, and to borrow from the Noh theatre of Japan. The opera was to be a drama with masks, which fall away to reveal moral truth beneath the ruin of social pretence. I was taken by the idea, which seemed to me to be decidedly operatic, while permitting singers to play dual roles. But I could not persuade any of my composer friends to take an interest in it. Composers seem to be inherently suspicious of librettists, perhaps because they believe, with Wagner, that the libretto and the music must come from a single source. And maybe that goes some way to explaining their curious habit of pouring beautiful music into libretti so absurd that even a child's pantomime contains more by way of drama. Great musicians like Rameau, Weber, even Verdi have been guilty of this fault, and composers still seem to choose libretti as a condemned man might choose his noose.

Hence my crazy idea of writing a libretto gave rise to the even crazier idea of writing the music. I devised a few leitmotifs, allotted them to situations, moods and characters, and began to compose. To my amazement the music took shape before my ears and eyes, and within a few months I had a complete piano score. The first thing I discovered was how easy it is to make bar follow bar, theme follow theme and chord follow chord, when all are hung out on the line of dialogue. The *Gesamtkunstwerk* easily declines to its opposite: music that has only a borrowed order, and dialogue too weak to stand alone. I thought constantly of the conclusion to the second act of *Figaro*, in which sustained symphonic writing creates a tension that is wholly musical, wholly dramatic and also wholly integrated with da Ponte's brilliant text. That remains my paradigm of opera: a dramatic idea expounded through a tonal argument.

I recalled my feeble attempts at a string quartet, how at every juncture the stitching came apart, the themes fell away from one another and the bridge passages crumbled to dust. This didn't happen in *The Minister*, but only because the music was held together by the dramatic imperative of 'Next!' Wrestling with this problem, trying to re-imagine the music as the engine of the drama rather than the trailer that it pulled, I learned more about music than at any time in my life before. I recalled Berg's habit of drawing attention to the musical forms explored by his orchestra – sonata form, theme and variations, fugue, gavotte, passacaglia, and so on – all neatly and almost academically explained in the score, while the raging melodrama on the stage drags the music into excesses that would be utterly senseless in a purely instrumental work. Berg is cheating his way to musical form, by borrowing the shape of a drama. Adorno, in his book on Berg, asserts that *Wozzeck*'s 'extremely taut construction ... never allows the dramaturgic argument a moment's latitude'. As so often, Adorno hits on the opposite of the truth. It is the drama's relentless onward drive that never allows a moment's latitude to the music, binding it into an argument that bears no relation to its would-be 'taut' construction. The Variations and Fugue that open the third act of *Wozzeck*, for example, move with ever-increasing urgency to their climax: but it is a dramatic climax, entirely dependent upon Marie's cries of vain remorse. The triumph that Brahms achieves in his Handel Variations, in which the music develops organically towards the fugue that completes it, is a triumph that Berg could never emulate, since it is a triumph of pure musical form. This is not to deny the power and inspiration of Berg's music, but to recognize the extreme difficulty of writing music in which musical and dramatic movement coincide. Mozart managed it in *Figaro*, Wagner in *Tristan* and *Walküre*, Puccini in the first act of *Madame Butterfly* and Janáček in *Jenůfa* and *Katya Kabanova*. But these are the high points of operatic art, achievements that only a fool or a genius would try to emulate.

Intimidated though I was by those masterpieces, and by the problem that even a master as great as Berg had been unable to solve, I arose each day in a state of anticipation, impatient to try out my waking thoughts on the piano. The music was tonal, beginning and ending in G, with excursions into C sharp whenever the going got hot. I concluded that it would be instantly damned by the critics, who would have history, my lifelong enemy, on their side. But I had a sneaking desire to hear it nevertheless, and when Jessica Douglas-Home suggested celebrating my fiftieth birthday with a private performance at her house in Gloucestershire, I was delighted. For several years Jessica had been my closest friend and collaborator, joining me in the adventures that she describes in *Once Upon Another Time*, and jeopardizing many carefully nurtured contacts in the London élite on account of her association with this weird conservative whom nobody knew. It was a further act of defiance on her part to celebrate my fiftieth birthday, at a time when the entire intellectual establishment was competing to show itself sound on the Scruton question. To my surprise she managed to fill her music room with a sufficient number of pariahs and outcasts, and the opera was greeted with real applause, even though we had no orchestra beyond two pianos and a keyboard.

At the time, with the memory of communism still fresh, my reputation in Central Europe stood somewhat higher than my reputation at home. Shortly after *The Minister*'s first performance I was awarded the First of June prize by the city of Plzeň – a prize given each year to celebrate the first genuine revolution against communism in 1953, when workers marched from the factories to the town hall and threw the resident statues of Lenin and Gottwald from the window. Those responsible for the outrage spent the rest of their lives in prison. But their gesture was remembered thereafter, and caused the city of Plzeň to make the first real attempt in the Czech lands to come to terms with communism – to acknowledge those who had resisted it, and to forgive those who hadn't. The other recipient of the prize was an old general, imprisoned for 20 years after the war, during which he had fought with the Free Czech Army for the liberation of his country from the Nazis – a crime that the communists could not forgive and which in Poland carried an automatic death sentence, so automatic that it was never preceded by a trial. The old general was too old and frail to attend the ceremony, so it fell to me to give the speech of acceptance, and to make the city feel good about itself – which is, after all, the real reason why cities give prizes, as Wagner brilliantly shows in *Die Meistersinger*. In return, those responsible for the award sponsored three performances of *The Minister*, in its full orchestral version, one in Plzeň, and two at the Kolowrat theatre in Prague.

Not since that first encounter with *Figaro* have I been so excited by an operatic performance. I was going to hear my own modest contribution to an art-form that for me stands higher than all others. Melody, harmony and words had issued from a single source, and there existed a chance – a slender chance but a real one – that they would come together in a music drama.

I had reckoned without the producer. Everything that admitted of interpretation was interpreted; every symbol was underlined; every reference to Noh was accentuated with masks and fans. Ideas that I had foolishly let slip in conversation appeared in brazen letters on the stage, and every gimmick of the producer was given prominence, with the music sounding shyly behind it like a whispered exchange between prisoners awaiting trial. In short, the action vanished behind the production, as it now invariably does. There was music, and a strutting on the stage. But there was no music drama, and therefore no opera.

I was grateful, of course, and flattered to be mistreated in the same way as Verdi and Wagner. But the experience confirmed my sense that opera is now so widely misunderstood that only those who avoid going to performances will know what it means. Only those who sit at home with a score or a recording will understand the sublime ideal of a drama that unfolds through music, and music organized by a dramatic idea.

Despite this experience, I was not cured of my obsession. I was emboldened to look back at my predecessors – philosophers who had made a mark, or a blot, with an opera. The greatest was Rousseau, whose *Le Devin du Village*, put together in illustration of his musicological theories, was performed over 400 times between 1752 and 1829, and earned the praise of no less a master than Gluck. I borrowed the score from a library, to discover that it never rises above the level of corny entertainment. Not an idea to be absorbed from it, not a question raised by it, and the plodding harmonies entirely without invention. It is, I acknowledge, a tuneful little piece, but – like everything Rousseau did – entirely indifferent to the standards to which a more modest person might aspire.

By contrast, however, there is *Undine*, the highly influential romantic opera by the man whose intellect I admire above all others – E. T. A. Hoffmann, who based his opera on La Motte Fouqué's story of the water sprite destroyed by her love for a mortal. This story was a favourite of Wagner's, and he read it aloud to his family in Venice on the night before he died. During the course of my life I have had ambitions to be a philosopher, a critic, a musicologist, a poet, a novelist, a composer and (when reading for the Bar) a judge. Hoffmann effortlessly achieved all of those, was active as a conductor and a music director, wrote choral and instrumental music as well as several other operas to his own libretti and, through his brilliant music criticism, made the romantic idiom into a new *lingua franca*, before dying at the age of 46. I listen to his works with humility, recognizing that – ordinary though they are when compared with the works of the many great composers whom he influenced – they were written by an instinctive musician, a musician of the same exalted order as Auntie Betty.

And then, of course, I recall that, in addition to the handful of philosopher-composers, there has been one great composer-philosopher, namely Wagner. True, Wagner does not express his philosophy with the clarity or the self-centred absoluteness of Rousseau. But he is far more wedded to the truth than Rousseau and no more obscure in his voluminous prose writings than Hegel, whose unconfessed disciple he was. In recent years I have tried to assuage my operatic yearnings by studying Wagner, and teasing out some of the philosophical ideas explored in his music-dramas. Maybe, if I am ever to make a real contribution to opera, it will be in this way, with a philosophical study of the meaning of *The Ring*.

Nevertheless, the old yearning revisits me from time to time, and meets with little real resistance. Two years after the Prague performances I even wrote another libretto – *The Beetle in the Box* – ruminating on Wittgenstein's celebrated private language argument, while presenting a *Pelléas et Mélisande*-like attraction between a university teacher and his student, each playing with a fantasy of the other. The music would not come, however, and I put the work aside. For a while it almost seemed as though I was cured.

I had reckoned without Jessica. She had often told me of her great aunt, Violet Gordon Woodhouse, protégée of Arnold Dolmetsch and Arthur Rubió, the English rival of Nadia Boulanger, perhaps the greatest harpsichordist of her day and the true founder of the authentic performance movement among English concert-goers. This remarkable woman, who lived with four men hand-picked from the English upper classes, who were destined by their love for her to leave no offspring, led a life that was a brilliant synthesis of English pastoral and flagrant *ballet russe*. Like Jessica herself, Violet was both entirely eccentric and quintessentially English, at ease in all societies and at home in only one. Her friends included Casals and T. S. Eliot, Diaghilev and Vaughan Williams, the Sitwells, the Sassoons and Dame Ethyl Smyth. Her life had been a scandal and an inspiration, and Jessica often felt a sudden breath of the love that Violet had inspired, which blew from that vanished epoch like the breath of the East over Suleika. Indeed Violet was herself a kind of Suleika, a transportation into English mists of an oriental princess, whose Sumatran origins were as mysterious as her ability to charm, capture, and sterilize the upper-class men on whom she alighted like some bright but poisonous butterfly.

For a long time Jessica had been poring over the papers rescued from Nether Lypiatt by her father, who had inherited the house from his Aunt Violet. These documents told a story so extraordinary, and so replete with the tragedy of the English landed class, that Jessica conceived an urge to write Violet's biography. The book had some success, and extracts from it were presented, with musical illustrations, as a kind of tableau, with the character of Violet brought brilliantly alive against a harpsichord background. Jessica staged this tableau in her music room – the very same room that had seen the first performance of *The Minister*. Emerging from the outlines, I envisaged a full-scale opera in which, within the comedy of Violet's life, the tragedy of England would at the same time unfold.

I sketched a libretto, and then set it aside. Over the next two years I wrote *England: An Elegy*, a book that attempts what Freud called 'the work of mourning', setting the object of love at a distance, but without denying the love. In the wake of this therapy I planned a libretto that would touch on the absurdity and the innocent perplexity of the English upper classes as they threw themselves and their country into a pointless war – the war from which England never recovered. Jessica was enthusiastic, but would not rest until I had begun to set the words to music. Once again I found myself waking each morning to long hours at the piano, searching for melodies and bridging passages, looking with despair at the operatic scores on my music shelf, at the magical turns of phrase, the subtle rhythms and imaginative vocal lines that I could not imitate, conscious of my presumption and yet unable to relinquish it.

Thanks to Jessica's tireless work, *Violet* is due to be performed later this year at the Guildhall School of Music. I would love to see it in its proper setting, with the familiar and constantly changing uniforms of the Edwardian gentry as they migrate from drawing room to dining room and back again, dropping one mask and picking up another in the hope that no one will accuse them of being who they are. But have I not declared myself opposed to the very idea of opera production, and do I not insist on attending only concert performances? A concert performance, it seems, is all that I shall be allowed. Drinks with the cast, a meal with friends, and then – perhaps – a final divorce between opera and me.

9
Drinks in Helsinki

In the last days of the Soviet Union, when only half-crazed prophets foretold the empire's collapse, we in Europe were mesmerized by Soviet power. Even those, like Margaret Thatcher, who most vehemently condemned the communists, looked on the world behind the wall with awe and trepidation. Those who worked with the opposition movements in Eastern Europe knew how weak they were, how disorganized and confused in their aims and aspirations. And the omnipresent eyes and ears, feeding information into a system whose very anonymity rendered it impervious to human appeal, seemed to have taken up their posts in perpetuity. If you escape punishment, they seemed to say, it is because we know what you are doing and know that it will make no difference, except possibly to bind you more tightly in your chains. Political scientists divided Europe into two spheres of influence. But those who travelled behind the Iron Curtain knew that the American sphere of influence faced a Soviet sphere of control.

Only in one country had the Soviet Union tried to impose itself while exerting something less than control, and that was Finland. The Finns were the unsung heroes of the war against communism; for they alone among the peoples of Europe had fought this war and remained undefeated. They had lost large parts of Karelia to Stalin's armies; but they had held on to their historic homelands, and forced the communists to agree to something less than conquest. That something was called 'Finlandization', and it was a mystery to me. What exactly had the Finns agreed to, and how was the agreement enforced? Were decrees sent out from the Soviet Embassy, were show trials mounted of anti-Soviet dissenters, was there Soviet censorship of the popular press? Or was there something else, something more subtle and more insidious, which might be tried with success on the rest of us, just as soon as the Peace Movement had crippled our defences? Conservative politicians uttered dark warnings to this effect; but none seemed able to tell us what Finlandization really was. When in 1987 an invitation came to visit the University of Helsinki, therefore, I welcomed the opportunity to complete my psychic map of modern Europe.

I learned nothing about Finlandization, except that the Finns had also learned nothing about it. But the society in which I found myself was so peculiar that I kept a diary during those six hectic days, hoping that one day, in retrospect, it would make sense to me – perhaps even that the secret of Finlandization would be revealed. But was it? Let the reader be judge.

22 September 1987

Helsinki. I am sitting in a large room – once part of a grand suite, but now divided by a partition from its neighbour – in the university guest house on Vironkatu. The enormous double-glazed window, which reaches to the ceiling, shows me a patch of grey uncertain sky and beneath it a long, slab-like apartment block, faced in pale green roughcast with traces of art deco detailing. From one of the windows, between badly tended potted plants, an old woman is leaning. She wears a loud red shirt and dribbles ash from her cigarette into the street below, enjoying the breeze as it lifts her thin hair in a silver plume around her features. In the window above her stands a seven-branched candlestick, and curious figures move secretly behind it, with the tiny intimate movements of those who believe themselves unseen. Almost all the windows of the block contain something – a potted plant, a vase, a statue, a lamp, and what seems to be an old brass samovar – as though each household must declare some part of itself, and allow just so much to the curiosity of strangers. The people in the streets walk past each other silently, and all life is indoors. There is a strange, flat, inward-turning atmosphere, like communist Europe: people aware of one another, but moving always away, creeping into holes and crevices, creating in the midst of all movement some little place where only domestic impulses can be tried and brought to completion. They talk quietly, even in whispers, as Poles do.

My host is Johan Wrede (of Ilamaar – a barony bestowed on Johan's ancestor by Charles IX, whose life was saved in battle against the Polish armies by a self-sacrificing Wrede).[10] He is, as that fragment of history implies, a Swedish Finn, Professor of Swedish Literature at the university. Small in stature, with a wiry, bearded face, he has difficulty in catching from the air the ideas, and the words, necessary for public communication: therefore he laughs continuously, a slightly mad but thoroughly good-natured laugh, over which his thin, fragile sentences stretch like filigree bridges over a turbid river. He meets me at the air terminal and takes me in his car – a family car, neat, clean, with a household order, each seat occupied by the ghost of a child, emitting negative electricity at the usurping stranger – to the square before the Lutheran cathedral where, in the kind cool yellow light of a Nordic autumn sunset, he answers my questions (he having no questions for me) on Finnish history.

What an uncanny shelf of civilization is this square, the cathedral surmounting it and the city below – a neat well-dusted shelf, on which pots of culture have been placed by a housemaidenly hand: a meeting room here, a doll's parliament there, here a kitchen-clean Lutheran church, there a big, bothersome Orthodox Cathedral; here a university, strapping and fit like a Boy Scout headquarters, there a school, all dinky and dimpled, like a story-telling aunt. Law-abidingness lawfully abides; the air is replete with shy good manners, from which the soul of man hurries away in search of darkness, that ever-open door the way to which is so obscure that only the lamp of alcohol, burning with its bluish light, can guide you. In the parks the drunks lunge and totter, their fish-eyes vainly scanning the air, sinking beyond redemption, unless they strike that hidden path.

We made our way to Vironkatu via a spaghetti of streets, past the fortress-like Soviet Embassy, as vast and dictatorial as that in Warsaw, by the naive and open embassy of the United States, and past the Presidential Palace, a shy and cosy lodge of stucco which shrugs its shoulders at the sea. Johan tells me that Keikonen, the

[10] The episode is recounted in Juttikala and Pirinen's *History of Finland*, p. 81.

last President, was so ashamed to find himself with a few more rooms than he needed that when a student wrote to him, saying, 'look at the space you have, and look at me, who has no lodgings!', he promptly installed the student in his palace, which since that time has maintained quarters for two undergraduates from the university. Eventually I am established in Vironkatu, and promptly taken away to a Russian restaurant – the Kazhak, where we are served with *filet à la Catherine la Grande* (fillet steak with mushroom sauce, served on a pile of garlicky potatoes) and thick red Georgian wine, which tastes of tar. My history lesson continues, and I am embarrassed by my lack of appetite. The restaurant dates from the Russian Revolution; rather touching oil paintings, of a Russian Sunday-ish kind, clutter the walls, including one, dominating everything, of Czar Nicholas II, who clearly has not heard of Finlandization. In another portrait a sad but manly youth, sporting a moustache and wearing red Cossack trousers, leans his chin pensively on his hand, which is propped by the arm on a cloth-covered table. He stares out at the painter with a strange look of utter uncertainty, as though anything might happen to him – death, a kiss, an arrest, a gherkin – a picture of the Russian soul, lying in the gutter, waiting for Lenin to pick it up.

I am tired from the journey, and find it difficult to ply Johan with the questions that are necessary to justify his laughter. Long pauses begin to supervene, during which the noise of an American businessman from the next-door table sweeps across the silence like rubbish-filled waves across a beach. At last we are joined by Ilkka Niiniluoto, a philosopher from the university, with a soft, fleshy youthful face, wide-set unsettled eyes, and a downy beard that he pulls at with embarrassed fingers. He must be about 40, since he speaks of an adolescent son; but his locks of brown hair and untempered eyes give him the appearance of a novice in the school of life, who is astonished and dismayed at every turn. I give a speech – I don't know why – about politics and aesthetics, and the relation between them. We begin a discussion: formless, tangential, but nevertheless a kind of self-renewing excuse for our encounter, for which each of us is grateful. They tell me of developments in Finnish philosophy. Apparently it is becoming more 'applied', with an emphasis on 'burning issues', which turn out to be the usual ones – the environment, abortion, feminism etc. As in America, philosophy is retreating to its erstwhile position as the slave of theology – the theology, now, of the godless.

I tell them of British philosophy, which bores me, and we are happy in each other's company, with that vague and transferable solidarity of academics, joint dependents on the bounty of the liberal state, secure in our conviction that we have the better part of the deal. I learn that 20 per cent of Finnish students take their degrees ten years after the start of their studies, and that of the remainder a great proportion remains unaccounted for. I learn that most students do not receive a single tutorial during their years of study, and enter the examination room in the condition of people who are about to put pen to paper for the first time – and this in a language with 13 case endings! I learn that the Students' Union, far from being a forum of left-wing agitation, is a long-established *Burschenschaft*, with endowments from the last century that make it one of the great Helsinki property owners. It has a neo-classical club house in the centre of town, and behind it a department store whose profits pay for all the student societies and more besides. I ask about Finlandization, and my hosts refer darkly to 'agreements', 'conditions', 'circumstances', but seem unable to explain further. It is as though they were talking about it for the first time, like a bereavement put out of mind.

We walk across town, beside the sea shore, through quiet streets, and then into a main thoroughfare with trams and drunks and silent, stationary figures. Drunks here serve the function of policemen in the streets of London: periodic reminders of the precariousness of urban life, pointers to the chasm that lies beneath your feet as you spring along. They stare at you and through you, and their visions punctuate your thoughts.

We pass a hamburger stall, and then, by a garish cinema, we stop at a glass door. Two half-uniformed men open to us, take our coats in Central European fashion, and beckon to an uncrowded room of art deco tables, the walls of which are hung with morose paintings in curdled, earth-coloured oils. This is the Kosmos, where the Finnish intelligentsia get drunk together while discussing the higher life. A few unattractive women frown into half-empty beer glasses set upon white, meticulous tablecloths. A light of loneliness haloes them, driving away the groups of bearded men, who buttonhole one another with truncated stabbing gestures.

We take a table, and are served by a square-faced iron maiden, who nods at our order and then stops for a long discussion at the next-door table before fulfilling it. She smiles grimly at my attempt to say '*kiitos*', and bangs the glass of *koskenkorva* (a fiery Swedish grain spirit) on the cloth before me. I offer some outspoken conservative sentiments, so as not to hear, for a few blessed moments, the arches of sentiment going nowhere, so as not to climb on to broken-backed bridges that leave you scared and rescue-less above the roaring nothingness below – and again we are happy, as the kaleidoscope shifts into symmetry around us.

A fat, youngish man, with bulging glasses and a snotty pullover that once was scarlet, bumps drunkenly into our table. After a few words of Finnish he stumbles onwards to an empty place saying, in English, 'A philosophical discussion! I understand! I will go away! Go away! No hard feelings; no hard feelings at all! No!' But he does not settle at an empty table. His eyes continue to swim behind their lenses, until he lights upon a company that seems to tolerate their proximate gaze. I am told he is a famous film critic.

To the casual observer it is as though people come to the Kosmos not in order to overcome their loneliness, but in order to experience it to the full, to chase it into the depths of their souls, pouring glass upon glass of spirits after it, so as to fix it and fuel it below. I am told, however, that we visited the place at an unusually unfrequented time; normally it is next to impossible, late at night, to find a seat at the thronging tables.

23 September

Breakfast in the guest house, where there is a room reserved for that meal. I share a table with two large Russian ladies from Karelia, members of a group, who are excitedly discussing an article on Stalin in one of the Finnish weeklies.

I settle down after breakfast to write this journal, knowing, however, that my programme begins at 9.30. At 9.30 precisely there is a quiet knock on the door, and a creature in a faun mackintosh slides sideways through it. His shoulders are hunched, and he seems to keep his head in his inside pocket, from which it emerges shyly and curiously, like the head of a tortoise. Tiny, close-set eyes behind thick distorting lenses probe the air in my direction, and the beak-like mouth opens and closes soundlessly. The head is crowned by a tonsure of boyish fair hair, cropped close round the ears; this imparts, from the curious angle at which it is observed (half-hidden by the lapel of the raincoat) an appearance of youth. But the appearance is belied by the awkward, shambling gait of the body, which is that of an old man, as is the slow, uncertain speech, as it announces itself to be Yrjo Sepanmaa, expert in 'environmental aesthetics', who is to take me to the 'Technical Research Centre of Finland'. After a day in Sepanmaa's company I can still assign no definite age to him, but prefer to think of him rather as a timeless incarnation of the spirit of Finland, a shy, retreating creature that lives somewhere in a damp intimacy of vegetation, and that crosses the path of humans only reluctantly, in the course of inscrutable business of its own. Seeing him in this way I was able, by the end of the day, to come to terms with a shyness so absolute, so much a matter of rigid principle, as to amount to a constant affront. All the same, I cannot help recalling Alfred Gilbey's remark that shyness is really selfishness, a sign that you value yourself too highly to offer others a share.

We take a taxi to Tapiola. I assume there to be something of special interest to the student of aesthetics in that place made famous by Sibelius – some hideous modern building, perhaps, poking sharp edges through a veil of gloomy pine trees; or a collection of wooden shacks of advanced design, where Finns yet shyer than my guide can live secluded over the lake, plunging into the water whenever human beings are sighted. Tapiola is the home of the wood sprite in the Kalevala, and I discover that the name has been borrowed to denote an advanced modern suburb, planned on scientific principles, in which nature and buildings are to stand side by side in a harmony such as has never previously been seen. It is as hideous as that implies.

The Research Institute is a collection of white concrete buildings, rising on either side of the road and arching over it, so that buses and taxis gather in its rainless underpatch. It has the appearance of an international airport in some small, neglected country without a tourist trade – although even that implies a certain level of urgency, and in the Research Institute there is no urgency at all. Not a human form is visible, and the few waiting vehicles look as though they were placed there by the architect, in order to anticipate a future life that never materialized.

I am led down long white corridors, past rooms full of expensive-looking equipment, with here and there a mouse-like Finn busying himself about some fairy task. Sepanmaa's office is bare, without books or pictures, but with folders of papers and reports neatly arranged on clean pinewood shelving. From the window you see concrete paths leading to other clean white buildings, the whole fringed by mournful, windless trees. It is beginning to rain, and a creeping sadness like a mist is covering everything.

A woman enters and holds out a hand; her large clumsy face, with a wide oblong mouth that moves mechanically like the mouth of a dummy, attempts a smile indicating all conceivable welcomes. She has staring glassy eyes. 'Welcome,' she says, 'welcome. I am Hilkka Lehtonen, acting research professor in this laboratory. Welcome.'

Having come to the end of her prepared speech she continues to hold her face in a smile, but is clearly more and more uncomfortable in that posture and uncertain how to move to another one. 'Welcome,' she says again. 'You had a good journey into Finland? Yes? Welcome from our Institute. Welcome from Tapiola.'

We stand around for a while, Professor Lehtonen shifting awkwardly from one leg to another, but stretching her mouth in a smile that has become permanent, since something in the mechanism has clearly jammed. At last, by some process of tacit communication, we are back in the corridors, padding along in the direction of a 'laboratory' where the research in aesthetics is conducted. The silence, the neatness, the lack of books, the remoteness of every object and gesture from anything in the world of scholarship as I have known it, generate a feeling of acute anxiety. I am obviously here on false pretences; it is only a matter of minutes before they discover that I am not the Professor Scruton they wished to meet, the international expert on urban aesthetics and post-industrial design problems in a forward-looking research context, but someone else of the same name, a bumbling romantic whose real interests are old books and old buildings and whose behaviour towards his colleagues is far from correct and indeed positively inappropriate. All my anxieties over my name return, as I am ushered like a condemned man into the laboratory.

There is no equipment apart from an overhead projector – no sinks against the walls, no Bunsen burners, no retorts, test tubes or glass-stoppered bottles; no computers, tape recorders, word processors, video screens; only a great expanse of white Formica desktop, which circles the room under a noticeboard covered in newspaper cuttings. There are no objects on the desk-top apart from some plastic coffee cups, a plate of biscuits and a thermos flask – the entire subject-matter of today's experiment.

'Welcome from our laboratory,' says Professor Lehtonen, 'please to sit down. Here is coffee. Now other colleagues come to meet you and we explain you our works.'

The smile, with the exertion required by travel, has at last subsided, and her face now wears a blank expression, waiting to be re-programmed.

'This is the Laboratory of Urban Planning in our Centre for Land Use and Building Design,' she announces, emphasizing the capital letters, 'and here we research Quality Improvement of physical environment in a Future-Orientated way.'

One by one the mice enter from neighbouring burrows: a sour-faced creature in a navy pullover, a sprightly field mouse in a suit and tie with a neatly barbered beard and a nervous giggling boy mouse in Boy Scout shirt and camping slacks, who is the resident expert in philosophical aesthetics. They do not speak to me, but come up as close as they dare, point their faces in my direction and sniff the air with quick nervous vibrations of the nostrils. The silence is broken at last by Professor Lehtonen, who tells us to sit down.

'Now I explain you,' she says, and switches on the overhead projector. 'Once we were two laboratories, for Land Use, and for Building Technology Problems. Now we have project together. So we combine, to discuss new Planning Techniques, using Information Technology and Computer Design.'

I recall the Centre for Land Use and Built Form in Cambridge, and the controversy from which my book on architecture arose.[11]

[11] In 1976 I was asked to review *The Architecture of Form*, edited by Lionel March, in the *Cambridge Review*. The book was a compilation of essays by pseuds connected with the Centre for Land Use and Built Form in

Here I am, back in that world, or rather in an innocent microcosm of that world, inhabited by strange troglodytic creatures who startle at the scent of human flesh.

Professor Lehtonen switches on the projector, and a collection of boxes appears on the screen, linked by arrows whose significance is wholly obscure. The project, I read, is aimed at 'quality improvement of the physical environment, future studies and the development of new planning techniques'. There will be a new understanding of development needs, due to CAD systems and 'optical information medias'.

'The project,' Professor Lehtonen says, 'is divided into groups: the first is mainly qualitative orientated, the second group in economics, and the third technical aspects of architecture. Also there is a group working with expert systems and information technology.'

I nod politely and turn back to the screen, where a new box has appeared that says: 'Especially the aesthetic viewpoints are considered with respect to the introduction of new information processing techniques in planning.'

More boxes and arrows, everything feeding into everything else, to produce at last a glorious outcome: 'An enhanced evaluation of aesthetic qualities in decision-making and usage,' and 'an enhanced form-giving process in planning tasks.'

At the bottom of the chart it is declared that 'the project is financied by private foundations' – a nice synthesis of 'financed' and 'fancied'.

The display is finished, and I am in a panic, not knowing what on earth to say in response to it; but Professor Lehtonen makes a gesture to the members of her little team, and they all straighten up and begin to cough.

'Now we all explain you separate interests. You criticize perhaps.'

The bearded field mouse begins, telling me that his work is with CAD and expert systems, working to synthesize the

cont.

Cambridge. In those days I believed that reason, in any conflict with ambition, would prevail. I wrote *The Aesthetics of Architecture* in defence of truths that I had been taught by my father (see Chapter 11), and which the authors of *The Architecture of Form* seemed not to have encountered.

components of the building problem. He is particularly concerned to extract aesthetic rules from given forms so as to work them into a computer program. He finishes, and looks at me with shy expectancy. At last it occurs to me to say that perhaps aesthetics should not be reduced to rules – though it will always be part of the problem, perhaps the whole of the problem. He shakes his head and smiles secretly to himself.

'No, not the whole problem. We have made some progress. Now we understand aesthetics as just one component. There is a democracy of problems: function, utility, aesthetics, economics.'

He snuffles quietly and then falls silent. So it goes on round the table. Each mouse produces some piece of half-digested thinking – Wittgenstein on rules from the Boy Scout, William Mitchell on 'shape grammar' from Professor Lehtonen, Monroe C. Beardsley and the aesthetic point of view from Sepanmaa – all thrown together like a hasty catalogue of undergraduate reading, and all followed by an expectant silence as I reflect on my expert opinion, merely to find that I have none. Only the sour-faced man in navy blue seems to have any sense of the impossibility of the thing. He is clearly suffering from an habitual hangover, and his English is even worse than that of his colleagues. He ruminates sadly on his experience in Libya, on the problems of integrating traditional and modern logic, on the nature of the courtyard as a semi-public space. But all is delivered in a tone of such defeat and melancholy, with a constant painful blinking of his watery red-rimmed eyes, and a kind of prickle of anxiety over his red-tinged features, that I cannot draw any optimistic conclusions, or suppose that he will condense his thought into anything so definite as a statement, or stand in the name of architecture against the pseudo-scientific vandalism of his colleagues. Clearly, however, he hates them all.

I am taken to another laboratory, this time full of instruments, including a periscopic camera that can patrol around the model of a building, and project on to a video screen a pedestrian's (or, more accurately, motorist's) perception. There is a video programme that imposes people, trams and vegetation on the background provided by a model. And I am shown a computer graphics program that enables one to feed a building into a computer, and to receive print-outs of plans, cross-sections, projections, video pictures showing the effect of light and shade, and so on – in other words, a complete substitute for visual education. (All this can be found in the works of W. J. Mitchell et al.)

The expensive machinery is operated by docile middle-aged technicians, and the mice pad backwards and forwards in front of it without a touch or a glance. It too exists in another world for them. Far from being the kind of chatty computer buffs whose communications are translations out of Fortran, they regard the computers as natural objects, whose creations are of no special concern and may be just as meaningless as everything else. From this experience too they may at any moment scamper back into their holes.

The ordeal at the Research Institute lasts three hours. I emerge exhausted, my soul cramped by politeness, wishing to stretch myself spiritually in a prolonged mental scream, but in fact confined with mouse Sepanmaa in a taxi, which takes me to the university and my meeting with the Rector. As a matter of fact, I am told, it is not the Rector who will grant me an audience, but the Vice-Rector, who is none other than Johan Wrede. I am shown into his antechamber by solemn uniformed lackeys who add a strangely medieval touch to the long concrete gallery, lying behind a neo-classical façade, on which the Rector's office is situated. Not I, but we are shown in; for mouse Sepanmaa is still attached to me. For the past 40 minutes he has been at my elbow, explaining that this is the largest bookshop in Helsinki, that is the university accounts building, this the way to the Swedish department, that to the department of philosophy. His presence is particularly irksome in that I have an armful of books and pamphlets, and now is the perfect opportunity to read them. On the walls of the antechamber hang portraits of vanished dignitaries, most of them with peasant features, alcoholic eyes, and rough fat fingers that lie relaxed on their thighs.

At last Johan comes, the mouse vanishes into a hole, and I am conducted into a panelled office, with more old portraits of people of whom little can be sensed apart from a quiet patriotism and a total absence of left-wing opinions. Some leather-bound books stand in a glass case, and the centre of the room is occupied by a desk which is clearly never used for study or writing. We sit in brown leather armchairs of a vaguely functionalist design and contemplate two objects on a round Bauhaus-ish black table: a visitor's book, which I must sign, and a blue box containing secrets. Johan, dressed in a dignified suit and twinkling Faust-like from his slightly mad eyes, waves his arms like a magician over the box, descending slowly in his words like a bird spiralling downwards from a great height, and awakening, it must be said, the liveliest interest in his eventual target.

'Well, Roger, it is, I must say, I really mean, such a remarkable event, such a very, well a special honour, and, well, an honour which I must say I worked hard . . . to bring about . . . a quite real and special privilege, and so well worth the effort of exerting myself, getting the Rector to invite you and, well, to put it briefly, to put you in the very special category of visitors, not as an ordinary lecturer but as one of those who, you understand, is, I mean, a guest of the Rector himself, so to speak, and on whom, well, we wish, the university wishes, to bestow a special honour, in fact its second-highest honour which is, I may say, you know, the bronze medal of the University of Helsinki . . .'

Seizing the box, he opens its blue mottled lid, to reveal what seems to be an Olympic medal, with two socialist-realist faces, one male, one female, and neither in the first flush of youth, over whom a fairy hovers, bearing an olive branch, and gesturing to the distant university building, which the two figures do not see since they are staring intently towards some rather grim and exacting future which occurs invisibly beyond the perimeter of the medal. The fairy, I am told, is Athene. The whole composition is a masterpiece of ineptitude, designed, I learn, by some extremely distinguished man, whose heirs are now perhaps working somewhere with computers to produce objects equally representative of the deep Finnish embarrassment at the idea of meaning something.

I make many noises of gratitude, and am indeed touched by Johan's simple pleasure in the whole business; and being touched I feel an access of guilt – maybe I have not worked hard enough to deserve this honour. Maybe the scrappy lectures I have prepared will be a poor return for Johan's honest labour.

I leave the office in a changed frame of mind, but still without the possibility of doing the work that is so evidently required of me, since Johan is beside me and we are walking through the market place towards the hideous modern building (the Palace) that dominates and destroys the south harbour. Here we are due to have lunch in an Italian (sic) restaurant. The lunch is on the official programme of my visit; it is to be attended by Ingmar

Porn, who is professor of philosophy in the Swedish philosophy department (i.e., the department that teaches philosophy in Swedish). As we walk Johan tells me, rather curiously, that the Finns are indeed shy, but that this shyness is also a virtue, and is what leads them, when they finally offer their friendship, to heights of steadfastness and generosity rarely seen among other nations. He incidentally mentions how gratifying it would be if he could be invited to give lectures in England – or just brought over, as an official guest, for a conference, say, or a seminar.

Lunch is a strange affair, Porn laughing but saying little, while I eat a strange concoction of salmon and cèpes cooked in red wine. (On the market there are great piles of chanterelles, and as for the salmon, I have never seen such quantities, or beasts of such phenomenal size.) I learn more about the university, its lack of tutorial structure and its enormous intake of students. We discuss philosophical developments in Britain and Scandinavia, and I give a résumé of *Sexual Desire*. A pleasant simulacrum of conversation is established, and it is pleasant too to look from the window across the harbour, as the little boats go to and from the islands, and to see the great red-brick bell of the Orthodox Cathedral, fallen athwart the peninsula like an ornament from some giant Christmas tree that towers unseen above us in the mist. But I want urgently to return to the guest house, to catch that precious hour of rest and reflection before my lecture on the classical vernacular, which is to take place at the Technische Hochschule in Tapiola. Alas, it is not to be. Mouse Sepanmaa, whose shyness now seems to me to conceal a considerable calculating shrewdness, has appeared, and shuffles purposefully towards us across the restaurant floor. A surreal dialogue ensues:

'May I join you?' asks Sepanmaa.

'Yes of course,' Johan replies, 'and you must have a cognac.'

'No, I cannot, there is not time.'

'Surely there is time!'

'I think not. No, there definitely is not time. We must go by taxi soon to the Technical University.'

'No,' Johan insists, 'I think there is time.'

'Ah! You are right! I have made a mistake about the time.'

'A mistake about the time! What a scholar!'

'Sometimes I misread my watch. It happens to me. But now I cannot sit down.'

'Cannot sit down? Why not?'

'You see, I have not taken off my coat.'

'But then take it off, dear fellow.'

'But I must take it off over there. It has to be given to the lady who looks after the coats.'

'Ah so.'

'Yes. So I will now take my coat to her, if you will excuse me.'

'Of course.'

'So, I will return very shortly. Please, just one minute, while I take my coat.'

Will the lady also keep his head, I wonder, or is there space for it in his inside pocket? He returns with his head tucked beneath the lapel of his brown tweed jacket.

'So now I will sit down. But later we go to the Technical University.'

'And you will have a cognac?'

'Yes, perhaps I will have a cognac, thank you. But later we must take a taxi.'

'Professor Scruton, I think, would like a walk.'

The head turns slowly towards me and protrudes to the maximum extent from its nest of twine.

'You would like a walk? Then I must fetch my coat. From the lady who keeps the coats.'

'No,' I say, 'please stay a while. To drink your cognac.'

'Ah yes. I will drink this cognac. Where would you like to walk? I think it is raining. You will need a coat.'

After ten minutes of this, when I am on the verge of insanity, we make our way to the vestibule, where mouse Sepanmaa elaborately puts on his coat, takes it off, and then puts it on again from another direction, patting the head into place behind the coat-flap. Johan and Porn disappear towards the university, while Sepanmaa leads me stumblingly in the direction of the observatory, which is in a little public park above the harbour. Our silence is deafening; we seem to be melting irresistibly into the damp grey air. On the hill of the observatory a drunk is conducting an invisible orchestra in what seems to be a Mahler symphony. He tries in vain to include us among the trombones, pointing urgently as our cue arrives. We stumble on in embarrassment. I think: perhaps I do not exist, perhaps I have become a mouse, perhaps all my thoughts and feelings have been translated into a troglodytic language beyond my understanding. My legs are weak, my head wet, misty, sinking into unwanted sleep. I am barely conscious of mouse Sepanmaa as he urges me to follow him as fast as I can towards the taxi rank at the bottom of the hill.

Tapiola: more introductions, more silent sniffings, a long wait in bookless concrete, and at last the event: the slides are mounted, the lectern waits, I must go down to it. A curse on the day when I agreed to this. What shall I say? How shall I make contact with those closed sad faces? The first slide comes up; their eyes swing across to it, and I talk unobserved. A discussion follows. By Finnish standards, I am told, it is very lively. That is to say, two people speak besides myself.

And then I am given a conducted tour of Tapiola, with Professor Lehtonen, mouse Sepanmaa and the giggling Boy Scout. A garden city of white concrete, some of it veneered with white lavatory tiles. Hominoid sculptures stand meaninglessly on concrete pathways, and ranks of senseless fountains spout expensively into air that is already wetter than air can be. A square block, without windows on three sides, is the church. Houses and apartments are thrown down at illogical angles among dreary trees. Here and there a kiosk, a bicycle shop, even a hotel. Cheerless, sanitary, cold and yet random, a picture of modernist gloom. It was designed by the great Aarne Ervi and his equally great colleagues, according to future-orientated scientific programmes for the infinite prolongation of human happiness. A municipal launderette, where each washing machine contains some trapped white human form.

Only at 7 p.m. am I dropped off back at the hostel, utterly weary and with a kind of mist permanently settled in my brain.

25 September

Yesterday morning a walk around Helsinki, visiting the sparse white dome of the cathedral, the streets around the harbour, the lively market with its baked and smoked fish, and its stalls piled high with mushrooms and berries, and then the main thoroughfares. Most interesting from an architectural point of view are the art nouveau apartment blocks. Something in the Finnish imagination was evidently stirred by art nouveau, whose clumsy and disordered details permit ornament without form or harmony, and give rise to a kind of fairy architecture that is indistinguishable after dark from a gloomy forest of pines.

City regulations have for over a century set a maximum height for all buildings other than churches, and the blocks fit snugly under the virtual ceiling like children's bricks in a toy box. A few lines and dots break out towards the highest floors (usually there are five or six), and here and there a daring window sweeps into a corner or bursts through a sloping roof. For the most part, however, the buildings are flat, plain, fitted to the leaden, lightless sky by their grey, green and terracotta roughcast, which absorbs what little light comes down to them and gives to the street the character of a tunnel cut through the earth. All architectural character is confined to this tunnel, where astonishing rustications jut out into the pavement and assault the passer-by. Huge blocks of undressed granite crowd about the doorways, with here and there some short fat column, swelling and sausage-like, squeezed between them. The rustication often rises over the door, making a narrow pointed arch of stone, a kind of cave entrance, leading as a rule to some tiny wooden door in varnished pine, with a bas-relief of trees and animals above it. These are gnomes' dwellings, and the Finns retreat into their fairy doorways with all the appearance of going underground into a world of their own.

In the afternoon a lecture on the meaning of music, to a room full of blank young faces. Every now and then a student gets up and leaves with an ostentatious clatter. Strangely, however, in a peculiar reminiscence of good manners, each one turns back at the doorway, and bows graciously towards the podium as an old-fashioned Anglican bows towards the altar before leaving a church. I realize that the lecture (already in the press for the *Journal of Aesthetics and Art Criticism*) is badly written, obscure, self-referential and in short an episode in the decline of scholarship that I spend my days lamenting. As I read it I try in vain to detach myself, to improvise words that will be more truly meant, to speak from the heart at least, if not from the head. But I cannot do it, and begin to break out in a sweat, as once I did in Lublin, lecturing then to a room of young Catholics under an imaginary portrait of St Thomas Aquinas. After a while my attention wanders, I enter a dream-like state born of anxiety, and the words issue somnambulistically from my lips.

This room too is full of portraits: Finnish dignitaries, with hands folded and professorial suits lying stiff and itchy over their shapeless bodies. The faces have the same rigid closedness as the living faces in the hall. Behind both, however, there is an accumulated mass of energy awaiting the moment – which no doubt will never come, or come only once in a moment of drunkenness when it cannot be seized – to change the world utterly. This thought reconciles me to my situation, as another and larger group of students leaves the hall.

I am to have dinner with the philosophy department. In the event only two of them – Ilkka Niiniluoto and Esa Saarinen – turn up, in Saarinen's old Volkswagen, bringing with them Saarinen's mistress, whom he calls the Queen. Saarinen has long flaxen hair, flapping around his large-featured face, in which youth is mounting its last struggle with age – he is in fact 34, but looks ten years older. He wears hippy clothes, and affects a laid-back manner – he has already caught my attention after the lecture, with his reference to the 'low-profile' attitude of the Finns. He seems also to have a sense of humour – a precious commodity here, where laughter occurs rarely, and only as a kind of mad outrush of air, used like the ink of the squid to confuse the enemy.

The Queen is a tall, sexy Laplander, older, I should say, than Saarinen, with flowing red hair, leopardskin tights and a miniskirt. Her face is plastered with make-up, and her mouth, puckered all round with tiny wrinkles, is like a wound whose stitches have broken. She says very little, but laughs much. In fact her one topic of conversation, indeed her one interest, function and raison d'être, is sex, which she embodies so fully and grotesquely as to stand out among these embarrassed and sexless people like a peacock in a chicken run. Esa Saarinen, whom she refers to always by his surname, as though there have been too many Esas already for her to distinguish him in any other way, is clearly besotted with her. She carries a rose that he has given her – his daily tribute – and at every pause in the flow of life around them they exchange little pecking kisses, often turning to us in the course of their osculations to say how little they slept last night and how exhausted they are from their bedroom adventures. However, the Queen adds at one point, she does not like doing it at night: far better in the morning, or in the middle of the day.

Therefore we must make the evening last, so that Saarinen goes to bed exhausted and awakens refreshed to his duty.

Ilkka (whom she calls Niini) nods politely to such remarks and often, as he endeavours to say gentle and forgiving things about everybody and everything, she takes his hand, laces her fingers in his, and strokes his downy cheeks with a smile.

Our first stop is an art gallery, where a philosopher-painter is having a vernissage. The people are drunk already, apart from a few dignified old couples whom Saarinen knows and to whom he talks in a relaxed and charming way, while his hand quietly explores the contours of the Queen's bottom. In the first room there are some heath-coloured, lightless paintings, autumnal, leaden and suicidal, by Olavi Hurmerinta, apparently a famous artist, who stands among them in a smart velvet jacket, his flowing white hair ablaze in the criss-crossing light. Their prices range from 1,000 (for little gouaches) to 30,000 marks (the latter sum being about £4,000). Mr Humerinta must be about 70, a small, civilized-looking man who greets people genially and seems to be playing with precision the part of artist as this was conceived during the 1930s.

In the back room the philosopher-painter has set up his works, and he explains them to me in execrable English. His language, like his conception of painting, was acquired during a year in New York. The works are of plywood, stuck with plaster rosettes, with sections scooped out and filled with stars of birch bark, bands of red or black paint occasionally crossing them. He is very excited by a square hung at an angle and wrapped by two black ribbons of glossy paint, with a plaster rose at their crossing point. His broad, bony face shines with enthusiasm, and a kindly light enters his pale yellow eyes as he explains the virtues of this composition. Apparently it refers to Mondrian, while at the same time making an abstruse and extremely complicated comment on Mondrian's hatred of ornament and distaste for unfinished things. Serving punch in plastic cups is the only attractive girl in Finland, but nobody seems to notice her.

Our second stop is the Sea Horse, a drinking house famous for its authenticity. Behind a dull fifties façade a little corridor sinks into the channelled darkness of a long, narrow room, with cloth-covered tables arranged along its sides. Light, of a kind, issues from coloured lamps against the wall and falls over the unsmiling faces of the people, many of whom are sitting alone, clutching their glasses of beer or *koskenkorva* and staring grimly before them into space. Others talk quietly, or raise their voice in a sudden bark, as drunkards do. Grim-faced waitresses ply between the tables, receiving orders as though they were insults, and putting down drinks like farmhands throwing down pigswill. Saarinen is concerned that the full impact of Finnish drinking has yet to be made on me and therefore, after a couple of *koskenkorvas* we beat a retreat, crossing the town to a more modern and brighter place. Here there are one or two people smiling, though silently. At one table young executives are eating crayfish, and celebrating some event with set silent faces. After a while one of them, a fat boy in a ridiculous peacock-blue pullover, begins to talk, raising his glass repeatedly and leaning on his neighbours with a show of gritty affection. They exchange fierce determined looks, like warriors about to go together into battle.

Saarinen discourses on the Finnish habit of repressing emotion. In all social gatherings, he argues, a Finn feels himself to be ridiculous, since he cannot really make contact with his neighbour. In order to live with this feeling, he makes himself yet more ridiculous – wearing paper hats and necklaces, dancing lugubriously, or telling inappropriate stories. Plunging ever deeper into social failure his loneliness grows until, in a last explosion of absurdity, he may run from the room with a cry, strike his neighbour, or stalk quietly and manfully into the forest and shoot himself in the head.

Our dinner is in a nearby restaurant, sparsely frequented, but known for its Finnish cuisine. A few people sit in distant corners. At one point Tawaststjarna, the biographer of Sibelius, enters with his pianist son and pianist daughter-in-law (who is Japanese). He is a fine old man who lifts his hat to us with a gracious and antique gesture, like a dream sequence in a Bergman film. He ushers his family before him with a proud, quiet smile on his face – the very opposite of the Finnish mentality as Saarinen had described it. But then, he is Swedish, and writes in Swedish – apparently very finely, adapting his style to his subject, so as to describe each Sibelius symphony in its own peculiar idiom.

We have whitefish caviar served on Finnish blinis, which are a kind of greasy waffle of unappetizing texture; then wild duck in a cream sauce with pickled mushrooms, and finally an ice cream made from cloudberries – the small yellow-pink raspberries that grow in northern forests.

The most interesting part of our conversation concerns the 'Theatre of God', a group of four students in the university drama school, all boys, who, in protest against the world in general, and the fact of being Finns in particular, had taken to mounting situationist spectacles, beating each other's naked bodies, and recreating the anti-bourgeois postures familiar from Armand Gatti and the Living Theatre in the sixties. They decided that the time had come to arrange an important confrontation with the establishment. Their plan was to interrupt the theatre festival that takes place every January in Oulu in the North Midlands, and which is attended by critics, professors, authors and people prominent in the literary world. For a week they prepared themselves, sitting in silence in a darkened room, until ready for the moment of sacrifice. Then, taking a train, from which they removed the fire-extinguisher required by their script, they arrived after a day's journey in Oulu, proceeding at once to stage their *coup de théâtre*. In the middle of one of the productions, in protest against the state subsidy granted to such mediocre stuff, they appeared in the auditorium naked and screaming, their bodies smeared with shit, lashing each other, and also the occasional member of the audience, with long leather whips. One of them directed the fire extinguisher here and there into the crowd while another, finding an honourable bourgeois who refused to flee before the outrage, sat in his lap and smeared his clothes with excrement.

The Finns responded in character, withdrawing from the theatre in melancholy puzzlement, and leaving the four young men to make their way back to their stopping place, clean themselves up, and repair to a restaurant for a well-earned meal. There they were discovered by the police, who took them into custody. They were held, as Finnish law apparently permits, for 11 days without communication with the outside world. Meanwhile the fame of their exploit, observed and suffered by the highest critics in the land, spread immediately over the whole of Finland. Leading articles and TV interviews discussed the affair, and Professor Turkka, professor of drama in the University of Helsinki and a well-known scourge of the establishment, added to the uproar by giving an interview in which he said 'the boys did a good job'. The students of the drama school also wrote to the newspapers, defending the aesthetics of the action in Oulu and arguing that, with the end of structuralism and post-structuralism and the entry of Western culture into its post-modern period, it has been conclusively established that words no longer mean anything, that reference is impossible, and that only actions performed without commentary have any aesthetic significance. In illustration of this thesis, they organized a meeting in order to break the furniture of the drama school and hurl it through the windows. The meeting was quite well attended, despite the fact that the students had difficulty entering the building, the four members of the Theatre of God, by now released from custody and awaiting trial, having chained themselves to the doors in protest against a commission that had been appointed to examine their case.

The papers were now full of demands for the closure of the drama school and for prosecution of the Theatre of God, not only on grounds of criminal activity likely to endanger life (which charge has now been laid by the public prosecutor) but also on grounds of blasphemy, a charge justified by their name, and also by previous productions consisting of a silent crucifixion, howling flagellation and assorted obscenities. This prompted an intervention from the Lutheran Archbishop of Helsinki, a young and go-ahead clergyman, who asserted that there is not and could not be such a crime as blasphemy, and who knows whether these authentic cries of protest do not ring more sweetly in God's ears than all our hypocritical acts of worship? Others joined the battle, denouncing the culprits as 'terrorists' and the first, moreover, to make their mark on Finnish soil. To this the *bien pensants* of the university replied, not at all, these young men are attempting to express and neutralize the destructive energies that have accumulated through decades of repression, energies that would otherwise most certainly express themselves, as they have expressed themselves elsewhere, in acts of terror.

Discussion of the case continues unabated, and the trial has now begun, the four young men proving to be almost entirely incapable of speech and with no justification to offer for their actions. Indeed, they have pleaded guilty on all counts, whatever they might be, and shown no interest in the proceedings, while their disconcerted lawyers have continued to argue that their plea is not sincere and that in any case they are innocent, for all the reasons which have been so carefully spelled out by the *bien pensants*.

After dinner we repair to a dance hall, again of authentic Finnish character, the name of which I have forgotten: a vast L-shaped space, wrapped around the corner of a city block, with a band playing in the crook of the L. There are the usual cloth-covered tables, occupied by single women and single men, with here and there a group or a couple. We enter by a flight of stairs; a gagging girl rushes past us to the toilets, her hand held tight to her mouth.

Inside there is no conversation. Ugly people eye one another, swallowing drink after drink until suddenly, in an access of madness, one will get up, home in on the woman of his choice, seize her around the waist, and lurch without a word on to the dance floor. On Thursdays, I am told, there is a ladies' night, in which women can take the initiative. Since we are here on a Wednesday, this dubious improvement is not in operation. The music is slow, drooling and fubsy. A sad, speechless knot of people drifts on the dance floor like a clot of rubbish on a pond. They do not dance but smooch aimlessly about, holding each other at arms' length, or occasionally burying their heads like hatchets in their partner's neck.

Then suddenly the music changes; the band plays a *humpa* and then a *yenka* – two *echt*-Finnish versions of the polka, composite dances reminiscent of the schottische. The Queen has already taught me the steps in the restaurant, and, the rest of our party being drunk by now, we take to the floor together, while the sad couples separate and go their lonely ways to the perimeter.

So the evening ends, with me bouncing round the floor in a crazy polka-step, the Queen, all soft and cuddly and oozing sexuality, pressing herself against me with a mad look in her eye.

All that happened yesterday. Today I take a quick walk through the town, to collect some more of the quite unnecessary money which has been allocated to me from the university budget, and to see the railway station built by another Saarinen, the famous architect from the 1920s, whose style lies halfway between art nouveau and Bauhaus.

From the outside, the main entrance, with its decorated arch flanked by four sexless herms, gives a disconcerting impression – half Nazi in its affirmation of Nordic purity and discipline. The four faces are blank Finnish faces, with cropped hair that lies in ridges over their heads like a regiment of folded napkins, and a clean-shaven stiffness of feature, like people who have learned to shave but not been told the reason why. (Incidentally, what *is* the reason?) Each holds in his hands an empty globe of lead-framed glass, symbol perhaps of that unanswerable 'why?' that you can read in the faces themselves, as though to say, this is what travel amounts to, always the same, no end and no result. But the pink granite stonework, set everywhere with wood and metal details, has a surprising lightness, and the whole is so brilliantly thought through, down to the tiniest details of door handles, clocks and window frames, that you are compelled to accept it as one of the fullest architectural *conceptions* of our century. Of course, it would never have been possible without *Jugendstil*, which seems to have had a greater influence here even than in Central Europe. The restaurant in particular, a great barrel-domed hall, in which every detail answers to the festive conception, must be one of the finest modern interiors in Europe, far superior to the Obecní Dům in Prague, whose superfluity of effect and richness of ornamentation it does not attempt to emulate. The clever fluctuating mouldings are of a design that I have seen nowhere else, snugly wrapping themselves around the wooden doors and metal window frames. The pilasters are veneered with a green moulded porcelain, in which forest lights travel ever upwards, and the modest brass lamps cast a warm daylight radiance over everything, as though the building were translucent. There is a roulette table in the restaurant, and railway workers drift constantly in and out to gamble at it, buying their chips from a busy girl croupier.

A man comes to me holding out a box for donations. He is sturdily built, with a wiry, weathered sailor's face, and tough-looking lumberjack clothes. He wears the cap of some uniform, like the Salvation Army. Everybody seems to be giving to him, and I ask him in English what I must give. 'Ah English!' he says, lifting a finger in the air before him. He fumbles in his pocket and puts a card on the table. It says 'A worth card: Life Insurance. John 3:16. Payed in advance. Can't be cancelled. For God so loved the world that he gave his only begotten Son, that whosoever believeth in him should not perish, but have EVERLASTING LIFE.' I pay three marks for this life that is promised me, and he seems well pleased.

Saarinen's furniture, in beechwood and pine, matches the curving movements of the building, and is scattered everywhere, as though the building were alive and had dropped these seeds of itself all around. In a corner of the booking hall there is even a little table with leather armchairs, as though for the use of some passing businessman eager to write out a deal. One of the striking features of Finland is the overt respect for property and the decorum with which it is used. Valuable furniture can be scattered at random about this public space and, failing the rejuvenating presence of the Theatre of God, it remains where it was put, undamaged, almost unused. If this is Finlandization, let's have more of it.

Another building also impresses me – Pohjola Kullervo, now a Japanese bank, but bearing the name thickly chiselled on its grey stone porch. (Pohjola Kullervo is the mysterious 'North Farm' of the Kalevala.) This is a perfect example of Finnish *Jugendstil*, situated in Alexander Street and facing the pavement with a massive, completely rusticated façade of grey granite, sculpted with gnomes and woodland animals. The heavy porch, raised by troglodytic gargoyles, gives, as always, on to a small secret fairy-land door, in bronze, brass and oak, embossed, engraved and squeezed all over with animals and ferns. I push the door open to find a tiny entrance hall, narrowing to an even tinier stone staircase, just tall enough, it would seem, for a rabbit to pass, which spirals upwards out of sight, lit by a stained-glass window: a most wonderful fairy effect, which completely forbids any member of the human race from proceeding further.

One of the best things about the Finns is their quiet patriotism. This sentiment – a loyalty both to the place and to its institutions – causes them to commemorate all their great and not-so-great men, to put up plaques, busts and statues on every corner, and to hang in all the rooms of the university the portraits of its parted dignitaries. Every professor, I learn, has his portrait painted on retirement, and there is no evidence that the portraits are abused or mocked by unruly students. On the contrary, everybody seems quietly to accept that they must be there, and that the university is rightly proud of them.

Elias Lonnrot, compiler of the Kalevala, is of course the quintessence of the Finnish patriot, a man to whom all Finns ought to be, and I think are, forever grateful, and whose character is painted by Aarne Anttila in the *Big Encyclopedia* (*Iso Tietosanakirja*) in a way that corresponds to my perception of the Finns – although with the curious addition of a 'sense of humour'. Maybe Finns are not very accurate observers of their own national character, since Anttila ends his article thus:

'As a human being Lonnrot is the epitome of a Finn, and even if one tries, it is hard to find in him any objectionable traits; indefatigable assiduity and power of concentration, a quiet firmness and a kindly sense of humour under all circumstances, reasonableness and tolerance, extreme unpretentiousness, and truly Christian humility were characteristic of him.'

There is no doubt that the Kalevala is quite the most extraordinary phenomenon thrown up by the national revivals in Europe. In one book there is a photograph of some of the singers, assembled with kaleles in their hands: old mad-eyed people, hollow trees in which a vanished wind still hums, singing husks from which the seed has been borne away.

In the National Gallery there are the graphic, almost Disney-like Kalevala paintings of Akseli Gallen-Kallela – stirring, evocative, almost other-worldly, and yet at the same time kitsch. There is also another tradition of Finnish painting, and one remarkable for the number of women who have taken part in it. Helene Schjerfbeck's *Convalescent* is, for all its sentimentality, a powerful work, while Fanny Churberg's strenuous impressionist landscapes must be among the most challenging paintings from the brush of a nineteenth-century woman. In the end, though, it is the melancholy symbolists who make the greatest impact – and in particular Hugo Simberg (1873–1917), whose early death is prefigured in all that he did.

28 September

I speak to Johan about the Theatre of God. He tells me that Finns have a particular love of theatre; official statistics indicate that there are as many theatre attendances as there are attendances at spectator sports. The reason, he suggests, is that theatre is absolutely necessary to them, the sole release from inhibition that is not also a dangerous act of self-exposure. Just to see others shouting sometimes makes the difference between life and death. In a shop window I see an old leather-bound work, probably from the late nineteenth century, in four volumes: a history of Finnish theatre in Finnish.

In the evening I give a lecture to the Finnish Aesthetics Society, which meets in the old house of estates, a beautiful neo-classical building, decorated outside in a terracotta stucco, and inside with intricate Italianate Renaissance patterns. Sixty silent faces, in a quiet, dignified room. But one of them is animated – almost like an English student, nodding and shaking his head, and waiting for the moment when he can express his views. After a while I recognize him as my former student from Birkbeck, Daryl Taylor, whom I now remember as a 'Finnomane', and who has evidently fulfilled his obsession by coming to live in his adopted country. Over dinner afterwards I ask him to explain Finlandization. He laughs and says that it is a myth, invented by sabre-rattling conservatives in the West. It turns out that he is a radical and a peacenik, and his joining us for dinner would have been somewhat irritating were it not for the fact that the quota of official Finns creates such a burden of silence that I need to unite his energy to mine in order to carry it. Besides, two American girls tag along and one of them is a robust Republican of the Reaganite school, whose black and white vision gives contours to our grey on grey.

After midnight I walk home down the esplanade. Crowds of drunken, silent young people, teenagers mostly, and of both sexes, moon helplessly around, leaning against one another, like a herd of sheep in a winter landscape. No laughter, no smiles, no talk – just a melancholy drifting in no direction, an absolute will-lessness, fed on drink and sex and drugs. Perhaps this is what is meant by Finlandization. But if so, I cannot think that we shall escape it.

10
Impressions d'Afrique

In a once-famous novel the surrealist writer Raymond Roussel described in meticulous detail rituals and customs from a continent that he never visited. His invented Africa was both more interesting and less threatening than the reality, and the pity is that indigenous Africans know nothing of *Impressions d'Afrique*, which might otherwise have served them as a guide through the post-colonial jungle. Just as Spain was made in Paris by Mérimée, Bizet, Chabrier, Debussy and Ravel, so might Africa have been made in Paris by the followers of Roussel. Alas, Africa today is not the fantasy of the *Impressions*, but the horror observed by Conrad, a place where gangsters boasting of their anti-imperial record pile corpse upon corpse as proof of the evils of imperialism.

My own visits to Africa began at school, when I would sit with my physics master, ex-Assistant District Commissioner Guy Granville-Chapman, during evenings at his home, listening to stories of his time among the Nigerian Ibos. Mr Chapman was one of the first to draw a map of Iboland, and every minute of his time there, when he was charged with the administration of the province, remained in his memory as a self-vindication, proof beyond doubt that his life had been worthwhile. I loved and admired Mr Chapman, whose character I described many years later in *England: An Elegy*. On the surface he was the 'sweet, just, boyish master of the world' praised in those words by Santayana; underneath he was a sad and troubled man of action, severed from the sphere of his achievements and surrendered to the rule of fools.

I began work on my *Impressions d'Afrique* as an undergraduate.

The novel was called *Mr Patterson*, and was based on things I had learned about Iboland from Mr Chapman, with a few details thrown in from Conrad and Greene. I had also spent two weeks in Egypt, to which country I had made my way after hitch-hiking to Greece with my schoolfriend Tom. I had spent one week suffering from a kind of dysentery in an empty empire hotel in Alexandria, and a second week recuperating in the youth hostel in Ghiza. There I met Martin Seymour-Smith (at least I think it was he) on his way to visit Robert Graves in Majorca. And I spent my evenings with learned professors from Al-Ahram University, visiting the youth hostel to enjoy the company of its enlightened warden, whose passion was philosophy. From those raw materials I constructed an Africa of mud huts and heat-logged villages, of trampled pathways and scant savannahs, of mosquitoes, malaria, mayhem and madness, with somewhere in the background old men chanting suras from the Holy Koran.

I rewrote the novel during my year as lecteur in the Collège Universitaire of Pau. By now it was called *Uranus*, and was built around the myth of the old god overthrown and castrated by his son. The chapters on Africa had shrunk to a few scenes in the hero's memory, and eventually these too were excised and the book rewritten under its original title. The novel made its way, in due course, to the bottom of my box of manuscripts, and there it remains, calling to me from time to time in the thin self-important voice of adolescence, but shrinking from my touch when I open the lid.

However, my visits to the dark continent did not cease. Every so often, maybe once in five years, I gather some part of myself into a character, a situation or a story and project it across the wrinkled sea to Africa. There, on that distant shore, removed from living trouble, the shades and phantoms move in a quiet *perpetuum mobile*. New experiences, new relationships, new troubles often end up there. But so do old and familiar things, which I send off as missionaries in the hope that they will end in the stomach of a cannibal. Whenever, in my novels, I touch on autobiography, as in the description of Jennie Fortnight and her atrocious death, or in that of the schoolteacher Mr Ferguson, I know that I am also in the heart of darkness, picking my way with careful words through a place of nightmares. Happier far those invocations of imagined things, of the pure heart of Zoë Costas in

A Dove Descending, of the robust kindliness of Xanthippe and the saucy sensuality of Phryne the Courtesan. Roussel was right: imagination demands its own continent.

Sometimes, however, the dreams will not be exported. Advancing through the everyday world we fall victim to fancies that have no place in our mature self-image. When this happens to me I am torn. Roger tries to be grown up; Vernon retreats in confusion. In one such episode I acquired a new name entirely: Papa el-Niño, the wrinkled child, whose feelings for a young woman led him into a fantasy-filled jungle, she rebutting all intimacy with an apt word of rebuke, Papa el-Niño wandering on the edge of her mysterious life until its otherness was utterly clear to him and the fantasy vanished. We remain the best of friends and here, in a sequence of poems on the subject of Miss Hap, as I call her, is the reason why. Incidentally Variation 3 (Hoop) is the longest palindrome that I know, being twice 40 letters. It emerged spontaneously, with just the meaning required. Of course, there is all the difference in the world between inspiration and a lucky accident. But Miss Hap was a lucky accident too.

1 Miss Hap

The Argument

Papa el-Niño, alone, middle aged, encumbered with knowledge, but a child at heart, encounters a young girl from another planet. She is Miss Hap, a Polish-born American, who has been sent to warn him against herself. He struggles with the paradox, trying every version of 'perhaps'. He is defeated. He laughs. His end is happy.

Theme: Hap

You call me hapless – yes,
But what is hap, and when is less?

Is hap what happens
When hope still flows?
Is less then hopeless,
As one who *knows*,
And draws a close
To happiness?

Less hap, perhaps,
Is handicap – which hops
To a defeat
Called victory by those
Who pity it.

More hap was yours – the heap
Of opportunities, the leap
Of happenstance,
The closing doors

Before my chance.
So yes –
My hap was less
Than yours.

Variation 1: Hope

(See Jerrold Levinson, 'Hope in the Hebrides', in his *Music, Art and Metaphysics*.)

Can hope exist without
The thing that's hoped?
Can heart and head steal out
Like those who once eloped

To nowhere, trusting love
Alone to light them?
It could be, if above
Our hopes some God of love
Decides he will requite them.

Hope exists in music: hope for what?
The hoped-for in itself
Is anacoustic,
And melody is all we've got.

But melodies can point
As in *The Hebrides*,
Whose spraying notes anoint
Imaginary eyes
That fix the Pleiades:

The cellos ride B minor
And charm it into D;
Young Felix wrote no finer
Theme, and if it hopes
Then hope exists in melody.

Stand then, Hapless,
At the helm:
No shapeless
Wave shall overwhelm
Your ship;
No stormy cape
Extinguish hope –

Just make your boat
Of music staves,
For then you'll float
On waves
Of sound; those dancing naiads
Are really triads,
And every sea change
Just a key change,
Your ballast just a note.

'But can I steer
This ship to port
And find the thing I hope?'

The answer's clear:
Yes sure, in thought;
But in the real world, nope.

Variation 2: Hip

What in you entices
To join you on your trip:
The adolescent crisis,
The flutter of the lip?

The fact that I am Pisces
And you the Crab, whose nip
In ocean depths suffices
To hold me in its grip?

Those blue-grey Polish eyes – is
That the cause? The quip
You made about my glasses
That meant 'He's not a drip'?

No: each of your devices
Unravels like a zip
To show that paradise is
Just a motion of the hip.

Variation 3: Hoop

(**A palindrome**)

On ho!
Hoop!
Oo, oo, or even
Oooo!
On – in – leap!
Apostrophe, eh?
Port?
So, Papa el-Niño:
Oooo!
Never: ooo, oo, pooh!
Oh no!

Variation 4: Hop

I'm getting there –
Just one hop
To where
Your mouth will stop
Mine with a kiss – my share
Of your pop-
bothered tear-
away heart: a cop-
y-cat affair
From some dumb soap
I'm not aware
Of. But you'll stop
One day and stare:
'We're at the top,'
You'll say, 'from here
You'll have to drop
Downhill.' 'Don't care!' –
A malaprop
Since all I do is care;
But now you lop
Me off, declare
You've shut up shop,
Have nothing spare
To keep me up –
The stuff's too rare:
Not a drop
Of love or care
Or all that crap
Your par-
ents spouted. Pop!
You've gone: one hop
To nowhere!

Do I dare
To plant that crop?
I'd better stop.

Variation 5: Harp

Your fingers abound
In American 'Can do!'
With instant glissando
They forage.

But your eyes, kid, astound
With a Pole's innuendo:
A scene in a window,
Like marriage.

And then I came round:
You were playing Nintendo,
Your face all intent too,
Like porridge.

I happed on – I found –
(And I didn't intend to)
A diminuendo
Of courage.

Variation 6: Hype

I practised like Praxiteles until
You came out from the stone, a real
Goddess, work of highest skill,
A walking, talking doll – a steal

At any price. Just look:
Those Tintoretto flesh-tints, smoky eyes
Like early morning mist above a brook,
One arm half raised, expression of surprise

On lips that tremble like a leaf in spring;
A nose that twitches, girlish as a Greuze,
A dancer's feet, small hands that touch and cling,
A graceful neck, the pose of *La Liseuse* . . .

I've hyped you up, I've breathed you out,
Exhaled you like a mist across the mirror;
He's wiped you off, you're up the spout,
And now the glass looks back at me in terror.

Variation 7: Harp

(Harping on)

The stretch of strings
And other things
Attunes you to yourself;

But when they're plucked
You're either fucked
Or left there on the shelf.

Variation 8: Heap

Take a grain of sand, then take another,
Another grain, and yet another still,
Pile grain on grain on grain together
Add more and more and more, until

Your hand and arm and back are aching,
Your throat is dry, your fingers numb,
Your brain is half asleep, half waking,
And every grain's a pain in the bum,

You'll make no heap of sand – no never,
Thus Greek philosophers have shown
By reasoning so very clever
The answer to it's still unknown.

For take some arbitrary number
And call it 'n' (since that's what's done):
If n is not a heap, the sombre
Thought must be: nor's n + 1.

For is one grain of sand enough
To make what's not a heap a heap?
Of course not! Reasoning, however tough,
Will reach this point, go on the bleep,

And stay there. The paradox is deep

As soul is, or the Trinity:
Since 1's no heap, then nor is 2,
Nor any number to infinity:
The world is heapless – and the same is true

Of everything we've hoped for and are due.

Coda: Hup!

He: 'Cap, kip, keep, coop?'
She: 'Cop, cope, cup.'
He: 'Sap, sip, seep, soup?'
She: 'Sop, soap, sup.'
He: 'Pap, pip, peep, poop?'
She: 'Pop.'
He: 'Pope?'
She: 'Pup!'
He: 'Hap, hip, heap, hoop, hop, hope –'
She: 'Hup!'

2 Murdochiana

Iris Murdoch's way with words was rough and casual and her plots sometimes far-fetched. But her prodigious imagination inspired me and I constantly return to her novels in the hope of absorbing some of their creative zest. Her characters inhabit a realm that, while superficially an exact copy of England, with all its snobberies and pieties, contains mysterious doors in its dumb façades. Her formidable intelligence is always at work, jumping into the midst of her characters as they peel each other raw with heartless dialogue, and pushing them sideways through one of those doors – doors that open into Africa. And there, like English roses in the wilting sun, they wither to their tiny crusts of poison. Iris records each wrinkle as the living surface dries, not with a scientific coldness but with a strange and god-like compassion – the 'sharp compassion of the healer's art'.

Bad things have been written about this excellent woman. But to me she was a sage and a fount of kindness. She looked into my timid heart, liked what she saw and told me so, at a time when my life stood still. She read what I wrote and encouraged me; she listened to my woes and helped me to face them with the only shield that works, which is the shield of forgiveness. She directed towards me a selfless sympathy that was neither pitying nor distant but full of a lively endorsement of the thing that I was. Aquinas describes love in that way: as willing another's existence. Just such a love was Iris's and although I moved only on the edge of her life her sun-like smile in my direction dispelled the clouds of melancholy.

Everyone knows about her illness, on account of John Bayley's excellent book and the film that was subsequently made from it. This illness cut me off from someone who understood without agreeing and endorsed without sharing. She was, in life as in art, an example of love who also inspired it. This was borne out by her illness, which served, in its early stages (the stages when character still shows) to enhance her gentle desire to sit on the edge of things while helping them along.

Serious illness is a catastrophe not only because it destroys our joy and comfort, but also because it tempts us to think that the human soul is after all an illusion, that the body is everything, and that the body is now in charge. Nor is this the result of mental decline only. A person who is too weak to move at will, whose bodily functions are no longer controllable, whose mind is clouded by pain, who has no joy in eating and for whom conversation is an unbearable strain – such a person is apt to appear, in his own eyes as well as in the eyes of others, as little more than a piece of decaying flesh. The soul evaporates like a mist, blown away by the harsh reality of illness, so that nothing remains save mortal débris. It is this catastrophic loss of the sense of self and soul that leads to the thought of suicide. For it induces in the patient a kind of shame – shame not for any act or omission, but for his own existence. He cannot look others in the eye, because he cannot look himself in the I. There *is* no I, only a great It, whose triumph can be read in all the daily humiliations that he undergoes, as his dependence increases, and his ability to control himself declines.

Iris, however, decided to have no part in that terrible process. She got out of her life before it ended, leaving the ungoverned body to coast to its grave like a plane from which the pilot has ejected. Somewhere among the heavenly hosts Iris looked down on this 'It' and on those who cared for it. And all were aware of her blessing. Here are two vignettes, one from the beginning of our friendship and before the onset of Alzheimer's disease, the other from the days when her spirit was faintly waving goodbye.

24 December 1989

I arrive in Cromwell Gardens on my bicycle and am padlocking it to the railings, staring down distractedly at the twinkling lights of a Christmas tree in the basement window, when that very window is angrily thrown open, and a severe middle-aged man pokes his head through the gap.

'You are not intending to leave that bicycle there for long, I hope?'

'Long enough to have lunch,' I reply.

He purses his lips as though debating in himself whether to stretch a point or whether on the contrary to take a principled stand.

'On second thoughts, I shall attach it to a more friendly set of railings.'

I push the bicycle along to the next house, as he furiously slams the window.

I ring the bell and Iris's voice comes at once down the intercom. 'Roger!' she cries, though, because she seems to see so deeply into things, I would not be surprised to hear 'Vernon!' instead. The door opens on to five flights of red-carpeted stairway. It is a grand Victorian house, and the Murdochs inhabit the top floor. (I always think of them as the Murdochs, rather than the Bayleys, as though she had once ridden like a knight to his rescue.) But how, given their age and manifest physical unfitness, they ever get past the first landing, God only knows.

Iris is standing at the door, and shows me into a garret of exemplary shabbiness, consisting of three rooms with a bed in each, no books, but heaps of paintings by friends stacked here and there against the walls and hanging in conspicuous but somehow inappropriate places. The floor of the back room is scattered with John's papers, punctuated by bottles of wine – these stand also here and there on window sills, mantelpieces and tables, providing the only ornaments apart from the grim lightless abstracts in which John and Iris have probably never seriously believed. John works in an armchair, with an old-fashioned portable typewriter on a low table beside it. I can't imagine a less comfortable way of writing. And yet everything in the flat is as it is because that is how they have shaped it, through a rigorously sustained indifference to anything save immediate human need.

The view from the rear window is striking: a fine Victorian church, terraced streets, Barkers and, in the distance, the Post Office Tower. But an air of parsimony and improvisation inhabits the interior. The main room has a ceiling covered in horrid polystyrene tiles – perhaps to avoid the cost of replastering after a leak. The furniture is shabby without being old or elegant, and Iris is much exercised by the fate of the tablecloth, since the last one was ruined, she says, by the builders, who had not only drunk her red wine illicitly in her absence, but also unforgivably placed the bottles, rimmed with red juice, on the tablecloth and left them to greet her on her return from the country – an unforgettable trauma that she is clearly still re-living, despite the fact that the old tablecloth, visible beneath a new one that has been reluctantly provided to cover it, was quite as cheap and hideous as its successor, and probably looked marginally more attractive for a stain or two.

John offers me a glass of revolting white wine – Yugoslav Riesling, of a vinegary complexion – and tells me how nice it possibly is, while leaving me quite free to disagree. His whole conversation, in fact, is a matter of leaving you free to disagree, and his wonderful theatrical stutters, which come always on the most surprising words, so as to forbid you the luxury of anticipating the completed sentence, serve the same function, of maintaining discourse suspended between affirmation and denial. It makes me think of a great teacher, offering thoughts of a sublimity that his pupils could not encompass unaided, and then inviting the pupils to claim them as their own, or else to go, as they are free to go, down some other and drearier path towards extinction.

A plate of 'sardine pâté' stands on the table – tinned sardines mixed with curry powder, which we spread on fingers of somewhat damp and defeated toast. After this delicacy John ferries in a plate of Woolworth's sausages, with a tube of Coleman's mustard to flavour them. With them is the pièce de résistance, of which he is particularly proud: cold kidney beans out of a tin, with cold tomato juice poured over them – a kind of failed imitation of baked beans. A crust of cold pasta lies over this concoction, giving to it the character of a mushy wound beneath blanched dead skin. There is salad too – soggy lettuce with a sweet dressing into which aftershave seems to have been spilled. To round off the meal there is processed cheese in packets of tinfoil, John having his own special rations of Dutch gouda in a plastic bag. I am not able to eat any more, but Iris insists that I put a disc of soft Bel Paese and a shiny apple into my pocket.

The wine has changed to John's favourite Beaujolais Nouveau, which he drinks with relish. Iris constantly refuses it and then, having done so, urgently asks for more, so that by the time the meal is over they are well into the second bottle, despite the fact that I have drunk very little. During all this John potters up and down, expending great efforts in the kitchen in order to deliver his delicacies in perfect condition to the table. While out of the room he talks to himself quietly. 'Really must stop smoking with this cold,' I overhear him say, and 'They would of course, that's absolutely the way they are.' There is an atmosphere of extraordinary serenity, while the food has a wartime air, reminding me of those festive meals in communist countries when the diet of potatoes is suddenly relieved by a tin of stale Spam. John recounts with pride Freddie Ayer's comment on *The Sea, the Sea*, which won the Booker Prize when Ayer was presiding over the panel of judges: 'I liked everything in the book except for the food, which was disgusting!' For it was John who invented those weird recipes, expressed in such unjustified imperatives, with which the hero, Charles, endeavours to maintain a semblance of order in the midst of his self-imposed chaos.

Conversation is very agreeable. We speak of hospitality, and its gradual disappearance. 'There are no longer hostesses among the younger generation of wives,' I say, 'partly because they are wives only provisionally, and only on their way to some other station in life.' John concurs, adding that the young rush into each other's laps like puppies and then away again, so that all sense of a social world, and of the duties involved in maintaining it, evaporates.

'Mind you,' he adds, 'we are not very good ourselves. We never give dinner p-p-parties, do we darling?'

And he peers up at Iris through his thick glasses, through which his eyes stare wide and still and grey like the eyes of an owl.

'Perhaps at your age,' I say politely, 'you can decently argue that the duty is no longer yours, that you have generously retired from the business of hospitality in order to give the next generation a chance.'

'What a good idea,' he says, rolling his head in manifest enjoyment; 'that's what we'll say, won't we darling? We're giving the n-n-next generation their chance!'

Iris, who is quiet, tolerant and a liberal-minded conservative in most things, makes an exception when it comes to the Catholic Church, having a deep-seated hatred of popery in general, and the Pope in particular. No doubt this stems from her Protestant Irish upbringing. She maintains this fierce hatred without any sense that there may be a tension with the metaphysically based – if somewhat agnostic – Christianity that informs her moral views. I take what I suppose is the Devil's part, and argue that there is nothing that would hold me back from the entire catechism, except the major premise of God's existence; and that when it comes to matters like sex, abortion, homosexuality – concerning which Iris has liberal Bloomsbury-ish views – I cannot see alternatives, once you have accepted that premise, to the Pope's rigid conclusions. Iris defends abortion, and laments the fact that men can abandon women, leaving them with the entire responsibility for the children that they have made between them.

'But Catholic morality forbids that too,' I reply. 'The problem comes only when you uphold *half* of the morality – the half that is binding on women – and leave men to escape the duties that are theirs. These problems surely arise because we seek to base a new morality on free choice alone – and then we build on sand. Of course, without God, maybe there *is* only sand.'

That makes it sound as though I was trying to score a point; in fact it is impossible to score points with the Murdochs, and certainly not with Iris. Conversation is entirely devoted to the matter in hand, and whether it be beans, Bach, beatitude or Beaujolais she sifts it over in a fair-minded and compassionate way, looking for what is good and just and durable. There is a saintly modesty about her, which causes me to search round frantically for topics that will show how right it is to be like her.

I describe to them Diana Phipps's dinner parties – last examples of the salon culture, in which Diana (no doubt soon to be Countess Sternberg again)[12] sits quietly at one corner of the table, hugely amused by the great male egos she has invited – Gore Vidal, Roy Jenkins, Harold Pinter – as they lock horns and growl over the upturned intoxicated faces of ladies carefully chosen to admire them. John likes this image, as does Iris. She thinks I have a central European sensibility – and we agree that the peculiarity of *Francesca* is that it is the product of a Central European mind, meditating, however, on a purely English experience. Where did I get that mind? Through an elaborate training, perhaps, in the art of being disinherited.

All their words and gestures, their surroundings, and the small unloved objects over which they stumble, bring my thoughts back to Iris's characters – little gods in musty shrines of their own devising, visited only by others equally hungry for a worship the habit of which has been long forgotten. And strangely pure, all the same – contaminated by nothing so honest as a job of work, a mortgage or a bill that cannot be paid.

Those thoughts remind me of my deadline, and I get up to go. The Murdochs wave goodbye from the top of the stairs, faces wreathed in smiles, the third bottle of Beaujolais open on the table behind them, its wet rim visibly staining the tablecloth.

From a letter, 17 June 1996

The most interesting episode has been the visit, this last weekend, of Iris Murdoch and her husband, John Bayley, for a house party. They travelled from Oxford by car, bringing their own provisions – sandwiches, biscuits, whisky and red wine in considerable quantities – and started to lay the table, just as soon as they were through the door. This laying of the table occurred many times, Iris having become slightly weak in the head, and finding solace from her

[12] This was shortly after the collapse of Communism in Czechoslovakia. Diana was already helping Havel to renovate the castle in Prague, where she had been given an apartment. A year later the castle of Častolovice (among others) was restored to her; she now lives there, trying to make ends meet by treating coachloads of American tourists to weekends in a real castle, with a real countess in charge. But, as Diana says, it is a virtual castle, a virtual countess, and the whole thing a fiction that makes her want to sit like a child in the kitchen, speaking Czech with the maid.

condition by carrying chairs from room to room, washing, drying and stacking plates, setting the table for some imaginary meal, and then smiling with pleasure when it appears from nowhere, vindicating her strategy. She was much exercised by the fact that I live in both London and the country, and her conversation at dinner consisted almost entirely of requests that I elucidate this strange state of affairs. John, a small man with a tiny mouth and round globular eyes behind his vast spectacles, talks incessantly, about every conceivable subject from Tennyson to radio masts, while striving desperately to agree with everyone within earshot. 'You may be right, my dear, I am sure you are right, perfectly right' – and every agreement is sealed with a cheerful toast to himself, from a glass which is constantly replenished with wine of whatever colour, so as to maintain a permanent rosé appearance. Nothing is demanded of Iris other than that she make noises so inflected that 'you are absolutely right, darling' sounds like a plausible response to them. And the gentle murmur of their conversation, combined with the constant popping of corks and glugging of wine in the bottle neck, as they sat outside in the sunshine, created the impression of a quiet stream, beside which all other guests sat with their dreams. At one stage John decided that it would be a good idea to swim in the pond: he would accept no argument against this proposal, but simply took off all his clothes, except for the glasses, and slipped onto the mud and into the water. Iris followed him, wearing her long white Victorian drawers, and emerging mud-stained and panting, her large boobs stuck to the cotton of her vest like palpitating fish that had been trapped there.

Their shapeless bags of smooth white flesh were strangely touching to behold, as they swam around in the muddy water with quiet angelic smiles. The carp meanwhile had made a dive for the bottom, and have only today re-emerged.

3 A Day in Soweto, August 1983

Julie is beautiful, with large dark eyes that rest gently on what they see like a settling butterfly. She is slightly taller than Yunus, who has planned this illegal outing and to whom she defers with the kind of grace that makes me want to take him aside and say 'Marry her, you fool!'. He is classified as coloured, she as Indian. Her mother, she tells me, wrote to P. W. Botha pleading with him to convert to Islam, for the sake of South Africa and also for the sake of his soul. Strangely, Julie's grandmother, whom we visit first, is classified as coloured, which means that she cannot live in the same quarter as her daughter, and must fend for herself in a shabby street of bungalows where only coloureds are allowed. The woman opposite is white, but has petitioned to be reclassified as coloured in order not to be moved. Yunus and I go to buy cream in tins at the corner shop: everything here is twice the price that would be paid in the city, since no one can go downtown without such trouble and expense that it is no longer worth it. Dogs bark everywhere and sometimes run at us, to be fended off by Yunus with a knobbly stick. It is a miserable wet day, with streets and pavements turning to mud.

Granny is called 'Ma', and is re-dressing as we arrive. In the room from which she eventually emerges in a multi-coloured foam of frocks a black servant is ironing and remains at her work throughout our lunch. Ma worked for many years in a hotel in Bloemfontein, cooking English and Indian dishes, and she has prepared a lunch of curried chicken, with home-made mango chutney and cauliflower pickle for which she gives me the recipe. Her passion is religion: she was brought up in the Calvinist church, converted to Islam aged 14, married the following year and became an amateur midwife as well as a cook. She has many small-scale enterprises, hates communism and all forms of atheism, and says her *namaz* five times a day, sometimes remaining in a trance, praying for the forgiveness of everyone while calculating the money owed to her through her various businesses. She is fat and, although only 63, has suffered four strokes, leaving one eye occluded and her face partly paralysed. Her accent is entirely South African and she is astonished when I begin to clear the dishes from the table: 'You English!' she says admiringly, and I feel a surge of imperial pride that we last products of the empire were brought up to serve.

Conversation veers several times towards religion, Yunus constantly kicking me under the table in fear that I shall let the side down. But Ma is pleased to discover that I know something of her faith and informs me that, being an obviously reasonable man, I will in time be converted. All the furniture is embellished with frilly-edged cloth in pastel colours. The seat of the loo, the top of the flush, even the toilet roll is wrapped up in its own little cook's hat of crinoline. The curtains are permanently drawn, here as in all the other houses on the street; the colours and designs are hideous beyond words. Real domesticity, real love, real kitsch.

After lunch we travel through the former mixed township of Western, near the centre of the city. It has pretty veranda'd houses, between which gaps have been deliberately made. The whole is to be demolished to make room for a new white area, the residents to be resettled 25 kilometres away in a prison-like compound of boxes like Ma's. I notice a little brass plaque on one of the doors, reading 'Dr Fong'. It is highly polished, though the house is a two-roomed shack with a bent tin roof. We pass through 'poor white' quarters to the old coloured township where Yunus was brought up: wonderful jumbled houses like the *gecekondu* of Ankara, put together out of scraps: ornamental columns, barbed wire, brick, oil drums, toothpaste etc., and often very *soigné*, with the same drawn curtains in ostentatious African colours. The building of Yunus's private school still stands. The school took people of all races, though it is now far too expensive for the neighbourhood and has gone elsewhere, leaving the empty building behind. The next school we come to is in a poor black quarter. Two white teachers had been sent there during a period of shortages, but no mercy was shown to them and they were replaced by untrained military 'education officers' with guns.

We enter the coloured township of Kliptown (of 'Freedom Charter' fame). We are standing in an open space of mud, surrounded by the same jumbled houses. I spend some time in conversation with a woman of some 60 or 70 years of age, who has sprayed her thin legs with aluminium paint and stacked her ankles with hundreds of thin metal anklets. She is convinced that I need the services of a witch doctor but explains her position in a mixture of Xhosa and Afrikaans, so I remain unpersuaded. Yunus catches sight of his uncle, who is wholly black. He calls me 'sir', which troubles me, but he is an easy-going, genial man and introduces me to his house guest, Isaq Hussein, who has apparently been British Heavyweight Champion and who boxes here under the name of Charka, having married a South African wife and spent a 'formative' weekend once in KwaZulu. He is visiting in order to spar with the reigning champion. He is a huge, soft-spoken black man from Dominica, with a squashed nose and missing side teeth, but, like so many boxers, very gentle and civil. I tell him I live in Notting Hill, and we talk about the Carnival, which has been peaceful this year, and about our shared hope that it will remain so.

Kliptown has a lively, scruffy market, with barrows piled high with vegetables and chickens in cages. It has the feel of rural Africa, a hereness and nowness that admit no passage of time. All voices are raised, and the sky seems to ring with the human sound beneath it. We visit Yunus's family box. His black grandmother is 84, wizened and with eyes almost closed. She talks angrily of the boxer, who won't stay in a hotel in town as he easily could. Yunus justifies him, saying that he rightly refuses to be classified as an 'honorary white'. Maybe, says Granny, but that doesn't excuse his behaviour: refusing to take the household food, cooking for himself, being under the roof but not belonging there. This is the greatest offence to an African, and she is very indignant. Yunus's other uncle, who lives with her and is also black, agrees, though moderates his anger with the observation that boxers have special diets. He resents the fact that the boxer doesn't pay for his stay, though if he wins the title he has promised to pay for Yunus to go to Zimbabwe. Granny is totally forthcoming about every possible grievance, and Yunus constantly interrupts her, saying 'Granny complaining again?' Gramophone and radio play at full volume through all conversations, which are maintained at the top of the voice so that even the mildest remark has the sound of anger. There is a small child, who is very shy of me, perhaps because I am white, but who is happy in Julie's arms, as who wouldn't be?

Afterwards we pass through a desolate coloured quarter known as Zombie Town. In one window there is a face that fixes me with a horrible accusing stare. It is the face of Gauguin's Spirit of the Dead. Then we cross over the railway line into Soweto. A notice says: 'Private Road. Entrance by permit only, to be obtained by application to the Department of Community Affairs'. A little mud town sprawls between the railway and the notice. There is a shebeen with a row of drunken women in its deeply shadowed porch. Helpless men stagger in the street, one of them beaten up and bleeding. Once into the township things improve. Many of the houses have been *embourgeoisé* with big brass numbers like 2017 nailed diagonally across the doors, in the style of the white suburbs. The numbers are fictions and chosen for their grandeur: all have four figures, since fewer would be downmarket, more arrogant. Bolas are burning in the street, to be taken in at night to prepare the evening meal, always posing a threat of asphyxiation, one of the most common causes of death in Soweto. In every street there is a herbalist. One has a drying monkey swinging over the door, with a hundred fetishes ranged along the outside of the window. There is a little clinic, a seedy building like an abandoned bunker, with 'Non-Europeans' in big letters over the door.

We drive through the mud streets in Yunus's old Fiat, worried that every car might contain a policeman. The police cars are not marked and contain white men: hence our car too is greeted with hostility and could at any moment become a target. Julie is frightened. It is raining and all the women wear blankets. The streets are endless, without lights, only spotlights as in a prison. The houses are without electricity and even 2017 is lit from within by candlelight. We pass through a comparatively open part of the township, where old houses have verandas looking onto the street and peaceable people wander in and out. Here the roads are surprisingly busy with cars, vans and lorries and occasionally we pass a shopping area with a rough 'supermarket' consisting of one dark room cluttered with tins, bottles, vegetables and dried fish. But army camps are hidden between each housing lot, and a prison is being built beneath the ground in one of them, with windowless cells lit only from above by the airholes.

We make it to the border without trouble and Julie relaxes. Back in Yunus's household she listens to my comments on Eastern Europe and takes comfort from her encounter with a woman from Mozambique who told her how lucky she is to be here and not there. (The woman had come to South Africa for an operation, as many do.) Yunus, however, is implacably bitter. He hates the university, and hates liberals more than anyone. A Boer, he tells me, is better than an Englishman, since he is straightforward and tells you that he dislikes the colour of your skin. I don't think this remark is directed at me; maybe I am an 'honorary black'. At least, I assure him, I am a pariah. He looks at me uncomprehendingly, and then squeezes my hand.

They need my help with their essays on representation in art. I have to use as my example the appalling primary colour picture of a mountain river and fir trees that hangs in the crowded living room, and I must speak over the constant pulse of the radio. Yunus says he can work only if he waits until 11, when everyone is in bed. The children are always screaming, the radio and the gramophone always playing. At the same time Yunus has an immense nostalgia for the intimacy of the old township where he was brought up, for the meddlesome clutter of bedrooms where six people sleep side by side, and for the constant sound of the rhythmical music of Zaire. In Soweto choruses of dogs bark through the night and only by becoming a dog yourself will you sleep.

Yunus's brother comes in: his hand is bandaged since he was in a fight when drunk, hitting both a man and a windscreen. Now he is being sued for damages. All at once there is peace in the household as everyone gathers round to express their unquestioning loyalty and support. 'Better a dish of herbs where love is, than a stalled ox and hatred withal.' The message can be clearly read in Julie's eyes, and that damned fool Yunus doesn't see it.

11
Returning Home

While Spengler, in *The Decline of the West*, composed his majestic evocation of the grandeur, strangeness and nature-defying rhythm of the 'city-as-world', the modern movement was already advocating a radical break with the city as we Europeans had known it – a rejection of all that had made the city a centre of life, worship, industry and exchange. Instead of streets – those 'long gorges between high, stony houses filled with coloured dust and strange uproar', as Spengler had described them – we were promised open parks. Instead of façades ranged along a public street or a public square, we were promised towers of glass, linked by aerial gangways across the unbounded lawns below. Architectural modernism rejected all attempts to adapt the old language of the city. It rejected classical orders, columns, architraves and mouldings. It rejected the Greek and Gothic revivals. It rejected the street as the primary public space and the façade as the public aspect of a building. It rejected every written and unwritten rule that had shaped the growth of our towns. Modernism rejected those things not because it had any well-thought-out alternative, but because it was intent on over-throwing the social order that they represented – the order of the bourgeois city, as a place of faith, festivity, commerce and spontaneous hierarchical life.

Of course, the modernists did not confess to such a purpose. Their project, they gave out, was not social but aesthetic. Le Corbusier, the Russian constructivists and Hannes Meyer, when director of the Bauhaus, claimed to be architectural thinkers in the tradition of Vitruvius and Palladio. However, the paltriness of what they said about architecture (compared with what had been said by the revivalists – for example by Alberti in his *Ten Books of Architecture*, by Ruskin in *Stones of Venice* and by Viollet-le-Duc in his two volumes of lectures) reveals this claim to be a sham. The modernist pioneers were social and political activists, who wished to squeeze the disorderly human material that constitutes a city into a socialist straightjacket. Architecture, for them, was one part of a new and all-comprehending system of control. True, they didn't *call* it control: socialists never do. Le Corbusier's project to demolish all of Paris north of the Seine and replace it with high-rise towers of glass was supposed to be an emancipation, a liberation from the old constraints of urban living. Those dirty, promiscuous streets were to be replaced with grass and trees – open spaces where the new socialist man, released from the hygienic glass bottle where he was stored by night, could walk in the sunshine and be alone with himself. The fact is, however, that Le Corbusier never asked himself whether people wanted to live in this new utopia, nor did he care what method was used to transport them there. History (as understood by the modernist project) required them to be there, and that was that.

Classical and Gothic buildings spoke of another age, in which faith, honour and authority stood proudly and without self-mockery in the street. Their styles and materials could no longer be used sincerely, the modernists argued, since nobody believed in those old ideals. The modern age was an age without heroes, without faith, without public tribute to anything higher or more dignified than the common man. It needed an architecture that would reflect its moral vision, of a classless society from which all hierarchies had disappeared, a society with no absolute, but only relative values. Hence it needed an architecture without ornament and without any other pretence to a grandeur beyond the reach of mortal beings, an architecture that used modern materials to create a modern world. The key words of this new architecture were 'honesty' and 'function'. By being honest, it was implied, buildings could help us to become so. The new city of glass, concrete and parkland would be a city without social pretence, where people would live in exemplary uniformity and be rewarded with equal respect.

This social agenda meant that architectural modernism was not an experiment but a crusade. Those opposed to it were regarded as enemies, members of a priesthood of pretenders and snobs. They were to be removed as soon as possible from positions of influence and power. When the German art historian Niklaus Pevsner and the Russian constructivist architect Berthold Lubetkin brought the crusade to London they set up shop as legislators, condemning everything that was not conceived as a radical break with the past. Both were travelling as refugees from modernism of the political variety – Nazism in Pevsner's case, Communism in Lubetkin's. But they brought with them the censorious attitudes of the regimes from which they fled. Nothing was more loathsome in their eyes than the would-be enchantment of a neo-classical school or a Victorian Gothic bank. To Pevsner, Arthur Street's great Gothic law courts, which are the centrepiece of London's legal quarter, and a fitting symbol of common-law justice and its daily work of reconciliation, were mediocre buildings of no consequence, whose fairytale pinnacles and marble columns were neither uplifting nor cheerful but merely pretence. By contrast the underground station at Arnos Grove, with its plain wrapped brickwork and its grim metal-frame windows, was a portent of a future and better world, in which modern life would be honestly portrayed and openly accepted.

When I discovered culture, it was not the culture of the past that interested me, but the culture of the present. I sought out modern music, modern poetry, modern painting and modern novels. But I rejected modern architecture. Gropius's claim that modern architecture is simply the architectural application of the modernist aesthetic – an aesthetic exemplified equally by Eliot's poetry, Joyce's prose, Schoenberg's music and the paintings of Matisse – left me entirely unpersuaded. And when, at Cambridge, I read Siegfried Giedion's *Space, Time and Architecture*, in which Einstein's theory of relativity is garbled into an apology for concrete, I threw the book across the room, amazed that such a charlatan should be published, let alone so avidly read. Others of my generation had the same response. Peter Fuller, drawn to the modern in everything else, could never bring himself to acknowledge modern architecture. For all his Marxist leanings, Peter was not an iconoclast. He saw the aesthetic project as Eliot had seen it: modern art must remake itself, not so as to destroy the tradition, but so as to reassume it. It must purify the artistic language, in order to repair the spiritual order that had been torn asunder by modern life. The vision that Eliot put forward in *Four Quartets* and in 'Tradition and the Individual Talent' was one that Peter found also in the great modern painters – and especially in those like Matisse, Ivon Hitchens and Ben Nicolson, who had seen abstraction not as an assault on the figurative tradition, but as an attempt to rescue that tradition from the cartoon and the photograph. Abstract art was, for Peter, the very opposite of the constructivist art which has since come to replace it. It does not play with pure forms and strident colours; it begins from things seen and felt, and distils from them the human essence, just as Raphael, Constable or Turner had done. When he founded the journal *Modern Painters*, it was from Ruskin that Peter took the title, and his intention was to restore an old and respectable idea of the modern, which he believed was still there in the collective consciousness, beneath the ignorant scribbling that had recently defaced it.

The reluctance to accept modernism in architecture has, I believe, a foundation in human nature. For many people, the best thing about modern music is that you don't have to listen to it, just as you don't have to read modern literature or go to exhibitions of modern painting. Architecture, however, is unavoidable. It is not a transaction between consenting adults in private, but a public display. The business of architecture is the building of a home – not my home and your home only, but the home of the community that includes us. The modernists conceived design in terms appropriate to the intimate arts of music, literature and painting. Their buildings were to be individual creative acts, which would challenge the old order of architecture and defy the tired imperatives of worn-out styles. They believed that originality – which is the *sine qua non* of communication in music, painting and poetry – was also a requirement of architecture, rather than a threat to it. Their egalitarian mission could be accomplished only by a daring élite, who built without respect for the tradition of popular taste – indeed, without respect for anything save their own redeeming genius. The paradox here is exactly that of revolutionary politics: human equality is to be achieved by an élite to whom all is permitted, including the coercion of the rest of us.

Peter Fuller was a very modern thinker, not only in his writings on art and psychoanalysis, but also in his conception of politics.

His socialist vision was adopted from the Marxist humanism of the sixties, which he had synthesized with T. S. Eliot, D. H. Lawrence and John Ruskin in an intoxicating call to redemption. It was not the revolutionary nature of architectural modernism that troubled him, nor its Leninist assumption of coercive powers; he was troubled, rather, by modernism's repudiation of the thing that he principally longed for and to which he saw Marxist politics as the indispensable means – namely, home. My father was an old-fashioned socialist of the English school, who hated revolutionaries, who believed that socialism would be accepted by anyone who took the trouble to understand it, and who abhorred coercion as a tool of the old ruling class. He rejected the monarchy, the Empire, the class system and the Anglican Church. He admired Oliver Cromwell and John Hampden, who in his version of events had tried to reclaim our country from the toffs who were destroying it. His vision of architecture sprang from the same Roundheaded attitude as his politics but, like Peter Fuller, whom he never met, he saw modernist architecture as the enemy of home.

Although he rejected the English establishment, Jack Scruton did not reject England. On the contrary, he was a passionate Englishman, who believed that his country persisted as a kind of spiritual presence behind the veil of old authority and usurping power. In his view of things, England had been betrayed by her rulers, but in herself was always there, a quiet but determined ghost, eager to reincarnate herself in living beings. His socialism was not the forward-looking, theory-driven machine that purred in our universities, waiting the countdown to zero. It was a home-grown local product, which had home-growing and local production as its aims. Its roots were in the Anglo-Saxon moots and witenagemots, in scutage and gavelkind, in the Peasants' Revolt and the Statute of Labourers, in *Piers Plowman*, Tyndale's Bible, and *Everyman*. My father's goal was not the classless society of the Marxists, but the tranquil order of the English country town, the order described by Thomas Hardy. When, in later life, he too discovered books (which were my books) he found in Hardy the image of all that he loved: the English landscape, the English weather, the English temperament, the English refusal to bow down to alien powers and insolent authorities. He admired all those who rose to protest from the ranks of the people and to say 'No' to official decrees. From the Peasants' Revolt to the trade union movement, Englishmen, he believed, had made 'no' into their national philosophy, and that philosophy was his.

When his turn came to say his own personal 'no' it was to architectural modernism, in the form that had been imposed during the sixties on the towns and villages of England. My father did not see modernism as a sign of social progress and, besides, it was not progress that mattered to him but people. Modernism, as he saw it, empowered the developer and disenfranchised the rest of us: it was the public face of private greed. And he was right. Developers, in league with corrupt town councils, were everywhere using modernist rhetoric to justify gigantic, self-interested and aesthetically outrageous schemes. They were ruthlessly destroying the organic townscapes that were the homes of real and living communities, and erecting faceless office blocks on their ruins. All the gentle contours of our towns were being levelled: Georgian terraces, medieval alleyways, Victorian pubs and – my father's particular source of anguish, since it was the townscape of his childhood – the workshops and back-to-backs of the old working class. Seeing this happen to High Wycombe, the centuries-old market town to which he had come with Bomber Command during the war, where he had met my mother and in whose pastoral surroundings he had courted her in the innocent fashion of those days, afterwards settling with her wherever he could afford in order to cling to this little piece of England and make it his own, Jack Scruton was awakened from the paralysed gloom in which he had been plunged by my mother's death. He looked out from his solitude at what was happening beyond the window of the living room (which had been her dying room) and declared uncompromising war on it.

'They' was the name that Jack had always used for the established powers, and it was 'they' who were at work beyond the living room window. 'They' had begun to demolish the High Street. 'They' were going to drive a road across the Rye, an ancient piece of common land that united the town with the River Wye and with the Chiltern woodlands that had provided the beechwood for the famous High Wycombe furniture. 'They' had in mind to demolish the old mills and half-timbered shops along the London Road, and to use the scheme to replace the higgledy-piggledy façades of a town that clustered around its market cross like a family of piglets around a sow, with a concrete plaza of which 'artistic impressions' already existed in glossy brochures. 'They' were going to bring to us citizens of Wycombe, whether we liked it or not and in any case without consulting our wishes in the matter, the full panoply of modernist benefits: wide roads, pedestrian zones, high buildings that would deface the sky and wide glass windows from which the new breed of post-industrial worker could stare over spaces as clean, straight and empty as the mind that surveyed them.

'They' had assumed that the residents of Wycombe would prove as docile and disorganized as those of Coventry, Winchester, Reading, Newcastle and every other place that had been turned overnight from an English community to an Antonioni film set. But 'they' had reckoned without Jack Scruton, who stood bareheaded on the Rye each Saturday, picking people from the crowd like the Ancient Mariner and not allowing them to proceed without appending their signature to his homespun petition. He went from neighbourhood to neighbourhood and house to house, jamming his foot in doorways and staring at victim after victim from hooded eyes that glowed in their caverns like the fires of crouching warriors. He addressed timid old ladies, loud Jamaicans, secretive Pakistanis and the resentful remnants of the old working class with words adjusted to their several conditions, always cajoling, always exhorting, and always reproving those for whom a private life seemed preferable to the arduous discipline of protest.

In this way he uncovered, to their mutual amazement, the quantities of studious and artistic people whom it was the virtue of such small English towns to possess: people who harboured in their hearts some version of the local patriotism and national grief that had bubbled up in my father's breast as he stared through the living room window and imagined the four-lane carriageway that would obliterate this piece of England forever, and along with it all the memories that he chose now (marked as they were by the most intense personal suffering) to treasure. And among the people whom he met were women for whom the encounter in the half-open doorway with those blazing eyes, those drawn cheeks lined by grief and that soft, confiding Northern accent which both announced calamity and promised help in averting it, was to be the decisive experience in a lifetime of hesitations. Marriages were jeopardized, domestic harmonies untuned, plans overturned and peaceable routines stirred to boiling point, in my father's pitiless journey through the suburbs. The personality that had lain dormant since the sad years of Sam the First had thrown off its mind-forged manacles and emerged into the light of day, bursting into those tranquil hallways with a sudden glare of charisma.

In mobilizing the people of Wycombe, therefore, Jack Scruton did what all such tribunes of the people do: he jeopardized his following. But it was worth it, because he won, defending his case before a Select Committee of Parliament and earning the respect even of the local MP, whose friendship Jack nevertheless spurned since it had never been permitted to a Scruton to be friends with a member of the establishment, still less with a Tory MP. And if my father's victory was, in a certain measure, a pyrrhic one (since the developers and their allies are always able to regroup against their unarmed opponents) it has remained in my feelings as a vindication of his time on earth, a proof not only of his energy, skill and conviction, but also of his goodness. The ruthless conquests that preceded his second marriage did not exactly cast credit on him. But they were a fitting rebuke to useless husbands who had neglected the first duty of a husband, which is to be a public as well as a private person. Jack uttered the lasting cry of the citizen – the cry to join in a shared life, to redeem a place and a time, to honour the community by honouring those who had built it over centuries. In the words of Jan Patočka (who, as first spokesman of Charter 77, paid for his public spirit with his life) Jack was inviting the people of High Wycombe to 'confess to history', and to take responsibility for a future that would die like a severed flower when cut off from its roots in the past. And in identifying architectural modernism as his target he showed his deep awareness of what is at stake in modern life – the very survival of a public world that is also a home. His warning to the people of Wycombe was that of Hans Sachs to the people of Nuremberg: it is not your town that is at stake, but your country, your culture, and your own survival as something more than a heap of atomic particles.

To this battle of my father's I made my own small contribution, with a lecture delivered in High Wycombe town hall on the aesthetics of architecture. Thus began an intellectual interest that has remained a source of consolation as well as the occasional channel for impotent rage. My thoughts grew, at length, into a book: not a polemical book, but a work of philosophy, in which I attempt to explore the roots of our relation to the built environment. *The Aesthetics of Architecture* appeared in 1979, just before *Morality and Architecture*, David Watkin's brilliant polemic against Pevsner and the modernist orthodoxy. David and I were, and remain, close friends, having been Fellows of Peterhouse together. We were products of the old Cambridge, in which it was assumed that authorities should be questioned and orthodoxies spurned. We observed at first with amusement, and then with mounting alarm, as our two books were put on trial and consigned to the flames. It was soon apparent that we were outside the fold of respectable opinion, so much so that we would not be permitted even to defend ourselves before the impromptu courts appointed to pass judgement on our work. One such was a day-long seminar mounted by the Bartlett School of Architecture in what was by then my own university of London. Neither David nor I was invited to attend, and the day consisted of paper after paper denouncing our two books as reactionary, immoral and intellectually worthless. And the voices that condemned us spoke in the name of progress and the common man.

Huge vested interests are at stake in architecture. My father was right to believe that these interests are financial, and that his opponents were among the most unscrupulous members of the rising capitalist class. What he did not perceive, however, since it challenged the moral basis of all that he thought and did, was that the capitalist class thrives best by pretending to be socialist. By clothing themselves in the ideology of equality, capitalists can neutralize the principal sources of opposition to their goals. This is what the modernist establishment had perceived. The money lies in gigantic schemes, mass destruction, the use of cheap and ill-understood materials, the reduction of architecture to engineering and the development of a language that requires no discipline of the heart or the soul, still less of the eye, for its efficient deployment. Modernism legitimizes those things, and dignifies visual and moral ignorance as a style. Align that style with the socialist ideology, and you will be able to bulldoze your opponents' arguments as easily as you bulldoze their cities.

Reflecting on my father's great campaign I have come to see that it was not, in fact, architecture that concerned him but something that lies deeper than architecture, deeper than building, deeper than history too. He was defending High Wycombe as a settlement, in which a collective impetus to dwell had for the time being triumphed over the entropy that brings all our hopes to nothing. In a brief fit of lucidity Heidegger wrote that it is only by dwelling that we build: building and dwelling are parts of a single enterprise, whereby we hunter-gatherers overcome our nature and begin the work of civilization, which has the temple, the market and the city as its goals. And Jack Scruton's campaign was a proof of that idea.

My father observed that most buildings, and most buildings that we truly love, are not the work of architects. The agreeable settledness of the old English town, he reasoned, was the work of local craftsmen, beings who had been lifted briefly from oblivion by Ruskin and Morris, but whose merely local patriotism and merely neighbourly ambitions had caused them to live and die unchronicled by the inventors of history. Architecture was, for Jack Scruton, not the cause of a healthy townscape but a disease of which towns must be cured. The true antibodies are the vernacular style, the craft tradition, the respect for scales and materials that had recommended themselves to ordinary builders in their collective attempt to settle in a home of their own.

Here, it now seems to me, is the true starting point for the aesthetics of architecture. And I would take my father's thought in another but complementary direction, which is to question not only the claims of the architect, but those of his client too. Most users of a building are not clients of the architect. They are passers-by, residents, neighbours: those whose horizon is invaded and whose sense of home affected by this new intrusion. The failure of modernism lies not in the fact that it produced no great or beautiful buildings – Le Corbusier's Chapel at Ronchamp, and the houses of Frank Lloyd Wright prove the opposite. It lies in the absence of any reliable patterns or types, which can be used so as spontaneously to harmonize with the existing urban decor, thereby retaining the essence of the city as a common home in which strangers live committed to strangers. The degradation of our cities is the result of a 'modernist vernacular', whose principal device is the stack of horizontal layers, with jutting and obtrusive corners, built without consideration for the street, without a coherent façade, and without intelligible relation to its neighbours. Although this vernacular has repeatable components, they are not conceived as parts of a grammar, answerable each to each, and subject to the over-arching discipline of the townscape. They are items in a brochure, rather than words in a dictionary. The old pattern books did not offer gadgets and structures. They offered matching shapes, mouldings and ornaments: forms that had pleased and harmonized, and that could be relied upon not to spoil or degrade the streets in which they were placed. They were used to great effect in New York and Boston, and could be used even now to restore the civility of those much damaged neighbourhoods. The only obstacle – and in this Jack Scruton was surely right – is the vast machine of patronage that puts architects, rather than the public, at the head of every scheme.

In American cities we can still witness the effect of the pattern books (such as that published by Asher Benjamin in Boston in 1839). Whole areas of agreeable and unpretentious dwellings, the architects of which are no longer remembered and perhaps never existed, have been saved from demolition on grounds of the charm imparted by their syntax: Beacon Hill and the Back Bay area of Boston, Greenwich Village, the Upper East Side, much of Brooklyn, and the terraced streets of Harlem are well-known American examples. We have the English equivalent in the East End of London, as it was before the bombing, in the industrial towns of the North, and in Georgian Bath – though the last, on account of the eager involvement of professional architects, shows the creation of novel and indigenous patterns handed down from the works of genius.

Bath is a city in which the original architects conformed to rules of scale, detail and material that every builder could imitate. Hence an unassuming vernacular grew side by side with the stylish Adam circles, crescents and squares, borrowing details and filling in gaps to produce a seamless web of stone-faced streets and alleyways. The result was much loved by the residents, who maintained Bath as a live cultural centre, even during the days when such things were hardly subsidized. The urbane and gentle streets inspired the thing that Plato saw as the true aim of the city: 'the care of the soul'. And it was wholly fitting that the great

Yehudi Menuhin should choose Bath as the location for his annual musical festival.

Bath therefore became an urgent project of the modernist establishment. Such a city should not exist, or if it did exist, it should not be loved. Thanks to a corrupt town council, the architectural knights, led by Sir Hugh Casson, moved in to destroy the city, rapidly pulling down as much as possible of the organic centre, erecting Gropius towers on the hillsides, and mutilating the street plan with blocks that conceded nothing to their neighbours. This extraordinary episode, in which modernist malice worked side by side with capitalist greed, has been documented by Adam Fergusson.[13] It marked a turning point in the history of urbanization. Henceforth it became common knowledge that modern architecture is at war with the city.

Meanwhile, the desperate residents of Bath had formed the Bath Preservation Trust, in an effort to save what they could of their city. One of the trustees – Timothy Cantell – was sent to lecture to the High Wycombe Society, and fell under the spell of Jack Scruton, who taught him how to mobilize people and to make them – whatever the level of their understanding – willing partners in a relentless campaign. Later it was the turn of the Bath Preservation Trust to exert its spell over a Scruton, when the young Sophie Jeffreys found work as the Trust's curator. I would visit her in her office, at the very top of the Building of Bath Museum. Balustrades and attic stories have a singular beauty: it is as though the classical builder seeks to shape the air with stone, and to make a final temple to the light. To find the woman I had dreamed of, lodged there in the dappled sunlight, like the soul of the stone – this was my turn for home.

Pattern-book housing bears the mark of civilization, even when it has degenerated, through poverty, neglect and speculative renting, into a slum. This too you learn from Bath, whose Victorian additions – once the Trust had secured their future – quickly recovered their dignity. It needs only private ownership and the prospect of security for the residents to respond to the call of their surroundings, and once again to take pride in them. The

[13] *The Sack of Bath*, London, 1973. The story is retold and updated by Sophie Jeffreys, 'Planning and the Citizen', in Anthony Barnett and Roger Scruton, eds, *Town and Country*, London, 1998.

modernist housing estate, built on the model recommended by Le Corbusier and Gropius, never rises from its inevitable decline, for the simple reasons that it is not a home where you dwell, but a shelter to which you flee from the surrounding devastation. When (usually within 20 years) the tower blocks and their barren surroundings become areas of 'social deprivation', there is no solution to the problem except dynamite. And already the modernist intrusions into Bath, for which lasting and invaluable streets had been sacrificed, are scheduled for demolition.

Pattern-book architecture is possible only because of the intellectual and visual labour that made the patterns. Some of this labour was collective – a far-reaching activity of trial and error, leading to easily managed designs. But just as important as this collective labour has been the inspiration that conjures new and living details, and which transforms our perception of form. Stylistic breakthroughs create a vocabulary of dignifying details. Gothic mouldings, the classical orders, Serlian arches, Palladian windows, Vignolesque cornices – these great artistic triumphs become types and patterns for the ordinary builder, and all of them can be witnessed in the vernacular architecture of New York, with its standardized window- and doorframes, its rusticated quoins and pressed-tin cornices. Our best bet in architecture is that the artistic geniuses should invest their energy as Palladio did, in patterns that can be reproduced at will by the rest of us. For the fact remains that most of the architecture that surrounds us is bound to be uninspired and uninspiring, and that its most important virtue will be that of good manners – a virtue that goes unnoticed, since that is its point.

Modernism began with manifestos: Le Corbusier, Gropius and the Russian Constructivists all issued pages of exhortations crying 'Down with the past!'. But nothing is more dangerous in architecture than a manifesto, whose purpose is to excite people to be bold and radical, in circumstances where they should be modest and discreet. Millennia of slowly accumulating common sense were discarded, for the sake of shallow prescriptions and totalitarian schemes. When architects began to dislike the result, they ceased to be modernists and called themselves postmodernists instead. But there is no evidence that they drew the right conclusion from the collapse of modernism – namely, that modernism was a *mistake*. Postmodernism is not an attempt to avoid mistakes, but an attempt to build in such a way that the very concept of a mistake has no application. Modernism was severe – it had to be, since it was taking a stand against popular taste, hunting down 'pastiche' and 'cliché' in their fetid lairs and dousing them with the cultural equivalent of carbolic acid. Postmodernism announces itself as a liberation; its aim is not to take the side of high culture against kitsch, but to play with both of them. Postmodernist art is 'non-judgemental': at home with affluence, advertising and mass-production, as tolerant of popular taste as of the modernist contempt for it. We are living beyond judgement, beyond value, beyond objectivity – so the postmodernist movement tells us. We are not in the business of forbidding things but in the business of permitting them. It turns out, however, that everything is permitted except the thing of which we stand most in need – namely, a return to the centuries-old conception of building, as a practice bound by a publicly accepted grammar. This is ruled out of court as much by the postmodernists as by their censorious predecessors. Any return to the values of the classical vernacular, with its emphasis on the street and the façade, is seen as a betrayal of history, a retreat into 'nostalgia', and in any case no better than pastiche.

Following the stern, cast concrete forms of modernism, therefore, there has been a new kind of flamboyant building: brightly coloured girders exposed to view, tubes and wires rioting over the surface, ornaments stuck anyhow on to surfaces of transparent perspex or shimmering tiles. The effect shows a freedom from constraint that reminds you why constraints are a good idea. At its most aggressive – and it is usually aggressive – it may involve the deliberate 'deconstruction' of the forms and values of the classical tradition, in the manner of Tschumi's student centre at Columbia, of the monstrous yet culpably vague designs by Peter Eisenman for the redevelopment of the West Side of New York, or of the lopsided spiral proposed by Daniel Libeskind for the Victoria and Albert Museum in London. If a justification is required, then the project will be backed up with pretentious gobbledygook in the style of Peter Eisenman, offering abstract ideas in the place of visual logic. Often these ideas are derived from modern science, referring to 'fractals', 'relativity' and 'quantum logic', in the spirit of Siegfried Giedion's original defence of modernism as the natural child of Einstein.[14] But the pseudo-science does not hide the visual ignorance, and there is no doubt in my mind that the postmodernist archetypes will prove as unacceptable to ordinary people as those inflicted on their eyes and souls by Gropius.

Nevertheless, gobbledygook is at a premium in public debate and belongs to the *lingua franca* of public patronage. Hence the way to win commissions is not to propose a building that will fit into its place as though it had always stood there, but to invent something outrageous, insolent and unignorable, and to sell it with a pretentious description in the style of Derrida. This explains the flamboyant anti-architecture of Gehry and Libeskind: architecture that eschews the vertical, breaks out in untamed edges or undetailed curves and, instead of decently hanging back from us, hangs over us like a curious intruder from a place outside the city.

Postmodernism in Britain has been associated with the name of Richard Rogers – the architect who, together with the modernist Norman Foster, receives all the important commissions, and sits on all the important committees. Rogers belongs to the generation of post-war architects trained in modernist rhetoric, who were taught very little about style and everything about public relations, and who have controlled the schools of architecture and the Royal Institute of British Architects, using their power to ensure that classicists, gothicists and other 'reactionaries' are excluded from public commissions. Recognizing the public hostility to modernism, many of these architects have hastened to declare modernism officially dead, and to welcome the new era of freedom of which they are the champions and the providers.

Rogers made his reputation in partnership with Peano at the Centre Beaubourg (Centre Pompidou) in Paris. This building, dumped without visual explanation in the city, is decorated with functionless tubes and scaffolding whose decorative effect depends upon being perceived as functional, like the chrome-plated exhaust of a racing car. Its colours are not those of the materials used to build it, but those of the paints that veneer them. Its joints and load-bearing parts are concealed, and nothing is really visible which is not surface. It is a slap in the face for the

14 See Nikos Salingaros, *Anti-Architecture and Deconstruction.*

modernist principles of honesty, truth to materials and functional transparency. In this respect you might very well be taken in by Rogers's claim that modernism is a thing of the past.

In fact, however, the Centre Beaubourg is the first real triumph in Paris of the modernist idea. It is a step towards achieving Le Corbusier's goal of razing the city to the ground. The Centre Beaubourg required the demolition of a vast and beautiful tract of stone-built classical vernacular, and the imposition of a recreational purpose on what had previously been a living *quartier* of the city. It was guided by a social vision – namely, to exchange the quiet self-sustaining life of bourgeois Paris for a fast-moving, multi-media 'happening' that would be maximally offensive to bourgeois taste. Its loud colours and in-your-face externals, its shape, size and materials, above all its windowless and doorless sides that warn you away with metallic imperviousness – all these are signs of a profoundly motivated effrontery, a desire to uproot and disenchant the domestic life of the world's greatest city, and to replace both work and home with an undisciplined playground.

This is not the socialist project, however, and in this at least we are a long way from the Bauhaus and Le Corbusier. The modernist programme was focused on work, discipline and the regimented life of the new proletariat. Le Corbusier's definition of a house as a 'machine for living in' says more about his conception of life than his ideal of architecture. Life, for the modernists, was all work and no play, with just an occasional stroll outside for medicinal reasons. The Centre Beaubourg is a celebration of play, randomness and indiscipline. It is a machine for playing in, and the machinery is part of the joke.

The postmodernist project has also visited London, with the same effect. Perhaps the most impressive symbol of the old city of London and its institutions was Lloyd's insurance company. This began life in 1668, among the club of merchants who were in the habit of meeting at the Edward Lloyd Coffee House, and who decided to establish an institution with which to protect each other from bankruptcy. English commercial enterprise relied upon bonds of honour that fell critically short of intimacy, which could therefore be extended far and wide through the world of strangers. Hence institutions like Lloyd's could appeal for capital from outside the community of City traders. The 'names' who provided this capital to the underwriters were people of wealth and standing, who implicitly trusted this institution run by gentlemen, and who thought nothing of placing their entire possessions in the hands of a discreet and well-spoken stranger.

The solid well-furnished buildings of Lloyd's were treated as clubhouses; its routines were shrouded in mystery like the rituals of a church; and the old bell of the frigate *Lutine*, captured from the French in 1793, sounded eerily through its hallway to announce the loss or arrival of a strategic merchant vessel. It was the very image of the safety that the English associated with their homeland, and its well-bred clientele somnolently assumed that such an institution would last forever, an unsinkable rock amid the tides of misfortune that visited lesser men. When a new board of directors decided to demolish the Victorian clubhouse, and to erect a grotesque piece of postmodernist cliché by Rogers in its place, the 'names' continued to dream in their country houses, unaware that the bottom had fallen out of their world, and that the proof of this was now standing on top of it.

One glance at Rogers's building, constructed at vast expense, and functioning so badly that it is the subject of continuous expensive repair, ought to have awoken the 'names' to what had happened. This tower, ridiculous as architecture, is manifestly part of a social project: it is an affront to the old conception of the City and a harbinger of the new world of corporate finance; a vertical playground, with the childish metalwork and intergalactic shapes familiar from the Centre Beaubourg, and transparent external lifts carrying the whiz-kids high above the streets of old London. It is a sign that probity and trusteeship are things of the past; from now on everything is fun. And part of the fun will be to deprive those trusting old gentlemen of their family fortunes.

Shortly after the erection of this building Lloyd's collapsed, the English squirearchy faced ruin, and the City institutions joined the Church of England and the Tory Party as things of the past. Richard Rogers, meanwhile, was knighted, and subsequently raised to the peerage, by a Labour Party grateful for his assaults on the old establishment and eager to make him part of the new. Accordingly the first attempt by Mr Blair to confront the problem of our inner cities, devastated by centrifugal development and modernist housing schemes, was to appoint a commission of enquiry into urban renewal, with Lord Rogers at the head of it. Meanwhile my father's greatest social ambition – the ruin of the English upper class – had been effortlessly accomplished, not by a Trade Union coup d'état nor by a Peasants' Revolt, but by the capitalists and the modernists, rebranded as postcapitalists and postmodernists, and advancing behind a shared rhetoric of social progress.

But perhaps the culminating postmodernist project has been the Millennium Dome, the Babylonian temple to Nothingness built by Rogers in Greenwich, and which is again both nugatory as architecture and eloquent as the expression of a social idea. Until very recently, great public projects were designed to last. Even the exhibition architecture of the nineteenth century, such as the Grand Palais and Petit Palais in Paris, was given a ceremonial and permanent exterior, and was conceived as a celebration of a city and its achievements, and a contribution to the public life that would be lived in its shadow. The Millennium Dome was conceived from the beginning as temporary – a vast tent, whose purpose would expire when sufficient numbers had bought their tickets and wandered in baffled crocodiles around its exhibits. Void of all architectural signifiers, impressive, if at all, only as a work of engineering, this fleeting visitor from another planet was part of the same broad social programme as the Centre Beaubourg – the programme of disestablishing the old culture of our cities, and putting a fun-filled playground in its place. Hence its very temporariness was integral to its effect. Nothing endures, it told us; nothing has meaning beyond the moment. The exhibits matched the architecture: the past of our country, its achievements in conquest and war, its institutions, monarchy and religion, its imperial triumphs and its leading role in the spread of law and democracy – these were either reduced to insignificance or ignored. All was fun – but fun with a vengeance. Even the crowning exhibit – the body zone, in which two humanoid creatures towered to the roof – found nothing meaningful to say about the human figure. All you were given was a lesson in pop physiology, with a tour through the inner organs of a faceless ape.

The Prime Minister often referred to the Dome as though he had ways of making us enjoy it; he had dismissed its critics as lacking in patriotism, and piled more and more public money into servicing the debts of a project that attracted just as much attention as arrogant nonsense deserves. The politically correct exhibits had one overriding purpose, which was to flatten out the landscape of our national culture, and to put a bland 'inclusive' multiculture in its place. Its greatest box-office success was 'Domosexual day', when the dome, flooded with pink light, was packed by London's partying gays. In order to revive its flagging fortunes the Dome company employed Pierre-Yves Gerbeau, former executive of Disneyland Paris, to draw in the crowds. What was to have been a celebration of Britain and its people for the millennium became a Franco-American fun palace, complete with ushers disguised as Coggsley and Sprinx – comic-strip characters in supermarket colours, professional lowerers of the tone who performed the function of Goofy and Donald Duck in Disneyland.

In the temple of the Dome we encountered what Joyce might have called God's funferall. My father, had he lived to see it, would have viewed it as the final triumph of capitalist consumerism. He believed that cities are built, and civilizations sustained, from the human need for permanence. The post-modernist project is an attempt to deny that need – to deny it collectively, like the dance of the Israelites around the Golden Calf. The frivolity of postmodernist architecture is of a piece with its spiritual idolatry. It exalts the present moment, defies the past and mocks the future. Nor is it bound by any law. In the face of this, it seems not only that modernism was a mistake, but that postmodernism compounds the mistake by removing the one thing that might rectify it – namely, the desire for permanence. Such, at any rate, would have been Jack Scruton's judgement, and it is one that I endorse.

It is one of the marvels of the modern world that human beings, having proceeded along a path that leads manifestly to error, can yet not turn back, but must always exhort themselves to go further in the same direction. It is with modern architecture as it has been with sexual liberation: those who defend it draw no other lesson from its failure than the thought that it has not yet gone far enough. Our present need is not for the uncoordinated and dislocated architecture that the postmodernists would wish on us, but for an architectural grammar that would permit talentless people once again to build. You could undo the work of modernism tomorrow by a simple expedient, namely by downgrading the role of the architect, equipping builders with the pattern books that created Beacon Hill, Doncaster, Helsinki or Lower Manhattan, and laying down regulations governing heights, depths and street lines. In this respect, however, the message of the postmodernists is the old one: that we must always be new. If modernism has failed, then the answer is not to learn from the past like Quinlan Terry or Léon Krier, nor to soften the modernist edges with mouldings and shadows, in the manner of Venturi and Rauch, but to press on still further, into the anti-architecture of Eisenman, Gehry, Libeskind and Tschumi, or into the kitsch monumentality of Rogers.

Relations with my father never regained the equilibrium that had been lost during the years of Sam the First. But our shared love of the built environment might, with time, have brought us nearer to a reconciliation. I would have wanted to introduce Jack to the equally charismatic but far more gentle figure who has taken the lead in defending the vernacular cities of Europe and in showing how to continue the collective work that built them. Léon Krier is known to the public as the man who built Poundbury, on land belonging to the Duchy of Cornwall, and under instructions from the Prince of Wales. In fact Léon didn't build Poundbury at all: rather, he laid down the simple principles that would enable Poundbury to build itself. By designing the street as the primary public space, by encouraging vertical syntax rather than horizontal spread, by suggesting materials, details and the number of storeys, and by embellishing here and there to ease the eye, he created a townscape into which any vernacular builder can insert the product of his craft, and which will grow organically without ever offending the eye, the soul or even the pocket. All who visit Poundbury, other than members of the architectural profession, are delighted and moved by it. And it is one of the many ironies of my father's outlook that this illustration of his theories should owe its being to the old English establishment, to the royalty that he loathed, and to a cultured conservative who was born in Luxembourg and now lives in France.

Nothing is more striking about Léon Krier than the feature that distinguishes him among architects – his modesty. He quietly unfolds his schemes for the city of the future, seeking your agreement and appealing for suggestions. His large face and twinkling eyes radiate happiness, and his hands as they unroll his drawings of the imaginary *polis* are the hands of a father gently lifting his newborn child from the cradle. Although he abhors the modernist vandalism that has torn the hearts out of our cities, he never utters an uncharitable word about those responsible. His whole being is directed towards consensus, towards a democratic pooling of our collective energies, to create the urban environment where we will all be at home. And in his large but placid form you feel the presence of an indefatigable energy, expressing an undaunted love of ordinary humanity.

I was surprised to discover that the process whereby books, music and culture had entered my consciousness had occurred also in Léon, and that, starting from insignificant origins in a Luxembourg village, you could stumble into the same wondrous cathedral that I had discovered by accident in suburban High Wycombe. I learned that we share our heroes – Schubert and Wagner, Eliot and Proust, Alberti and Palladio – just as we share our belief in spontaneous order and living tradition as the sole reliable guides to the public realm. Here was another conservative, a Burkean like me, who had seen the deep connection between the laws of society and the order of the street. Had Jack Scruton come face to face with Léon – and there is no way of approaching Léon except face to face – he would have seen at last that the traditional townscape that he so much admired is of a piece with the natural and unequal society that appalled him. Both are attempts at home, in a world where we have no other destination.

12
Regaining my Religion

In the early 1990s, teaching a course on the philosophy of music at Boston University, I would make a point of listening to my students' music, remembering how important it had been for me to put Muddy Waters side by side with Schubert and to take the needle off Ray Charles in order to put it down on Bach. There is no art without judgement, I insisted, and if the stuff that they brought to the classroom could not be listened to, but only heard, then this was one sign that it was merely pretending to be music. Eric Clapton – who had already rescued himself from the heavy metal idiom of Cream and set out to rediscover music – offered the first step on the *gradus ad parnassum* that led, if I was lucky, to Mendelssohn or Bach. Many songs from my students' high school days were discarded as they climbed the steps: but one song had a particular meaning for them, and would retain its place in their affections to the very end of the course. It was called 'Losing my Religion', and was sung by Michael Stipe, leader of the group REM. Its confused but poignant words engaged with sentiments that were all but universal in adolescents who had come from small-town America to their cynical classes in sin. For this song was the record of a personal loss, although a loss emptied of its tragic overtones. The bottom had not, after all, fallen out of their world, since what they had taken for the bottom was merely a stage phantom, projected by strobe lights on the void. Worlds, the luciferian pop-star says, are bottomless: you are always falling but falling forever. In which case you don't really fall.

Of course the situation of my students was nothing new. Losing religion has been a regular adventure of the Western mind, since the Enlightenment first announced the need for it. Wave after wave of Romantic and post-Romantic thinkers have looked on the world of faith from a point of view outside it, and listened, with Matthew Arnold, to that

melancholy, long, withdrawing roar,
Retreating, to the breath
Of the night-wind, down the vast edges drear
And naked shingles of the world.

Arnold wrote 'Dover Beach' in 1867, and his reflections on the dwindling of the Christian faith are marked by a very English melancholy, a not-quite-resigned attempt to fit the world of unbelief and scientific scepticism into the Gothic frame of Anglican culture. Twenty years later Nietzsche, in *Human, All-too-human*, while ostensibly throwing in his lot with the scientific atheists, espousing exhilarating and debunking explanations of the religious way of life, recognizes the enormous moral trauma that our civilization must undergo, as the Christian faith recedes. Faith is not simply an addition to our repertoire of ordinary opinions. It is a transforming state of mind, a stance towards the world, rooted in our social nature and altering all our perceptions, emotions and beliefs.

The distinction between Arnold and Nietzsche is the distinction between two kinds of loss. Arnold's loss of faith occurs in a world made by faith, in which all the outer trappings of a religious community remain in place, like the outward signs of holiness in a Gothic Revival church. Nietzsche's loss of faith is an absolute loss, a loss not only of inward conviction but of the outward symbols that make it possible. Nietzsche is foreseeing a new world, in which human institutions will no longer be shored up by pious habits and holy doctrines, but rebuilt from the raw, untempered fabric of the will to power. Loss of faith for Arnold is a personal tragedy, to be mourned but concealed. Loss of faith for Nietzsche is an existential transfiguration, to be accepted and affirmed, since the world no longer permits an alternative. The contrast between these two attitudes can be witnessed today, with the scientific optimists joining Nietzsche in welcoming our liberation from the chains of faith, and the cultural pessimists joining Arnold in his subdued lamentation.

Whatever our own position, we should acknowledge Arnold's

foresight in predicting something that Nietzsche hid from himself, namely:

> *a darkling plain*
> *Swept with confused alarms of struggle and flight,*
> *Where ignorant armies clash by night.*

That is surely an accurate prophecy of the godless century that was to follow. Nietzsche wrote at a time when doubt and scepticism were still a kind of luxury, and when the rot of unbelief had not spread far beyond the head. In retrospect his adulation of the 'free spirit', the *Übermensch* and the will to power show a blindness to what might happen, should these things begin to attract a politically organized following.

What exactly do we Europeans lose, as the Christian faith recedes from us? Is there any discipline that will compensate for that loss, and grant us consolation in the face of it? This question is not addressed to society as a whole, but to each of us individually. And the fact that the mass of mankind may be unable to live without religion, or may be liable, in the absence of religion, to stray into the terrible nihilism that has twice swept across our continent, is no proof that the loss that we have suffered is for each of us either unbearable or final, or that the loss is not offset by gains. In recent years I have constantly asked myself what *I* have lost, and whether the loss is irreparable. And by pondering my loss of faith I have steadily regained it, though in a form that stands at a distance from the old religion, endorsing it – but with its own reflected light.

Religion, as Durkheim pointed out in his great study of its elementary forms, is a social fact. A religion is not something that occurs to you; nor does it emerge as the conclusion of an empirical investigation or an intellectual argument. It is something that you join, to which you are converted, or into which you are born. Losing the Christian faith is not merely a matter of doubting the existence of God, or the incarnation, or the redemption purchased on the Cross. It involves falling out of communion, ceasing to be 'members in Christ', losing a primary experience of home. All religions are alike in this, and it is why they are so harsh on heretics and unbelievers: for heretics and unbelievers pretend to the benefits of membership, while belonging to other communities in other ways.

This is not to say that there is nothing more to religion than the bond of membership. There is also doctrine, ritual, worship and prayer. There is the vision of God the creator, and the search for signs and revelations of the transcendental. There is the sense of the sacred, the sacrosanct, the sacramental and the sacrilegious. All those grow from the experience of social membership and also amend it, so that a religious community furnishes itself with an all-embracing *Weltanschauung*, together with rituals and ceremonies that affirm its existence as a social organism, and lay claim to its place in the world.

Faith is not therefore content with the cosy customs and necromantic rites of the household gods. It strides out towards a cosmic explanation and a final theodicy. In consequence it suffers challenge from the rival advance of science. Scientific thinking brought Christian doctrine to a sudden check. Although religion is a social fact, therefore, it is exposed to a purely intellectual refutation. And the defeat of the Church's intellectual claims began the process of secularization, which was to end in the defeat of the Christian community – the final loss of that root experience of membership, which had shaped European civilization for two millennia, and which had caused it to be what it is.

The loss of faith may begin as an intellectual loss. But it does not end there. It is a loss of comfort, membership and home: it involves exile from the community that formed you, and for which you may always secretly yearn. Reading the great Victorian doubters – Matthew Arnold being pre-eminent among them – I am persuaded that they were not ready for this experience. Hence they attempted to patch up the social world while leaving the ecclesiastical crenellations intact on top of it. And the remarkable fact is that they were successful. Their loss of faith occurred against the background of a still perceivable religious community, whose customs they did nothing to disturb. They inhabited the same *Lebenswelt* as the believer, and saw the world as marked out by institutions and expectations that are the legacy of religion.

We witness this in the writings of nineteenth-century secularists such as John Stuart Mill, Jules Michelet or Henry Thoreau. Their world bears the stamp of a shared religion; the human form for them is still divine; the free individual still shines in their world with a more than earthly illumination, and the hidden goal of all their writings is to ennoble the human condition. Such writers did not experience their loss of faith as a loss, since in a very real sense they hadn't lost religion. They had rejected various metaphysical ideas and doctrines, but still inhabited the world that faith had made – the world of secure commitments, of marriages, obsequies and christenings, of real presences in ordinary lives and exalted visions in art. Their world was a world where the concepts of the sacred, the sacrilegious and the sacramental were widely recognized and socially endorsed.

This condition found idealized expression in the Gothic Revival, and in the writings of its principal high Victorian advocate, John Ruskin. Nobody knows whether Ruskin was a vestigial Christian believer, a fellow-traveller or an atheist profoundly attached to the medieval vision of a society ordered by faith. His exhortations, however, are phrased in the diction of the Book of Common Prayer; his response to the science and art of his day is penetrated by the spirit of religious inquisition, and his recommendations to the architect are for the building of the Heavenly Jerusalem. The Gothic style, as he described and commended it, was to recapture the sacred for a secular age. It was to offer visions of sacrifice and consecrated labour, and so counter the dispiriting products of the industrial machine. The Gothic would be, in the midst of our utilitarian madness, a window on to the transcendental, where once again we could pause and wonder, and where our souls would be filled with the light of another world. The Gothic Revival – both for Ruskin and for the atheist William Morris – was an attempt to reconsecrate the city as an earthly community united by real presences in sacred precincts.

Loss of faith involves a radical change to the *Lebenswelt*, as Husserl called it. The most ordinary things take on a new aspect, and concepts that inhabit the soul of believers and shape their most intimate experiences – concepts of the sacred and profane, of the forbidden, the sacramental and the holy – seem to make no contact with the world as it appears to the person who has lost hold of the transcendental. In response to this we might strive as the Victorians did to maintain and repair the faith community, to hope that the process of re-consecration would continue, refurbishing the image of humanity as god-like and redeemed. In short, we could go on stealing from churches. But it doesn't work – not now. More appropriate to our time is the response of

Rilke and Eliot, the two poets over whom I stumbled when first I discovered books. They did not hope for that enduring simulacrum of a religious community, but instead wished to rediscover the real thing, only lying dormant within us. Among the greatest religious poems of the twentieth century we must surely count the *Duino Elegies* of Rilke, and the *Four Quartets* of T. S. Eliot. In the first a private religion is created from the fragmentary offerings of intensely subjective experiences, which are gradually elaborated until they seem to contain the intimation of a personal redemption. In the second the poet is living in a world that refuses his religious yearning; he rediscovers, through a lost but imagined religious community, the experience of the sacramental from which he had been cut off. Both poets are restored in imagination to what they had lost in fact. There is a kind of belief there, but it is a belief that recreates the religious community out of memories, intimations and signs.

In the *Duino Elegies* the idea of the transcendental is embodied in the figure of the Angel, summoned into existence by the poet's need, and representing the triumph of consciousness over the world of fact. In all of us, Rilke believes, there is the deep need to transform fact into thought, object into subject, Earth into the idea of Earth: the Angel is the being in whom this transubstantiation is complete. He is like the soul released into Brahma, who has translated matter to spirit so as to be co-terminous with his world. We emulate this process of translation, but we must begin from the fragments of our earthly experience where the sacred can take root – the places of love, heroism, death and memory, in which Earth beseeches us to take conscious note of her, to ingest her into our own transcendental presence, which is also an absence. For Rilke the experience of the sacred is saturated with the image of community, with the full, conscious rejoicing of the tribe, now dormant in all of us, and resurrected in imagination in the tenderness of sexual love:

Look, we don't love as flowers love, out of
a single year; there rises in us, when we love,
immemorial sap in the arms. O girl,
This – that we loved in ourselves, not one yet to be, but
the innumerable ferment; not a single child
but the fathers resting like ruined mountains

in our depths –; but the dry river-bed
of former mothers –; but the whole
soundless landscape under its clear
or cloudy destiny –, this, girl, came before you.

In that passage Rilke finds in the intense longing of erotic love the intimations of a religious community – one dedicated to its own reproduction. The transcendental is contained in the moment – the moment of desire that summons past and future generations as witnesses to the present passion. Angels live like this always; we only sometimes, in those moments when we recognize our own mortality and embrace it.

Eliot had another vision, one nearer to that of the Gothic Revival – though his is a Gothic Revival of the imagination, in which the effort of renewal takes place inwardly, in the subjective experience of the suffering poet. His pilgrimage to Little Gidding, once the home of an Anglican community dedicated to the life of prayer, leads him to the following thought:

If you came this way,
Taking any route, starting from anywhere,
At any time or at any season,
It would always be the same: you would have to put off
Sense and notion. You are not here to verify,
Instruct yourself, or inform curiosity
Or carry report. You are here to kneel
Where prayer has been valid. And prayer is more
Than an order of words, the conscious occupation
Of the praying mind, or the sound of the voice praying.
And what the dead had no speech for, when living,
They can tell you, being dead: the communication
Of the dead is tongued with fire beyond the language
of the living.
Here the intersection of the timeless moment
Is England and nowhere. Never and always.

This is a very different vision from Rilke's, of course. Not for Eliot that *unvordenklicher Saft in die Arme*: the erotic has been banished from his world; or rather, it never intruded there. Instead we have a search for the 'timeless moment' – and, stated thus briefly, it sounds like a chocolate-box platitude. But the context clarifies the thought. Eliot has found his way to a sacred place, and imagined himself into the community that made it holy. He is in communion with the dead, has passed over to them from the empirical world, and is kneeling beside them in that transcendental region. He has rediscovered the sacred, in a world that seemed to exclude it from view.

Eliot's redemption at Little Gidding involves the imagined recovery of the old Christian community. Rilke's self-made redemption through the society of Angels involves the invention of a community that is not of this world. Both are quintessentially modern responses to the loss of religion – attempts to recuperate the transcendental and the sacred from the raw experience of the solitary self. But they cannot compensate for that other and greater loss, which is that of the religious community itself. For that community contained a vital store of moral knowledge – knowledge collectively generated and collectively deployed.

The moral knowledge that I have in mind is manifest in our response to other people, in our social projects and in our sense of ourselves. It is also manifest in our ability spontaneously to understand and to act upon human realities. Moral knowledge is a practical, not a theoretical acquisition. It does not consist in the knowledge of truths. Nevertheless it may open the way to such knowledge. For there are certain truths about the human condition that are hard to formulate and hard to live up to, and which we therefore have a motive to deny. It may require moral discipline if we are to accept these truths and also to live by them.

For instance, there is the truth that we are self-conscious beings, and that this distinguishes us from the rest of the animal kingdom. There is the truth that we are free, accountable and objects of judgement in our own eyes and in the eyes of others. There is the truth that we are motivated not only by desire and appetite, but by a conception of the good. There is the truth that we are not just objects in the world of objects, but also subjects, who relate to each other reciprocally. There are all the other vital truths that I have discovered through growing up with Sam. To the person with religious belief – whether Christian or Muslim, whether monotheist or polytheist, whether a believer in the afterlife or not – those truths are obvious, and their consequences immediately apparent. Religious people may not express the truths as I have done, since I am adopting a secular idiom. Nor will they normally be aware of the philosophical reasoning that would defend those truths against modernist and postmodernist doubt. Nevertheless that is how they see the world. For them the 'human form divine', as Blake described it, is set apart from the rest of nature. Our form bears, for them, the marks of its peculiar destiny; it is capable of sanctity and liable to desecration, and in everything it is judged from a perspective that is not of this world. That way of seeing people enshrines the fundamental truth of our condition, as creatures suspended between the empirical and the transcendental, between being and judgement. But it deploys concepts that are given to us through religion, and to be obtained only with the greatest effort without it.

If you see things in that way you will find it difficult to share the view of Enlightenment thinkers that religious decline is no more than the loss of false beliefs; still less will you be able to accept the postmodernist vision of a world now liberated from absolutes, in which each of us constructs guidelines of his own, and that the only agreement that counts is the agreement to differ. The decline of Christianity, I maintain, involves, for many people, not the freedom from religious need, but the loss of concepts that would enable them to assuage it and, by assuaging it, to open their knowledge and their will to the human reality. For them the loss of religion is an epistemological loss – a loss of knowledge. Losing that knowledge is not a liberation but a fall.

Loss is fundamental to the human condition. But civilizations differ in their way of accommodating it. The Upanishads exhort us to free ourselves of all attachments, to rise to that blissful state in which we can lose nothing because we possess nothing. And flowing from that exhortation is an art and a philosophy that make light of human suffering, and scorn the losses that oppress us in this world.

By contrast, Western civilization has dwelt upon loss and made it the principal theme of its art and literature. Scenes of mourning and sorrow abound in medieval painting and sculpture; our drama is rooted in tragedy and our lyric poetry takes the loss of love and the vanishing of its object as its principal theme. It is not Christianity that gave us this outlook. Virgil's *Aeneid*, ostensibly an expression of Aeneas's hope as he is god-guided to his great and world-transforming goal in Italy, is composed of losses. The terrible sack of Troy, the loss of his wife, the awful tale of Dido, the death of Anchises, the visit to the underworld, the ruinous conflict with Turnus – all these explore the parameters of loss, and show us that our highest hopes and loyalties lead of their own accord to tragedy.

For all that, the *Aeneid* is just as much a religious text as the Upanishads. The world of Aeneas is a world of rites and rituals, of sacred places and holy times. And Aeneas is judged by the gods, sometimes hounded by them, sometimes sustained, but at every moment accountable to them and aware of their real presence in the empirical world. It is for this reason that Aeneas can look his many losses in the face and also set them at the distance that enables him to gain from them. They come to him not as inexplicable accidents but as trials, ordeals and judgements. He wrestles with them and overcomes them as you might overcome an opponent. And each loss adds to his inner strength, without hardening his heart.

At the risk of sounding somewhat Spenglerian, I would suggest that the questing and self-critical spirit of Western civilization distinguishes it among civilizations and informs both the style of its losses and its way of coping with them. The Western response to loss is not to remove yourself from the world. It is to bear it *as* a loss, to mourn it, and to strive to overcome it by seeing it as a form of consecrated suffering. Religion lies at the root of that attitude. Religion enables us to bear our losses, not primarily because it promises to offset them with some compensating gain, but because it sees them from a transcendental perspective. Judged from that perspective they appear not as meaningless afflictions but as *sacrifices*. Loss, conceived as sacrifice, becomes consecrated to something higher than itself: and in this it follows a pattern explored by René Girard in his bold theory of the violent origins of the human disposition to recognize sacred things.[15] I think that is how people can cope with the loss of children – to recognize in this loss a supreme example of the transition to another realm. Your dead child was a sacrificial offering, and is now an angel beckoning from that other sphere, sanctifying the life that you still lead in the material world. This thought is of course very crudely captured by my words.

[15] René Girard, *La violence et le sacré*, Paris, 1972

Fortunately, however, three great works of art exist that convey it completely – the medieval poem *The Pearl* from the *Gawain* manuscript, Mahler's *Kindertotenlieder*, and Britten's church parable *Curlew River*.

In our civilization, therefore, religion is the force that has enabled us to bear our losses and so to face them as truly ours. The loss of religion makes real loss difficult to bear; hence people begin to flee from loss, to make light of it, or to expel from themselves the feelings that make it inevitable. They do not do this in the way of the Upanishads, which exhort us to an immense spiritual labour, whereby we free ourselves from the weight of Dharma and slowly ascend to the blessed state of Brahma. The path of renunciation presupposes, after all, that there is something to renounce. Modern people pursue not penitence but pleasure, in the hope of achieving a condition in which renunciation is pointless since there is nothing to renounce. Renunciation of love is possible only when you have learned to love. This is why we see emerging a kind of contagious hardness of heart, an assumption on every side that there is no tragedy, no grief, no mourning, for there is nothing to mourn. There is neither love nor happiness – only fun. For us, one might be tempted to suggest, the loss of religion is the loss of loss.

Except that the loss need not occur. This is the lesson that I draw from my own experience, and that has caused me to revisit the Christianity of my youth. I was brought up in the England of the fifties, in which it was generally assumed that, with the exception of the Jewish minority, you were either Nonconformist or Church of England. On official documents that required you to state your religion you wrote 'C of E' regardless. And you could be confident that God was an Englishman, who had a quiet, dignified, low-key way of visiting the country each weekend while being careful never to outstay his welcome. When Eliot addressed that God – the very God of the Anglican communion – with the *cri de coeur* of *Ash Wednesday* and the solemn psalmody of *Four Quartets*, we were shocked and also moved. Maybe, beneath those formal robes, there beat a real and living heart and one that cared for us! This possibility had not occurred to us before.

In the England of today God is a foreigner, an illegal immigrant, with aggressive manners and a violent way of intruding into every gathering, even in the middle of the working week. The Muslims in our midst do not share our impious attitude to absent generations. They come to us from the demographic infernos of North Africa and Pakistan, like Aeneas from the burning ruins of Troy, each with an old man on his shoulders, a child at his feet and his hands full of strange gods. They are manifestly in the business of social, as well as biological, reproduction. They show us what we *really* stand to lose, if we hold nothing sacred: namely, the future. In the presence of this new religious spirit the voice of the English churches becomes ever weaker, ever more shy of doctrine, ever more conciliatory and ill at ease. The idea that the British should be re-evangelized would be dismissed by most of the official clergy as an act of aggression, even a racist affront to our Muslim minorities. The Church is not there to propagate the Christian faith, but to forgive those who reject it.

Now of course it is one of the great strengths of Christianity that it makes forgiveness a duty and freedom of conscience a religious ideal. But Christians recognize the duty of forgiveness because they seek forgiveness too. Those brought up in our post-religious society do not seek forgiveness, since they are by and large free from the belief that they need it. This does not mean they are happy. But it does mean that they put pleasure before commitment, and can neglect their duties without being crippled by guilt. Since religion is the balm for guilt, those brought up without religion seem, on the surface, to lose the need for it.

But only on the surface. You don't have to be a believer to be conscious of a great religious deficit in our society. We saw its effect during the strange canonization of Princess Diana, when vast crowds of people congregated in places vaguely associated with the Princess's name, to deposit wreaths, messages and teddy bears. The very same people whose pitiless prurience had caused Diana's death now sought absolution from her ghost. Here was beauty, royalty, distinction punished for its fault, to become a sacrificial offering and therefore a saintly intercessor before the mysteries that govern the world. Forget the gruesome kitsch and liturgical vagueness – necessary results, in any case, of the decline of organized religion. We were in the presence of a primordial yearning for the sacred, one reaching back to the very earliest dream-pictures of mankind and recorded in a thousand myths and rituals.

Many religions focus on such episodes of sacrificial offering, often, as in Christianity and Shi'ism, through a re-enacted martyrdom, in a collective ritual that purges the believer of his sins. So widespread is the phenomenon that René Girard has seen it as the fundamental secret of religion. In Girard's view, the suffering of a victim is necessary if the accumulated violence of society is to be released and abjured. That is why we are moved by the story of Christ's Passion. It is we ourselves who nailed this man to the Cross, and the compassion that we feel for him is also a purging of our guilt. This guilt arises from the experience of society; it is the residue of the aggressions through which we compete for our thrills. In our post-religious society these aggressions are no longer sublimated through acts of humility and worship. Hence the sadistic forms of entertainment that dominate our media in Europe. But, if we accept Girard's view – and there is surely a lot to be said for it – we must also accept that Generation X is just as subject to the burden of religious guilt as the rest of us.

And indeed, as soon as we look at religion in that detached, anthropological way, we begin to discern its subterranean presence in European society. Although doctrine has no place in our public life, a fear of heresy is beginning to grip the countries of Europe – not heresy as defined by the Christian churches, but heresy as defined by a form of post-Christian political correctness. A remarkable system of semi-official labels has emerged to prevent the expression of dangerous points of view. And a point of view is identified as dangerous if it belongs to the old Judaeo-Christian culture, thereby reminding us of what we were when we actually believed something. Those who confess to their Christianity are 'Christian fundamentalists' or even part of the 'Christian fundamentalist right', and therefore a recognized threat to free opinion; those who express concern over national identity are 'far-right extremists' – a label attached to Holland's Pim Fortuyn, despite his impeccable left-wing credentials; those who question whether it is right to advocate homosexuality to schoolchildren are 'homophobic'; defenders of the family are 'right-wing authoritarians', while a teacher who defends chastity rather than free contraception as the best response to teenage pregnancy, is not just 'out of touch' but 'offensive' to his pupils. To criticize popular culture, television or contemporary rock music, even to press for the teaching of grammatical English in English schools – all these are proofs of 'elitism', whereby a person disqualifies himself from the right to speak. It is as though our society is seeking to define itself as a religious community, whose very lack of faith has become a kind of orthodoxy.

There is nothing new in this. Jacobinism and Communism both began life as anti-religious movements, and both bear the marks of the Enlightenment. But they recruited people in just the way that religions recruit them, offering inviolable orthodoxies, mysterious rituals, witch-hunts and persecutions. And that is why they were successful. Living as we do in an age without certainties, we like to believe that we can finally dispense with the religious instinct and coexist in open dialogue with people who dissent from the premises on which we build our lives. But we too need orthodoxies, we too hunger for rituals, and we too are apt to confront the critic and the dissenter with persecution rather than argument.

We even have gods of a kind, flitting below the surface of our passions. You can glimpse Gaia, the earth goddess, in the crazier rhetoric of the environmentalists; Fox and Deer are totemic spirits for the defenders of animal rights, whose religion was shaped by the kitsch of Walt Disney; the human genome has a mystical standing in the eyes of many medical scientists. We have cults like football, sacrificial offerings like Princess Diana and improvised saints like Linda McCartney.

On the other hand, we have abandoned those aspects of religion that provide genuine guidance in a time of spiritual need. The instinctive awe and respect towards our own being that the Romans called *pietas* has more or less vanished from the public life of Europe. And nowhere is this more clearly noticeable than in the officially Roman Catholic countries of France and Italy. Now that the Church has ceased to be a public voice in those countries, the culture is being colonized by secular ways of thinking. Discussions of embryo research, cloning, abortion and euthanasia – subjects that go to the heart of the religious conception of our destiny – proceed in once-Catholic Europe as though nothing were at stake beyond the expansion of human choices. Little now remains of the old Christian idea that life, its genesis and its terminus are sacred things, to be meddled with at our peril. The piety and humility that it was once natural to feel before the fact of creation have given way to a pleasure-seeking disregard for absent generations. The people of Europe are living as though the dead and the unborn had no say in their decisions.

The Romans warned against impiety not only because it would bring down judgement from heaven but because it was a repudiation of a fundamental human duty – the duty to ancestors and progeny. The ills of modern civilization have their origins in the loss of piety, and we should take a lesson from the Romans, who had such a clear perception of why piety matters. The important thing, in the ancient world, was not theological belief, which was hidden behind the plethora of gods, but the cult. Religion was first of all a practice, a habit of worship, a humble setting aside of self and a deep genuflection in the presence of the divine – as Apuleius, in *The Golden Ass*, finally bows down before Isis, and is reborn to the world. Faith may or may not step into the ensuing silence. But it is the silence itself that matters: the silence of the penitent soul. Regaining religion is a matter of preparation, a quiet waiting for grace.

Moving to the country ten years ago I went out of curiosity to our local church, no longer as a thief but as a penitent. And because the little church announced the use of the Book of Common Prayer – in whose idiom my prayers are invariably expressed – I joined the congregation, and volunteered to play the organ. The truth contained in the words of Morning Prayer and Holy Communion is not directly there on the page, but revealed in the silence of the soul that comes from speaking them. It is a truth that reaches beyond words, to the inexpressible end of things.

Perhaps there is no more direct challenge to secular ways of thinking than the famous Hundredth Psalm, the *Jubilate Deo*, as translated in the Book of Common Prayer. It was by reflecting on this psalm that I came to see how its pure and unsullied idiom contains the answer to the lamentations of Michael Stipe. The psalmist enjoins us to be joyful in the Lord, to serve the Lord with gladness and to come before his presence with a song. It is a notable fact of our modern civilization, in which duties to God are ignored or forgotten, that there is very little gladness and still less singing. 'Losing my Religion' is a moan, not a song, and the idiom of heavy metal expressly forbids its followers to 'join in' when the music starts.

Once we came before God's presence with a song; now we come before his absence with a sigh. The triumphs of science and technology, the vanquishing of disease and the mastery over nature – these things coincide with a general moroseness, the origin of which, I believe, is religious. Someone who turns his back on God cannot receive his gifts with gratitude, but only with a grudging resentment at their insufficiency. No scientific advance will bestow eternal youth, eternal happiness, eternal love or loveliness. Hence no scientific advance can answer to our underlying religious need. Having put our trust in science we can expect only disappointment. And seeing, in the mirror raised by science, our own aggrieved and sullen faces, we are turned to disaffection with our kind. That is why the singing stops.

The psalmist goes on to remind us of the remedy: 'Be ye sure that the Lord he is God: it is he that hath made us, and not we ourselves.' This sentence contains all of theology. It is reminding us first that our knowledge of God is a kind of personal acquaintance, summarized in a statement of identity. We know God by knowing that God is the Lord and the Lord is God. Christians believe that they have three ways of knowing God: as God the Father, God the Son and God the Holy Ghost. But they also believe that our knowledge of God is a matter of personal acquaintance, which cannot be conveyed in the language of science.

The psalmist is also reminding us that we did not create ourselves, nor did we create the world in which we live. Such is the presumption of modern science that it strives to deny even this evident truth. Scientists are endeavouring to unravel the secret of creation, so as to take charge of it and to turn it in some new direction. This project – hailed by all forward-looking people as promising the final victory over disease, suffering and even death itself – was foretold and rejected by Aldous Huxley, in his novel *Brave New World*. Huxley's message was really a religious one. If human beings ever unlock their own genetic code, he foretold, they will use this knowledge to escape the chains of nature. But having done so, they will bind themselves in chains of their own.

The chains of nature are those that God created. They are called reason, freedom, morality and choice. The human chains foretold by Huxley are of a quite different composition: they are made entirely of flesh and the pleasures of the flesh. They bind so tightly that reason, choice and moral judgement can find no chink in which to grow and corrode them. So completely do they encircle the human soul that it shrinks to a tiny dot within the organism. There is no suffering in the Brave New World; no pain or doubt or terror. Nor is there happiness. It is a world of reliable and undemanding pleasures, from which the causes of suffering have been banished, and with them all striving, all hope, and all joy.

But love is a cause of suffering; so too are freedom, judgement and choice. Hence these things too will disappear from the Brave New World. As a result, confronted with the inhabitants of this world, we do not recognize ourselves. We instinctively reject this new form of life as monstrous, inhuman, meaningless. And that is because we seek in vain for God's image, in a world where man has presumed to be in charge.

Finally, the psalmist says that God created us. For many people this proposition is the sticking point. They can accept that, if there is knowledge of God, then it is a kind of personal knowledge; they can accept that we did not create ourselves and even that the attempt to put ourselves in the position of self-creators is dangerous presumption. But they cannot accept that God created us. They have a better explanation, and that is Darwin's.

Thanks to the work of scientific popularizers like Richard Dawkins the debate between evolutionism and creationism, which once rocked the schools of theology, is now rocking the world. If we evolved from apes, and if the whole process of evolution is merely an outgrowth of the chemistry of carbon, what place is there for God? Can we not explain everything without that old and stale hypothesis? Such are the questions that animate contemporary discussions; and people seem eager to be taken in by them.

From a philosophical perspective, however, it is very strange that people should think that the psalmist and the scientist are mutually opposed. We are natural beings, part of the biological order. Natural beings exist in time and therefore change over time. That we should evolve is inevitable. If we ask the question how we humans came to be as we are, then any conceivable answer will refer to the unfolding of a process – and processes take time. The surprising fact is not that we should have evolved from the humble chemistry of the oceans but that it should have taken so long to discover this.[16]

Of course, one thing that prevented the discovery was the story of Eden, understood not as a parable but as a literal truth about creation. But the proposition that God created the world and the proposition that we evolved over time are not merely compatible; they arise in response to quite different questions. Evolution tells us *how* the world is spread out in time, the story of creation tells us *why*. The best that science can offer is a theory of the *how* of things; but it is silent about the *why*. When we ask for the why of the world we are seeking a point of view outside all time and change, from which we can view the world as a whole. Only God can obtain that point of view. Hence it is to him that we must look for an answer. That, surely, is what the psalmist meant when he said that it is he that hath made us, and not we ourselves.

What follows from this truth, however, and how does it affect our lives? The psalmist goes on at once to tell us, in a beautiful phrase: 'we are his people, and the sheep of his pasture'. God watches over us, as a shepherd watches over his sheep. And the world in which we live is a pasture. It was natural for the poet, living in a pastoral community, to use this imagery. And it is all the more emotive for us, in that we are conscious of the history that has severed us from the green pastures of our ancestors. We long, in our hearts, to return to a simpler and more pastoral way of life, just as we long to be united with God. Hence the psalmist's words have a dual function. They remind us that we depend on God's mercy and power. And they remind us of our fallen state, of our need for safety, and of the long history of human pride and arrogance that has sundered us from nature. Our world was intended as a pasture, and we have turned it into a junkyard.

The psalmist is reminding us, too, of other things. Like sheep we go astray; and like sheep we stray as a crowd. Moreover, sheep that stray from their pasture are making a huge mistake: they are venturing into territory where they are no longer protected. We, who have damaged the natural order, are in a like condition. We have emerged into a world much of the fabric of which has been deflected from its natural condition, so as to

[16] Though there are hints of Darwinian thinking among the Greeks, especially Anaximander.

depend upon us for its survival. And yet we haven't the faintest idea how to ensure that this world survives. We improvise from day to day, and each day we become more deeply mired in error.

And the process seems to obey a terrible and inexorable logic. We overcome the danger presented by cars by building better roads, which make the cars go faster, so increasing the danger. We try to rescue our towns from the frenzy with bypasses, and within a year or two they are twice as dangerous, since the bypasses have brought more traffic to the towns. We think we can make the streets safer with street lights, only to discover that we pollute the night sky and shut out the stars, so causing us to lie half-awake at night under a searing light that troubles our body rhythms. Every attempt to correct our mistakes seems merely to add to them. And those who tell us this are greeted with anger and vilification, since the one thing that people wedded to error cannot bear is the truth. Men who tell the truth are dangerous. They should be crucified.

To return, however, to the Hundredth Psalm. The right course for those sheep who have strayed into unknown territory is to go back through the hole in the hedge. This is the essence of the religious life: not progress and experiment, but the journey back to the place that protects us. It is a mark of our sinful nature that those who advocate this course are so often sneered at. Yet there is a way back to those cooling streams, which can be rediscovered at any time.

I don't mean to imply that the conservation of nature is the answer to original sin. But I do mean to suggest that the truth that is being brought home to us in the sphere of ecology applies equally to the rest of human life. The General Confession tells us that 'we have erred and strayed from thy ways like lost sheep', and thereby implies that the ways to which we are called are part of our nature and our destiny, and not to be improved upon. If you ponder the many ways in which people have recently tried to improve on the human condition – from sexual liberation to modernist architecture, and from television to junk food – you will surely come to see how true is that ancient vision of the sheep-like nature of humanity.

We have made an idol of progress. But 'progress' is simply another name for human dreams, human ambitions, human fantasies. By worshipping progress we bow before an altar on which our own sins are exhibited. We kill in ourselves both piety and gratitude, believing that we owe the world nothing, and that the world owes everything to us. That is the real meaning, it seems to me, of the new secular religion of human rights. I call it a religion because it seems to occupy the place vacated by faith. It tells us that we are the centre of the universe, that we are under no call to obedience, but that the world is ordered in accordance with our rights.

The result of this religion of rights is that people feel unendingly hard done by. Every disappointment is met with a lawsuit, in the hope of turning material loss to material gain. And whatever happens to us, we ourselves are never at fault. The triumph of sin thereby comes with our failure to perceive it.

But this world of rights and claims and litigation is a profoundly unhappy one, since it is a world in which no one accepts misfortune, and every reversal is a cause of bitterness, anger and blame. Misfortune becomes an injustice, and a ground for compensation. Hence our world is full of hatred – hatred for the other, who has got what is mine. Look at contemporary art, literature and music and you will find in much of it a singular joylessness, a revulsion towards human life. This revulsion is the inevitable reward of those who think only of what is owed to them, and not of what they owe.

That is why the psalmist enjoins us to direct our thoughts outwards, in praise and gratitude. 'O go your way into his gates with thanksgiving, and into his courts with praise: be thankful unto him, and speak good of his Name.' Once we have made the decision to turn back to the ways of duty, gratitude will flow naturally into us, and – so the psalmist reminds us – gratitude is the precondition of joy. Only those who give thanks are able to rejoice, for only they are conscious that life, freedom and well-being are not rights but gifts.

A gift is a reminder that others care for us. The doctrine of human rights is prompting us to forget that truth. And that is why it is leading to a world without joy. For if the good things of life are mine by right, why should I be grateful for receiving them?

Where there is no gratitude there is no love. Conversely, a world in which there is love is a world in which the good things of life are seen as privileges, not rights. It is a world where you are aware of the good will of others, and where you respond to that good will with a reciprocal bounty, giving what is in your power to give, even if it is only praise.

That is why we should say, even in the midst of suffering, that the Lord is gracious, his mercy is everlasting. After all, we might not have existed; precisely because we are finite, created beings, we endure from moment to moment by God's grace. It is not through our own efforts that we attain peace but through the great endowment of good will, which lays down for us commands that only a free being can obey. That is what is meant by 'everlasting mercy': not the constant forgiveness of sins, but the maintenance of an order in which free choice can guide our conduct, even through suffering and hardship.

However much we study the evolution of the human species, however much we meddle with nature's secrets, we will not discover the way of freedom, since this is not the way of the flesh. Freedom, love and duty come to us as a vision of eternity, and to know them is to know God. This knowledge breaks through the barrier of time, and places us in contact with the eternal. Hence the psalmist concludes by telling us of God that 'his truth endureth from generation to generation'.

Discovering this truth, we encounter what is permanent – or rather what is beyond time and change, the eternal peace that serves as the divine template, so to speak, for our brief homecomings here on earth. When we take those tentative backward steps that I mentioned earlier, trying to restore this or that little precinct of our mutilated Eden, we are creating icons of another pasture, outside time and space, where God and the soul exist in dialogue. We are prefiguring our eternal home.

If, therefore, I am called upon to express my much-amended but nevertheless regained religion, it would not be in the penitential words of Little Gidding, nor in the self-centred cries of Rilke to his Angel, but in the tranquil words of the *Jubilate Deo*:

> *O be joyful in the Lord, all ye lands: serve the Lord with gladness, and come before his presence with a song.*
> *Be ye sure that the Lord he is God: it is he that hath made us, and not we ourselves; we are his people and the sheep of his pasture.*

O go your way into his gates with thanksgiving, and into his courts with praise: be thankful unto him, and speak good of his Name.
For the Lord is gracious, his mercy is everlasting: and his truth endureth from generation to generation.

Index